OpenCV 3 Blueprints

Expand your knowledge of computer vision by building amazing projects with OpenCV 3

Joseph Howse

Steven Puttemans

Quan Hua

Utkarsh Sinha

BIRMINGHAM - MUMBAI

OpenCV 3 Blueprints

First published: November 2015

Production reference: 1281015

Published by Packt Publishing Ltd.
Livery Place
35 Livery Street
Birmingham B3 2PB, UK.

ISBN 978-1-78439-975-7

www.packtpub.com

Credits

Authors

Joseph Howse

Steven Puttemans

Quan Hua

Utkarsh Sinha

Reviewers

Demetris Gerogiannis

Li Jing

Walter Lucetti

Luca Del Tongo

Theodore Tsesmelis

Commissioning Editor

Julian Ursell

Acquisition Editors

Harsha Bharwani

Divya Poojari

Content Development Editor

Merwyn D'souza

Technical Editor

Pramod Kumavat

Copy Editor

Janbal Dharmaraj

Project Coordinator

Neha Bhatnagar

Proofreader

Safis Editing

Indexer

Priya Sane

Graphics

Abhinash Sahu

Production Coordinator

Komal Ramchandani

Cover Work

Komal Ramchandani

About the Authors

Joseph Howse lives in Canada. During the cold winters, he grows a beard and his four cats grow thick coats of fur. He combs the cats every day. Sometimes, the cats pull his beard.

Joseph has been writing for Packt Publishing since 2012. His books include *OpenCV for Secret Agents, OpenCV 3 Blueprints, Android Application Programming with OpenCV 3, Learning OpenCV 3 Computer Vision with Python,* and *Python Game Programming by Example.*

When he is not writing books or grooming cats, Joseph provides consulting, training, and software development services through his company, Nummist Media (http://nummist.com).

I dedicate my work to Sam, Jan, Bob, Bunny, and the cats, who have been my lifelong guides and companions.

To my coauthors, I extend my sincere thanks for the opportunity to research and write *OpenCV 3 Blueprints* together. Authoring a book is a lot of work, and your dedication has made this project possible!

I am also indebted to the many editors and technical reviewers who have contributed to planning, polishing, and marketing this book. These people have guided me with their experience and have saved me from sundry errors and omissions. From the project's beginnings, Harsha Bharwani and Merwyn D'souza have been instrumental in assembling and managing the team of authors, editors, and reviewers. Harsha has advised me through multiple book projects, and I am grateful for her continued support.

Finally, I want to thank my readers and everybody else at Packt and in the OpenCV community. We have done so much together, and our journey continues!

Steven Puttemans is a PhD research candidate at the KU Leuven, Department of Industrial Engineering Sciences. At this university, he is working for the EAVISE research group, which focuses on combining computer vision and artificial intelligence. He obtained a master of science degree in Electronics-ICT and further expanded his interest in computer vision by obtaining a master of science in artificial intelligence.

As an enthusiastic researcher, his goal is to combine state-of-the-art computer vision algorithms with real-life industrial problems to provide robust and complete object detection solutions for the industry. His previous projects include TOBCAT, an open source object detection framework for industrial object detection problems, and a variety of smaller computer vision-based industrial projects. During these projects, Steven worked closely with the industry.

Steven is also an active participant in the OpenCV community. He is a moderator of the OpenCV Q&A forum, and has submitted or reviewed many bug fixes and improvements for OpenCV 3. He also focuses on putting as much of his research as possible back into the framework to further support the open source spirit.

More info about Steven's research, projects, and interests can be found at `https://stevenputtemans.github.io`.

Firstly, I would like to thank my girlfriend and family for supporting me through the long journey of writing my first computer vision-based book. They stood by me at every step of the way. Secondly, I would like to thank the OpenCV Q&A community who have been supporting me with all the technical problems that arose while writing this book.

Quan Hua is a software engineer at Autonomous, a start-up company in robotics, where he focuses on developing computer vision and machine learning applications for personal robots. He earned a bachelor of science degree from the University of Science, Vietnam, specializing in computer vision, and published a research paper in CISIM 2014. As the owner of Quan404.com, he also blogs about various computer vision techniques to share his experience with the community.

I wish to thank everyone who has encouraged me on the way while writing this book.

I want to express my sincere gratitude to my coauthors, editors, and reviewers for their advice and assistance. Thank you, Neha Bhatnagar, Harsha Bharwani, and Merwyn D'souza for giving me a golden opportunity to join this project.

I would like to thank the members of my family and my girlfriend, Kim Ngoc, who supported and encouraged me in spite of all the time it took me away from them. They all kept me going, and this book would not have been possible without them.

I would also like to thank my teachers who gave me the knowledge in computer vision and machine learning.

Utkarsh Sinha lives in Pittsburgh, Pennsylvania, where he is pursuing a master's in computer vision at Carnegie Mellon University. He intends to learn the state of the art of computer vision at the university and work on real-life industrial scale computer vision challenges.

Before joining CMU, he worked as a Technical Director at Dreamworks Animation on movies such as *Home*, *How to Train your Dragon 2*, and *Madagascar 3*. His work spans multiple movies and multiple generations of graphics technology.

He earned his bachelor of engineering degree in computer science and his master of science degree in mathematics from BITS-Pilani, Goa. He has been working in the field of computer vision for about 6 years as a consultant and as a software engineer at start-ups.

He blogs at `http://utkarshsinha.com/` about various topics in technology — most of which revolve around computer vision. He also publishes computer vision tutorials on the Internet through his website, AI Shack (`http://aishack.in/`). His articles help people understand concepts in computer vision every day.

I would like to thank my parents for supporting me through the long journey of writing my first book on computer vision. Without them, this book wouldn't have been possible.

I am indebted to the technical reviewers and editors who have helped polish the book to be what it is now. Their efforts have really brought the book together — thinking of aspects such as planning and marketing. Harsha Bharwani and Merwyn D'souza have been linchpins in this project — managing the team of authors, editors, and reviewers. I am grateful to them for providing me with such an excellent opportunity.

My friends, teachers, and the computer vision community have helped me understand computer vision and have supported me by answering questions, and having good debates and discussions. This has been vital, and I would like to acknowledge and thank everyone for the efforts they put in.

I would also like to express my gratitude to the Packt community and OpenCV users. Computer vision is a very exciting place to be right now — and we're just getting started!

About the Reviewers

Walter Lucetti, known on internet as Myzhar, is an Italian computer engineer with a specialization in Robotics and Robotics Perception. He received the *laurea* degree in 2005 studying at Research Center E. Piaggio in Pisa (Italy), with a thesis on 3D mapping of the real world using a 2D laser tilted using a servo motor, fusing 3D with RGB data. During the writing of the thesis, he was introduced to OpenCV for the first time; it was early 2004 and OpenCV was at its larval stage.

After the *laurea*, he started working as software developer for a low-level embedded system and high-level desktop system. He deeply improved his knowledge about computer vision and machine learning as a researcher, for a little lapse of time, at Gustavo Stefanini Advanced Robotics Center in La Spezia (Italy), a spinoff of PERCRO Laboratory of the Scuola Superiore Sant'Anna of Pisa (Italy).

Now, he works in the industry, writing firmware for embedded ARM systems and software for desktop systems based on Qt framework and intelligent algorithms for video surveillance systems based on OpenCV and CUDA.

He is also working on a personal robotics project, MyzharBot. MyzharBot is a tracked ground mobile robot that uses computer vision to detect obstacles and analyze and explore the environment. The robot is guided by algorithms based on ROS, CUDA, and OpenCV. You can follow the project on its website: `http://myzharbot.robot-home.it`.

He has reviewed several books on OpenCV with Packt Publishing, including *OpenCV Computer Vision Application Programming Cookbook, Second Edition*.

Luca Del Tongo is a computer engineer with a strong passion for algorithms, computer vision, and image processing techniques. He's the coauthor of a free eBook called *Data Structures and Algorithms (DSA)* with over 100k downloads to date and has published several image processing tutorials on his YouTube channel using Emgu CV. While working on his master's thesis, he developed an image forensic algorithm published in a scientific paper called *Copy Move forgery detection and localization by means of robust clustering with J-Linkage*. Currently, Luca works as a software engineer in the field of ophthalmology, developing corneal topography, processing algorithms, IOL calculation, and computerized chart projectors. He loves to practice sport and follow MOOC courses in his spare time. You can contact him through his blog at `http://blogs.ugidotnet.org/wetblog`.

Theodore Tsesmelis is an engineer working in the fields of computer vision and image processing. He holds a master of science degree with specialization in computer vision and image processing from Aalborg University in the study programme of Vision Graphics and Interactive Systems (VGIS).

His main interests lie in everything that deals with computer science and especially with computer vision and image processing. In his free time, he likes to contribute to his favorite OpenCV library as well as to consult and help others to get familiar with it through the official OpenCV forum.

> With the chance that this part of the book provides me, I would like to thank Steven Puttemans and Neha Bhatnagar for the nice collaboration and opportunity that they provided me to participate in this project.

www.PacktPub.com

Support files, eBooks, discount offers, and more

For support files and downloads related to your book, please visit www.PacktPub.com.

Did you know that Packt offers eBook versions of every book published, with PDF and ePub files available? You can upgrade to the eBook version at www.PacktPub.com and as a print book customer, you are entitled to a discount on the eBook copy. Get in touch with us at service@packtpub.com for more details.

At www.PacktPub.com, you can also read a collection of free technical articles, sign up for a range of free newsletters and receive exclusive discounts and offers on Packt books and eBooks.

https://www2.packtpub.com/books/subscription/packtlib

Do you need instant solutions to your IT questions? PacktLib is Packt's online digital book library. Here, you can search, access, and read Packt's entire library of books.

Why subscribe?

- Fully searchable across every book published by Packt
- Copy and paste, print, and bookmark content
- On demand and accessible via a web browser

Free access for Packt account holders

If you have an account with Packt at www.PacktPub.com, you can use this to access PacktLib today and view 9 entirely free books. Simply use your login credentials for immediate access.

Table of Contents

Preface   **vii**

Chapter 1: Getting the Most out of Your Camera System   **1**

  Coloring the light   **4**

  Capturing the subject in the moment   **8**

  Rounding up the unusual suspects   **13**

  Supercharging the PlayStation Eye   **14**

  Supercharging the ASUS Xtion PRO Live and other

  OpenNI-compliant depth cameras   **19**

  Supercharging the GS3-U3-23S6M-C and other

  Point Grey Research cameras   **31**

  Shopping for glass   **49**

  Summary   **59**

Chapter 2: Photographing Nature and Wildlife with an

Automated Camera   **61**

  Planning the camera trap   **62**

  Controlling a photo camera with gPhoto2   **65**

    Writing a shell script to unmount camera drives   67

    Setting up and testing gPhoto2   69

    Writing a shell script for exposure bracketing   70

    Writing a Python script to wrap gPhoto2   72

    Finding libgphoto2 and wrappers   77

  Detecting the presence of a photogenic subject   **77**

    Detecting a moving subject   81

    Detecting a colorful subject   87

    Detecting the face of a mammal   93

Processing images to show subtle colors and motion	**98**
Creating HDR images	98
Creating time-lapse videos	100
Further study	**101**
Summary	**102**
Chapter 3: Recognizing Facial Expressions with Machine Learning	**103**
Introducing facial expression recognition	**103**
Facial expression dataset	105
Finding the face region in the image	**105**
Extracting the face region using a face detection algorithm	106
Extracting facial landmarks from the face region	108
Introducing the flandmark library	108
Downloading and compiling the flandmark library	110
Detecting facial landmarks with flandmark	111
Visualizing the landmarks in an image	111
Extracting the face region	112
Software usage guide	113
Feature extraction	**114**
Extracting image features from facial component regions	115
Contributed features	116
Advanced features	119
Visualizing key points for each feature type	120
Computing the distribution of feature representation over k clusters	121
Clustering image features space into k clusters	121
Computing a final feature for each image	123
Dimensionality reduction	123
Software usage guide	124
Classification	**125**
Classification process	126
Splitting the dataset into a training set and testing set	126
Support vector machines	127
Training stage	128
Testing stage	130
Multi-layer perceptron	130
Training stage	132
Testing stage	134
K-Nearest Neighbors (KNN)	135
Training stage	136
The testing stage	136

Normal Bayes classifier   137
  Training stage   137
  Testing stage   137
Software usage guide   138
Evaluation   **138**
Evaluation with different learning algorithms   140
Evaluation with different features   143
Evaluation with a different number of clusters   143
System overview   **143**
Further reading   **145**
Compiling the opencv_contrib module   145
Kaggle facial expression dataset   145
Facial landmarks   146
  What are facial landmarks?   146
  How do you detect facial landmarks?   147
  How do you use facial landmarks?   147
Improving feature extraction   147
K-fold cross validation   148
Summary   **148**

Chapter 4: Panoramic Image Stitching Application Using Android Studio and NDK   **149**
Introducing the concept of panorama   **149**
The Android section – an application user interface   **152**
The setup activity layout   154
Capturing the camera frame   155
  Using the Camera API to get the camera frame   157
Implementing the Capture button   160
Implementing the Save button   163
Integrating OpenCV into the Android Studio   **164**
Compiling OpenCV Android SDK to the Android Studio project   164
Setting up the Android Studio to work with OpenCV   167
  Importing the OpenCV Android SDK   167
  Creating a Java and C++ interaction with Java Native Interface (JNI)   168
  Compiling OpenCV C++ with NDK/JNI   170
Implementing the OpenCV Java code   173
Implementing the OpenCV C++ code   174
Application showcase   **176**
Further improvement   **178**
Summary   **179**

Chapter 5: Generic Object Detection for Industrial Applications 181

Difference between recognition, detection, and categorization 182
Smartly selecting and preparing application specific training data 186
  The amount of training data 186
  Creating object annotation files for the positive samples 189
  Parsing your positive dataset into the OpenCV data vector 193
Parameter selection when training an object model 195
  Training parameters involved in training an object model 196
  The cascade classification process in detail 200
    Step 1 – grabbing positive and negative samples 203
    Step 2 – precalculation of integral image and all possible features from the training data 203
    Step 3 – firing up the boosting process 204
    Step 4 – saving the temporary result to a stage file 205
  The resulting object model explained in detail 205
    HAAR-like wavelet feature models 207
    Local binary pattern models 209
    Visualization tool for object models 210
  Using cross-validation to achieve the best model possible 212
Using scene specific knowledge and constraints to optimize the detection result 212
  Using the parameters of the detection command to influence your detection result 212
  Increasing object instance detection and reducing false positive detections 215
Obtaining rotation invariance object detection 217
2D scale space relation 222
Performance evaluation and GPU optimizations 225
  Object detection performance testing 226
  Optimizations using GPU code 228
Practical applications 232
Summary 234

Chapter 6: Efficient Person Identification Using Biometric Properties 235

Biometrics, a general approach 236
  Step 1 – getting a good training dataset and applying application-specific normalization 236
  Step 2 – creating a descriptor of the recorded biometric 238
  Step 3 – using machine learning to match the retrieved

feature vector   238
Step 4 – think about your authentication process   240
Face detection and recognition   **241**
Face detection using the Viola and Jones boosted cascade
classifier algorithm   242
Data normalization on the detected face regions   244
Various face recognition approaches and their corresponding feature space 247
Eigenface decomposition through PCA   249
Linear discriminant analysis using the Fisher criterion   252
Local binary pattern histograms   255
The problems with facial recognition in its current OpenCV 3
based implementation   258
Fingerprint identification, how is it done?   **259**
Implementing the approach in OpenCV 3   260
Iris identification, how is it done?   **267**
Implementing the approach in OpenCV 3   269
**Combining the techniques to create an efficient
people-registration system**   **275**
Summary   **277**
Chapter 7: Gyroscopic Video Stabilization   **279**
Stabilization with images   **280**
Stabilization with hardware   **282**
A hybrid of hardware and software   **283**
The math   **283**
The camera model   284
The Camera motion   284
Rolling shutter compensation   285
Image warping   286
Project overview   **287**
Capturing data   **288**
Recording video   288
Recording gyro signals   297
Android specifics   **300**
Threaded overlay   300
Reading media files   311
Calibration   **316**
Data structures   317
Reading the gyroscope trace   318
The training video   321
Handling rotations   325
Rotating an image   325
Accumulated rotations   328

The calibration class   331
Undistorting images   337
Testing calibration results   339
Rolling shutter compensation   **339**
Calibrating the rolling shutter   339
Warping with grid points   341
Unwarping with calibration   343
What's next?   **345**
Identifying gyroscope axes   345
Estimating the rolling shutter direction   345
Smoother timelapses   345
Repository of calibration parameters   346
Incorporating translations   346
Additional tips   346
Use the Python pickle module   346
Write out single images   347
Testing without the delta   347
Summary   **347**
Index   **349**

Preface

Open source computer vision projects, such as OpenCV 3, enable all kinds of users to harness the forces of machine vision, machine learning, and artificial intelligence. By mastering these powerful libraries of code and knowledge, professionals and hobbyists can create smarter, better applications wherever they are needed.

This is exactly where this book is focused, guiding you through a set of hands-on projects and templates, which will teach you to combine fantastic techniques in order to solve your specific problem.

As we study computer vision, let's take inspiration from these words:

> *"I saw that wisdom is better than folly, just as light is better than darkness."*

> *– Ecclesiastes, 2:13*

Let's build applications that see clearly, and create knowledge.

What this book covers

Chapter 1, Getting the Most out of Your Camera System, discusses how to select and configure camera systems to see invisible light, fast motion, and distant objects.

Chapter 2, Photographing Nature and Wildlife with an Automated Camera, shows how to build a "camera trap", as used by nature photographers, and process photos to create beautiful effects.

Chapter 3, Recognizing Facial Expressions with Machine Learning, explores ways to build a facial expression recognition system with various feature extraction techniques and machine learning methods.

Chapter 4, Panoramic Image Stitching Application Using Android Studio and NDK, focuses on the project of building a panoramic camera app for Android with the help of OpenCV 3's stitching module. We will use C++ with Android NDK.

Chapter 5, Generic Object Detection for Industrial Applications, investigates ways to optimize your object detection model, make it rotation invariant, and apply scene-specific constraints to make it faster and more robust.

Chapter 6, Efficient Person Identification Using Biometric Properties, is about building a person identification and registration system based on biometric properties of that person, such as their fingerprint, iris, and face.

Chapter 7, Gyroscopic Video Stabilization, demonstrates techniques for fusing data from videos and gyroscopes, how to stabilize videos shot on your mobile phone, and how to create hyperlapse videos.

What you need for this book

As a basic setup, the complete book is based on the OpenCV 3 software. If a chapter does not have a specific OS requirement, then it will run on Windows, Linux, and Mac. As authors, we encourage you to take the latest master branch from the official GitHub repository (`https://github.com/Itseez/opencv/`) for setting up your OpenCV installation, rather then using the downloadable packages at the official OpenCV website (`http://opencv.org/downloads.html`), since the latest master branch contains a huge number of fixes compared to the latest stable release.

For hardware, the authors expect that you have a basic computer system setup, either a desktop or a laptop, with at least 4 GB of RAM memory available. Other hardware requirements are mentioned below.

The following chapters have specific requirements that come on top of the OpenCV 3 installation:

Chapter 1, Getting the Most out of Your Camera System:

- **Software**: OpenNI2 and FlyCapture 2.
- **Hardware**: PS3 Eye camera or any other USB webcam, an Asus Xtion PRO live or any other OpenNI-compatible depth camera, and a Point Grey Research (PGR) camera with one or more lenses.
- **Remarks**: The PGR camera setup (with FlyCapture 2) will not run on Mac. Even if you do not have all the required hardware, you can still benefit from some sections of this chapter.

Chapter 2, Photographing Nature and Wildlife with an Automated Camera:

- **Software**: Linux or Mac operating system.
- **Hardware**: A portable laptop or a single-board computer (SBC) with battery, combined with a photo camera.

Chapter 4, Panoramic Image Stitching Application Using Android Studio and NDK:

- **Software**: Android 4.4 or later, Android NDK.
- **Hardware**: Any mobile device that supports Android 4.4 or later.

Chapter 7, Gyroscopic Video Stabilization:

- **Software**: NumPy, SciPy, Python, and Android 5.0 or later, and the Android NDK.
- **Hardware**: A mobile phone that supports Android 5.0 or later for capturing video and gyroscope signals.

Basic installation guides

As authors, we acknowledge that installing OpenCV 3 on your system can sometimes be quite cumbersome. Therefore, we have added a series of basic installation guides for installing OpenCV 3, based on the latest OpenCV 3 master branch on your system, and getting the necessary modules for the different chapters to work. For more information, take a look at `https://github.com/OpenCVBlueprints/OpenCVBlueprints/tree/master/installation_tutorials`.

Keep in mind that the book also uses modules from the OpenCV "contrib" (contributed) repository. The installation manual will have directions on how to install these. However, we encourage you to only install those modules that we need, because we know that they are stable. For other modules, this might not be the case.

Who this book is for

This book is ideal for you if you aspire to build computer vision systems that are smarter, faster, more complex, and more practical than the competition. This is an advanced book, intended for those who already have some experience in setting up an OpenCV development environment and building applications with OpenCV. You should be comfortable with computer vision concepts, object-oriented programming, graphics programming, IDEs, and the command line.

Conventions

In this book, you will find a number of text styles that distinguish between different kinds of information. Here are some examples of these styles and an explanation of their meaning.

Code words in text, database table names, folder names, filenames, file extensions, pathnames, dummy URLs, user input, and Twitter handles are shown as follows: "You can find the OpenCV software by going to `http://opencv.org` and clicking on the download link."

A block of code is set as follows:

```
Mat input = imread("/data/image.png", LOAD_IMAGE_GRAYSCALE);
GaussianBlur(input, input, Size(7,7), 0, 0);
imshow("image", input);
waitKey(0);
```

When we wish to draw your attention to a particular part of a code block, the relevant lines or items are set in bold:

```
Mat input = imread("/data/image.png", LOAD_IMAGE_GRAYSCALE);
GaussianBlur(input, input, Size(7,7), 0, 0);
imshow("image", input);
waitKey(0);
```

Any command-line input or output is written as follows:

New terms and **important words** are shown in bold. Words that you see on the screen, for example, in menus or dialog boxes, appear in the text like this: "Clicking the **Next** button moves you to the next screen."

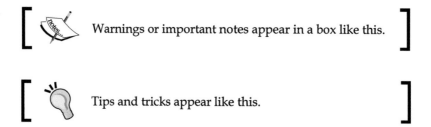

Warnings or important notes appear in a box like this.

Tips and tricks appear like this.

Reader feedback

Feedback from our readers is always welcome. Let us know what you think about this book—what you liked or disliked. Reader feedback is important for us as it helps us develop titles that you will really get the most out of.

To send us general feedback, simply e-mail feedback@packtpub.com, and mention the book's title in the subject of your message.

If there is a topic that you have expertise in and you are interested in either writing or contributing to a book, see our author guide at www.packtpub.com/authors.

Customer support

Now that you are the proud owner of a Packt book, we have a number of things to help you to get the most from your purchase.

Downloading the example code

You can download the example code files from your account at http://www.packtpub.com for all the Packt Publishing books you have purchased. If you purchased this book elsewhere, you can visit http://www.packtpub.com/support and register to have the files e-mailed directly to you.

The code is also maintained on a GitHub repository by the authors of this book. This code repository can be found at https://github.com/OpenCVBlueprints/OpenCVBlueprints.

Downloading the color images of this book

We also provide you with a PDF file that has color images of the screenshots/diagrams used in this book. The color images will help you better understand the changes in the output. You can download this file from https://www.packtpub.com/sites/default/files/downloads/B04028_ColorImages.pdf.

Errata

Although we have taken every care to ensure the accuracy of our content, mistakes do happen. If you find a mistake in one of our books—maybe a mistake in the text or the code—we would be grateful if you could report this to us. By doing so, you can save other readers from frustration and help us improve subsequent versions of this book. If you find any errata, please report them by visiting http://www.packtpub.com/submit-errata, selecting your book, clicking on the **Errata Submission Form** link, and entering the details of your errata. Once your errata are verified, your submission will be accepted and the errata will be uploaded to our website or added to any list of existing errata under the Errata section of that title.

To view the previously submitted errata, go to https://www.packtpub.com/books/content/support and enter the name of the book in the search field. The required information will appear under the **Errata** section.

Since this book also has a GitHub repository assigned to it, you can also report content errata by creating an issue at the following page: https://github.com/OpenCVBlueprints/OpenCVBlueprints/issues.

Piracy

Piracy of copyrighted material on the Internet is an ongoing problem across all media. At Packt, we take the protection of our copyright and licenses very seriously. If you come across any illegal copies of our works in any form on the Internet, please provide us with the location address or website name immediately so that we can pursue a remedy.

Please contact us at copyright@packtpub.com with a link to the suspected pirated material.

We appreciate your help in protecting our authors and our ability to bring you valuable content.

Questions

If you have a problem with any aspect of this book, you can contact us at questions@packtpub.com, and we will do our best to address the problem. Or as mentioned before, you could open up an issue on the GitHub repository and one of the authors will help you as soon as possible.

1

Getting the Most out of Your Camera System

Claude Monet, one of the founders of French Impressionist painting, taught his students to paint only what they *saw*, not what they *knew*. He even went as far as to say:

> *"I wish I had been born blind and then suddenly gained my sight so that I could begin to paint without knowing what the objects were that I could see before me."*

Monet rejected traditional artistic subjects, which tended to be mystical, heroic, militaristic, or revolutionary. Instead, he relied on his own observations of middle-class life: of social excursions; of sunny gardens, lily ponds, rivers, and the seaside; of foggy boulevards and train stations; and of private loss. With deep sadness, he told his friend, Georges Clemenceau (the future President of France):

> *"I one day found myself looking at my beloved wife's dead face and just systematically noting the colors according to an automatic reflex!"*

Monet painted everything according to his personal impressions. Late in life, he even painted the symptoms of his own deteriorating eyesight. He adopted a reddish palette while he suffered from cataracts and a brilliant bluish palette after cataract surgery left his eyes more sensitive, possibly to the near ultraviolet range.

Like Monet's students, we as scholars of computer vision must confront a distinction between *seeing* and *knowing* and likewise between input and processing. Light, a lens, a camera, and a digital imaging pipeline can grant a computer a sense of *sight*. From the resulting image data, **machine-learning (ML)** algorithms can extract *knowledge* or at least a set of meta-senses such as detection, recognition, and reconstruction (scanning). Without proper senses or data, a system's learning potential is limited, perhaps even nil. Thus, when designing any computer vision system, we must consider the foundational requirements in terms of lighting conditions, lenses, cameras, and imaging pipelines.

What do we require in order to clearly see a given subject? This is the central question of our first chapter. Along the way, we will address five subquestions:

- What do we require to see fast motion or fast changes in light?
- What do we require to see distant objects?
- What do we require to see with depth perception?
- What do we require to see in the dark?
- How do we obtain good value-for-money when purchasing lenses and cameras?

 For many practical applications of computer vision, the environment is not a well-lit, white room, and the subject is not a human face at a distance of 0.6m (2')!

The choice of hardware is crucial to these problems. Different cameras and lenses are optimized for different imaging scenarios. However, software can also make or break a solution. On the software side, we will focus on the efficient use of OpenCV. Fortunately, OpenCV's **videoio** module supports many classes of camera systems, including the following:

- Webcams in Windows, Mac, and Linux via the following frameworks, which come standard with most versions of the operating system:
    - **Windows**: Microsoft Media Foundation (MSMF), DirectShow, or Video for Windows (VfW)
    - **Mac**: QuickTime
    - **Linux**: Video4Linux (V4L), Video4Linux2 (V4L2), or libv4l
- Built-in cameras in iOS and Android devices
- OpenNI-compliant depth cameras via OpenNI or OpenNI2, which are open-source under the Apache license

- Other depth cameras via the proprietary Intel Perceptual Computing SDK
- Photo cameras via libgphoto2, which is open source under the GPL license. For a list of libgphoto2's supported cameras, see `http://gphoto.org/proj/libgphoto2/support.php`.

 Note that the GPL license is not appropriate for use in closed source software.

- IIDC/DCAM-compliant industrial cameras via libdc1394, which is open-source under the LGPLv2 license
- For Linux, unicap can be used as an alternative interface for IIDC/DCAM-compliant cameras, but unicap is GPL-licensed and thus not appropriate for use in closed-source software.
- Other industrial cameras via the following proprietary frameworks:
  - Allied Vision Technologies (AVT) PvAPI for GigE Vision cameras
  - Smartek Vision Giganetix SDK for GigE Vision cameras
  - XIMEA API

 The videoio module is new in OpenCV 3. Previously, in OpenCV 2, video capture and recording were part of the highgui module, but in OpenCV 3, the highgui module is only responsible for GUI functionality. For a complete index of OpenCV's modules, see the official documentation at `http://docs.opencv.org/3.0.0/`.

However, we are not limited to the features of the videoio module; we can use other APIs to configure cameras and capture images. If an API can capture an array of image data, OpenCV can readily use the data, often without any copy operation or conversion. As an example, we will capture and use images from depth cameras via OpenNI2 (without the videoio module) and from industrial cameras via the FlyCapture SDK by Point Grey Research (PGR).

An industrial camera or **machine vision camera** typically has interchangeable lenses, a high-speed hardware interface (such as FireWire, Gigabit Ethernet, USB 3.0, or Camera Link), and a complete programming interface for all camera settings.

Most industrial cameras have SDKs for Windows and Linux. PGR's FlyCapture SDK supports single-camera and multi-camera setups on Windows as well as single-camera setups on Linux. Some of PGR's competitors, such as Allied Vision Technologies (AVT), offer better support for multi-camera setups on Linux.

We will learn about the differences among categories of cameras, and we will test the capabilities of several specific lenses, cameras, and configurations. By the end of the chapter, you will be better qualified to design either consumer-grade or industrial-grade vision systems for yourself, your lab, your company, or your clients. I hope to surprise you with the results that are possible at each price point!

Coloring the light

The human eye is sensitive to certain wavelengths of electromagnetic radiation. We call these wavelengths "visible light", "colors", or sometimes just "light". However, our definition of "visible light" is anthropocentric as different animals see different wavelengths. For example, bees are blind to red light, but can see ultraviolet light (which is invisible to humans). Moreover, machines can assemble human-viewable images based on almost any stimulus, such as light, radiation, sound, or magnetism. To broaden our horizons, let's consider eight kinds of electromagnetic radiation and their common sources. Here is the list, in order of decreasing wavelength:

- **Radio waves** radiate from certain astronomical objects and from lightning. They are also generated by wireless electronics (radio, Wi-Fi, Bluetooth, and so on).

- **Microwaves** radiated from the Big Bang and are present throughout the Universe as background radiation. They are also generated by microwave ovens.

- **Far infrared (FIR) light** is an invisible glow from warm or hot things such as warm-blooded animals and hot-water pipes.

- **Near infrared (NIR) light** radiates brightly from our sun, from flames, and from metal that is red-hot or nearly red-hot. However, it is a relatively weak component in commonplace electric lighting. Leaves and other vegetation brightly reflect NIR light. Skin and certain fabrics are slightly transparent to NIR.

- **Visible light** radiates brightly from our sun and from commonplace electric light sources. Visible light includes the colors red, orange, yellow, green, blue, and violet (in order of decreasing wavelength).

- **Ultraviolet (UV) light**, too, is abundant in sunlight. On a sunny day, UV light can burn our skin and can become slightly visible to us as a blue-gray haze in the distance. Commonplace, silicate glass is nearly opaque to UV light, so we do not suffer sunburn when we are behind windows (indoors or in a car). For the same reason, UV camera systems rely on lenses made of non-silicate materials such as quartz. Many flowers have UV markings that are visible to insects. Certain bodily fluids such as blood and urine are more opaque to UV than to visible light.

- **X-rays** radiate from certain astronomical objects such as black holes. On Earth, radon gas, and certain other radioactive elements are natural X-ray sources.

- **Gamma rays** radiate from nuclear explosions, including supernovae. To lesser extents the sources of gamma rays also include radioactive decay and lightning strikes.

NASA provides the following visualization of the wavelength and temperature associated with each kind of light or radiation:

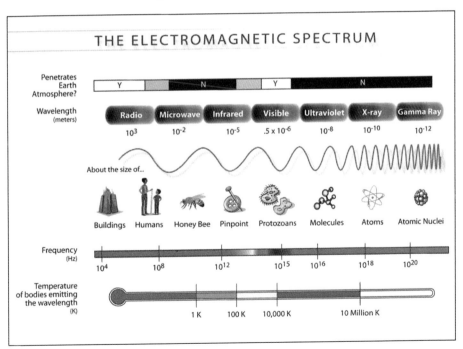

Passive imaging systems rely on **ambient** (commonplace) light or radiation sources as described in the preceding list. **Active** imaging systems include sources of their own so that the light or radiation is **structured** in more predictable ways. For example, an active night vision scope might use a NIR camera plus a NIR light.

For astronomy, passive imaging is feasible across the entire electromagnetic spectrum; the vast expanse of the Universe is flooded with all kinds of light and radiation from sources old and new. However, for terrestrial (Earth-bound) purposes, passive imaging is mostly limited to the FIR, NIR, visible, and UV ranges. Active imaging is feasible across the entire spectrum, but the practicalities of power consumption, safety, and interference (between our use case and others) limit the extent to which we can flood an environment with excess light and radiation.

Whether active or passive, an imaging system typically uses a lens to bring light or radiation into focus on the surface of the camera's sensor. The lens and its coatings transmit some wavelengths while blocking others. Additional filters may be placed in front of the lens or sensor to block more wavelengths. Finally, the sensor itself exhibits a varying **spectral response**, meaning that for some wavelengths, the sensor registers a strong (bright) signal, but for other wavelengths, it registers a weak (dim) signal or no signal. Typically, a mass-produced digital sensor responds most strongly to green, followed by red, blue, and NIR. Depending on the use case, such a sensor might be deployed with a filter to block a range of light (whether NIR or visible) and/or a filter to superimpose a pattern of varying colors. The latter filter allows for the capture of multichannel images, such as RGB images, whereas the unfiltered sensor would capture **monochrome** (gray) images.

The sensor's surface consists of many sensitive points or **photosites**. These are analogous to pixels in the captured digital image. However, photosites and pixels do not necessarily correspond one-to-one. Depending on the camera system's design and configuration, the signals from several photosites might be blended together to create a neighborhood of multichannel pixels, a brighter pixel, or a less noisy pixel.

Consider the following pair of images. They show a sensor with a Bayer filter, which is a common type of color filter with two green photosites per red or blue photosite. To compute a single RGB pixel, multiple photosite values are blended. The left-hand image is a photo of the filtered sensor under a microscope, while the right-hand image is a cut-away diagram showing the filter and underlying photosites:

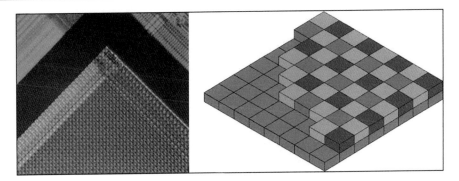

The preceding images come from Wikimedia. They are contributed by the users Natural Philo, under the Creative Commons Attribution-Share Alike 3.0 Unported license (left), and Cburnett, under the GNU Free Documentation License (right).

As we see in this example, a simplistic model (an RGB pixel) might hide important details about the way data are captured and stored. To build efficient image pipelines, we need to think about not just pixels, but also channels and **macropixels** — neighborhoods of pixels that share some channels of data and are captured, stored, and processed in one block. Let's consider three categories of image formats:

- A **raw image** is a literal representation of the photosites' signals, scaled to some range such as 8, 12, or 16 bits. For photosites in a given row of the sensor, the data are contiguous but for photosites in a given column, they are not.

- A **packed image** stores each pixel or macropixel contiguously in memory. That is to say, data are ordered according to their neighborhood. This is an efficient format if most of our processing pertains to multiple color components at a time. For a typical color camera, a raw image is *not* packed because each neighborhood's data are split across multiple rows. Packed color images usually use RGB channels, but alternatively, they may use **YUV channels**, where Y is brightness (grayscale), U is blueness (versus greenness), and V is redness (also versus greenness).

- A **planar image** stores each channel contiguously in memory. That is to say, data are ordered according to the color component they represent. This is an efficient format if most of our processing pertains to a single color component at a time. Packed color images usually use YUV channels. Having a Y channel in a planar format is efficient for computer vision because many algorithms are designed to work on grayscale data alone.

An image from a monochrome camera can be efficiently stored and processed in its raw format or (if it must integrate seamlessly into a color imaging pipeline) as the Y plane in a planar YUV format. Later in this chapter, in the sections *Supercharging the PlayStation Eye* and *Supercharging the GS3-U3-23S6M-C and other Point Grey Research cameras*, we will discuss code samples that demonstrate efficient handling of various image formats.

Until now, we have covered a brief taxonomy of light, radiation, and color — their sources, their interaction with optics and sensors, and their representation as channels and neighborhoods. Now, let's explore some more dimensions of image capture: time and space.

Capturing the subject in the moment

Robert Capa, a photojournalist who covered five wars and shot images of the first wave of D-Day landings at Omaha Beach, gave this advice:

> *"If your pictures aren't good enough, you're not close enough."*

Like a computer vision program, a photographer is the intelligence behind the lens. (Some would say the photographer is the soul behind the lens.) A good photographer continuously performs detection and tracking tasks — scanning the environment, choosing the subject, predicting actions and expressions that will create the right moment for the photo, and choosing the lens, settings, and viewpoint that will most effectively frame the subject.

By getting "close enough" to the subject and the action, the photographer can observe details quickly with the naked eye and can move to other viewpoints quickly because the distances are short and because the equipment is typically light (compared to a long lens on a tripod for a distant shot). Moreover, a close-up, wide-angle shot pulls the photographer, and viewer, into a first-person perspective of events, as if we become the subject or the subject's comrade for a single moment.

Photographic aesthetics concern us further in *Chapter 2, Photographing Nature and Wildlife with an Automated Camera*. For now, let's just establish two cardinal rules: don't miss the subject and don't miss the moment! Poor visibility and unfortunate timing are the worst excuses a photographer or a practitioner of computer vision can give. To hold ourselves to account, let us define some measurements that are relevant to these cardinal rules.

Resolution is the finest level of detail that the lens and camera can see. For many computer vision applications, recognizable details are the subject of the work, and if the system's resolution is poor, we might miss this subject completely. Resolution is often expressed in terms of the sensor's photosite counts or the captured image's pixel counts, but at best these measurements only tell us about one limiting factor. A better, empirical measurement, which reflects all characteristics of the lens, sensor, and setup, is called **line pairs per millimeter** (lp/mm). This means the maximum density of black-on-white lines that the lens and camera can resolve, in a given setup. At any higher density than this, the lines in the captured image blur together. Note that lp/mm varies with the subject's distance and the lens's settings, including the focal length (optical zoom) of a zoom lens. When you approach the subject, zoom in, or swap out a short lens for a long lens, the system should of course capture more detail! However, lp/mm does not vary when you crop (digitally zoom) a captured image.

Lighting conditions and the camera's **ISO speed** setting also have an effect on lp/mm. High ISO speeds are used in low light and they boost both the signal (which is weak in low light) and the noise (which is as strong as ever). Thus, at high ISO speeds, some details are blotted out by the boosted noise.

To achieve anything near its potential resolution, the lens must be properly focused. Dante Stella, a contemporary photographer, describes a problem with modern camera technology:

> *"For starters, it lacks ... thought-controlled predictive autofocus."*

That is to say, autofocus can fail miserably when its algorithm is mismatched to a particular, intelligent use or a particular pattern of evolving conditions in the scene. Long lenses are especially unforgiving with respect to improper focus. The **depth of field** (the distance between the nearest and farthest points in focus) is shallower in longer lenses. For some computer vision setups—for example, a camera hanging over an assembly line—the distance to the subject is highly predictable and in such cases manual focus is an acceptable solution.

Field of view (FOV) is the extent of the lens's vision. Typically, FOV is measured as an angle, but it can be measured as the distance between two peripherally observable points at a given depth from the lens. For example, a FOV of 90 degrees may also be expressed as a FOV of 2m at a depth of 1m or a FOV of 4m at a depth of 2m. Where not otherwise specified, FOV usually means diagonal FOV (the diagonal of the lens's vision), as opposed to horizontal FOV or vertical FOV. A longer lens has a narrower FOV. Typically, a longer lens also has higher resolution and less distortion. If our subject falls outside the FOV, we miss the subject completely! Toward the edges of the FOV, resolution tends to decrease and distortion tends to increase, so preferably the FOV should be wide enough to leave a margin around the subject.

The camera's **throughput** is the rate at which it captures image data. For many computer vision applications, a visual event might start and end in a fleeting moment and if the throughput is low, we might miss the moment completely or our image of it might suffer from motion blur. Typically, throughput is measured in frames per second (FPS), though measuring it as a bitrate can be useful, too. Throughput is limited by the following factors:

- **Shutter speed** (exposure time): For a well-exposed image, the shutter speed is limited by lighting conditions, the lens's **aperture setting**, and the camera's ISO speed setting. (Conversely, a slower shutter speed allows for a narrower aperture setting or slower ISO speed.) We will discuss aperture settings after this list.

- **The type of shutter**: A **global shutter** synchronizes the capture across all photosites. A **rolling shutter** does not; rather, the capture is sequential such that photosites at the bottom of the sensor register their signals later than photosites at the top. A rolling shutter is inferior because it can make an object appear skewed when the object or the camera moves rapidly. (This is sometimes called the "Jell-O effect" because of the video's resemblance to a wobbling mound of gelatin.) Also, under rapidly flickering lighting, a rolling shutter creates light and dark bands in the image. If the start of the capture is synchronized but the end is not, the shutter is referred to as a **rolling shutter with global reset**.

- **The camera's onboard image processing routines**, such as conversion of raw photosite signals to a given number of pixels in a given format. As the number of pixels and bytes per pixel increase, the throughput decreases.

- **The interface between the camera and host computer**: Common camera interfaces, in order of decreasing bit rates, include CoaXPress full, Camera Link full, USB 3.0, CoaXPress base, Camera Link base, Gigabit Ethernet, IEEE 1394b (FireWire full), USB 2.0, and IEEE 1394 (FireWire base).

A wide aperture setting lets in more light to allow for a faster exposure, a lower ISO speed, or a brighter image. However, a narrower aperture has the advantage of offering a greater depth of field. A lens supports a limited range of aperture settings. Depending on the lens, some aperture settings exhibit higher resolution than others. Long lenses tend to exhibit more stable resolution across aperture settings.

A lens's aperture size is expressed as an **f-number** or **f-stop**, which is the ratio of the lens's focal length to the diameter of its aperture. Roughly speaking, **focal length** is related to the length of the lens. More precisely, it is the distance between the camera's sensor and the lens system's optical center when the lens is focused at an infinitely distant target. The focal length should not be confused with the **focus distance** – the distance to objects that are in focus. The following diagram illustrates the meanings of focal length and focal distance as well as FOV:

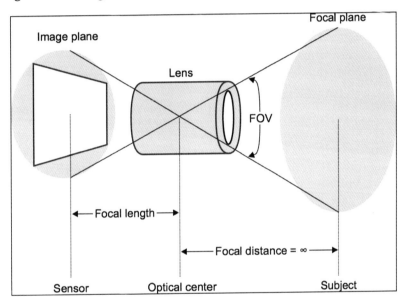

With a higher f-number (a proportionally narrower aperture), a lens transmits a smaller proportion of incoming light. Specifically, the intensity of the transmitted light is inversely proportional to the square of the f-number. For example, when comparing the maximum apertures of two lenses, a photographer might write, "The f/2 lens is twice as fast as the f/2.8 lens." This means that the former lens can transmit twice the intensity of light, allowing an equivalent exposure to be taken in half the time.

A lens's **efficiency** or **transmittance** (the proportion of light transmitted) depends on not only the f-number but also non-ideal factors. For example, some light is reflected off the lens elements instead of being transmitted. The **T-number** or **T-stop** is an adjustment to the f-number based on empirical findings about a given lens's transmittance. For example, regardless of its f-number, a T/2.4 lens has the same transmittance as an ideal f/2.4 lens. For cinema lenses, manufacturers often provide T-number specifications but for other lenses, it is much more common to see only f-number specifications.

The sensor's **efficiency** is the proportion of the lens-transmitted light that reaches photosites and gets converted to a signal. If the efficiency is poor, the sensor misses much of the light! A more efficient sensor will tend to take well-exposed images for a broader range of camera settings, lens settings, and lighting conditions. Thus, efficiency gives the system more freedom to auto-select settings that are optimal for resolution and throughput. For the common type of sensor described in the previous section, *Coloring the light*, the choice of color filters has a big effect on efficiency. A camera designed to capture visible light in grayscale has high efficiency because it can receive all visible wavelengths at each photosite. A camera designed to capture visible light in multiple color channels typically has much lower efficiency because some wavelengths are filtered out at each photosite. A camera designed to capture NIR alone, by filtering out all visible light, typically has even lower efficiency.

Efficiency is a good indication of the system's ability to form *some kind of image* under diverse lighting (or radiation) conditions. However, depending on the subject and the real lighting, a relatively inefficient system could have higher contrast and better resolution. The advantages of selectively filtering wavelengths are not necessarily reflected in lp/mm, which measures black-on-white resolution.

By now, we have seen many quantifiable tradeoffs that complicate our efforts to capture a subject in a moment. As Robert Capa's advice implies, getting close with a short lens is a relatively robust recipe. It allows for good resolution with minimal risk of completely missing the framing or the focus. On the other hand, such a setup suffers from high distortion and, by definition, a short working distance. Moving beyond the capabilities of cameras in Capa's day, we have also considered the features and configurations that allow for high-throughput and high-efficiency video capture.

Having primed ourselves on wavelengths, image formats, cameras, lenses, capture settings, and photographers' common sense, let us now select several systems to study.

Rounding up the unusual suspects

This chapter's demo applications are tested with three cameras, which are described in the following table. The demos are also compatible with many additional cameras; we will discuss compatibility later as part of each demo's detailed description. The three chosen cameras differ greatly in terms of price and features but each one can do things that an ordinary webcam cannot!

Name	Price	Purposes	Modes	Optics
Sony PlayStation Eye	$10	Passive, color imaging in visible light	640x480 @ 60 FPS 320x240 @ 187 FPS	FOV: 75 degrees or 56 degrees (two zoom settings)
ASUS Xtion PRO Live	$230	Passive, color imaging in visible light Active, monochrome imaging in NIR light Depth estimation	Color or NIR: 1280x1024 @ 60 FPS Depth: 640x480 @ 30 FPS	FOV: 70 degrees
PGR Grasshopper 3 GS3-U3-23S6M-C	$1000	Passive, monochrome imaging in visible light	1920x1200 @ 162 FPS	C-mount lens (not included)

 For examples of lenses that we can use with the GS3-U3-23S6M-C camera, refer to the *Shopping for glass* section, later in this chapter.

We will try to push these cameras to the limits of their capabilities. Using multiple libraries, we will write applications to access unusual capture modes and to process frames so rapidly that the input remains the bottleneck. To borrow a term from the automobile designers who made 1950s muscle cars, we might say that we want to "supercharge" our systems; we want to supply them with specialized or excess input to see what they can do!

Supercharging the PlayStation Eye

Sony developed the Eye camera in 2007 as an input device for PlayStation 3 games. Originally, no other system supported the Eye. Since then, third parties have created drivers and SDKs for Linux, Windows, and Mac. The following list describes the current state of some of these third-party projects:

- For Linux, the gspca_ov534 driver supports the PlayStation Eye and works out of the box with OpenCV's videoio module. This driver comes standard with most recent Linux distributions. Current releases of the driver support modes as fast as 320x240 @ 125 FPS and 640x480 @ 60 FPS. An upcoming release will add support for 320x240 @187 FPS. If you want to upgrade to this future version today, you will need to familiarize yourself with the basics of Linux kernel development, and build the driver yourself.

> See the driver's latest source code at `https://github.com/torvalds/linux/blob/master/drivers/media/usb/gspca/ov534.c`. Briefly, you would need to obtain the source code of your Linux distribution's kernel, merge the new `ov534.c` file, build the driver as part of the kernel, and finally, load the newly built gspca_ov534 driver.

- For Mac and Windows, developers can add PlayStation Eye support to their applications using an SDK called PS3EYEDriver, available from `https://github.com/inspirit/PS3EYEDriver`. Despite the name, this project is not a driver; it supports the camera at the application level, but not the OS level. The supported modes include 320x240 @ 187 FPS and 640x480 @ 60 FPS. The project comes with sample application code. Much of the code in PS3EYEDriver is derived from the GPL-licensed gspca_ov534 driver, and thus, the use of PS3EYEDriver is probably only appropriate to projects that are also GPL-licensed.

- For Windows, a commercial driver and SDK are available from Code Laboratories (CL) at `https://codelaboratories.com/products/eye/driver/`. At the time of writing, the CL-Eye Driver costs $3. However, the driver does not work with OpenCV 3's videoio module. The CL-Eye Platform SDK, which depends on the driver, costs an additional $5. The fastest supported modes are 320x240 @ 187 FPS and 640x480 @ 75 FPS.

- For recent versions of Mac, no driver is available. A driver called macam is available at `http://webcam-osx.sourceforge.net/`, but it was last updated in 2009 and does not work on Mac OS X Mountain Lion and newer versions.

Thus, OpenCV in Linux can capture data directly from an Eye camera, but OpenCV in Windows or Mac requires another SDK as an intermediary.

First, for Linux, let us consider a minimal example of a C++ application that uses OpenCV to record a slow-motion video based on high-speed input from an Eye. Also, the program should log its frame rate. Let's call this application Unblinking Eye.

Unblinking Eye's source code and build files are in this book's GitHub repository at https://github.com/OpenCVBlueprints/OpenCVBlueprints/tree/master/chapter_1/UnblinkingEye.

Note that this sample code should also work with other OpenCV-compatible cameras, albeit at a slower frame rate compared to the Eye.

Unblinking Eye can be implemented in a single file, UnblinkingEye.cpp, containing these few lines of code:

```cpp
#include <stdio.h>
#include <time.h>

#include <opencv2/core.hpp>
#include <opencv2/videoio.hpp>

int main(int argc, char *argv[]) {

  const int cameraIndex = 0;
  const bool isColor = true;
  const int w = 320;
  const int h = 240;
  const double captureFPS = 187.0;
  const double writerFPS = 60.0;
  // With MJPG encoding, OpenCV requires the AVI extension.
  const char filename[] = "SlowMo.avi";
  const int fourcc = cv::VideoWriter::fourcc('M','J','P','G');
  const unsigned int numFrames = 3750;

  cv::Mat mat;

  // Initialize and configure the video capture.
  cv::VideoCapture capture(cameraIndex);
  if (!isColor) {
    capture.set(cv::CAP_PROP_MODE, cv::CAP_MODE_GRAY);
  }
  capture.set(cv::CAP_PROP_FRAME_WIDTH, w);
```

```
    capture.set(cv::CAP_PROP_FRAME_HEIGHT, h);
    capture.set(cv::CAP_PROP_FPS, captureFPS);

    // Initialize the video writer.
    cv::VideoWriter writer(
        filename, fourcc, writerFPS, cv::Size(w, h), isColor);

    // Get the start time.
    clock_t startTicks = clock();

    // Capture frames and write them to the video file.
    for (unsigned int i = 0; i < numFrames;) {
      if (capture.read(mat)) {
        writer.write(mat);
        i++;
      }
    }

    // Get the end time.
    clock_t endTicks = clock();

    // Calculate and print the actual frame rate.
    double actualFPS = numFrames * CLOCKS_PER_SEC /
        (double)(endTicks - startTicks);
    printf("FPS: %.1f\n", actualFPS);
}
```

Note that the camera's specified mode is 320x240 @ 187 FPS. If our version of the gspca_ov534 driver does not support this mode, we can expect it to fall back to 320x240 @ 125 FPS. Meanwhile, the video file's specified mode is 320x240 @ 60 FPS, meaning that the video will play back at slower-than-real speed as a special effect. Unblinking Eye can be built using a Terminal command such as the following:

```
$ g++ UnblinkingEye.cpp -o UnblinkingEye -lopencv_core -lopencv_videoio
```

Build Unblinking Eye, run it, record a moving subject, observe the frame rate, and play back the recorded video, SlowMo.avi. How does your subject look in slow motion?

On a machine with a slow CPU or slow storage, Unblinking Eye might drop some of the captured frames due to a bottleneck in video encoding or file output. Do not be fooled by the low resolution! The rate of data transfer for a camera in 320x240 @ 187 FPS mode is greater than for a camera in 1280x720 @ 15 FPS mode (an HD resolution at a slightly choppy frame rate). Multiply the pixels by the frame rate to see how many pixels per second are transferred in each mode.

Suppose we want to reduce the amount of data per frame by capturing and recording monochrome video. Such an option is available when OpenCV 3 is built for Linux with libv4l support. (The relevant CMake definition is WITH_LIBV4L, which is turned on by default.) By changing the following line in the code of Unblinking Eye and then rebuilding it, we can switch to grayscale capture:

```
const bool isColor = false;
```

Note that the change to this Boolean affects the highlighted portions of the following code:

```
cv::VideoCapture capture(cameraIndex);
if (!isColor) {
  capture.set(cv::CAP_PROP_MODE, cv::CAP_MODE_GRAY);
}
capture.set(cv::CAP_PROP_FRAME_WIDTH, w);
capture.set(cv::CAP_PROP_FRAME_HEIGHT, h);
capture.set(cv::CAP_PROP_FPS, captureFPS);

cv::VideoWriter writer(
    filename, fourcc, writerFPS, cv::Size(w, h), isColor);
```

Behind the scenes, the VideoCapture and VideoWriter objects are now using a planar YUV format. The captured Y data are copied to a single-channel OpenCV Mat and are ultimately stored in the video file's Y channel. Meanwhile, the video file's U and V color channels are just filled with the mid-range value, 128, for gray. U and V use a lower resolution than Y, so at the time of capture, the YUV format has only 12 bits per pixel (bpp), compared to 24 bpp for OpenCV's default BGR format.

> The libv4l interface in OpenCV's videoio module currently supports the following values for cv::CAP_PROP_MODE:
> - cv::CAP_MODE_BGR (the default) captures 24 bpp color in BGR format (8 bpp per channel).
> - cv::CAP_MODE_RGB captures 24 bpp color in RGB format (8 bpp per channel).
> - cv::CAP_MODE_GRAY extracts 8 bpp grayscale from a 12 bpp planar YUV format.
> - cv::CAP_MODE_YUYV captures 16 bpp color in a packed YUV format (8 bpp for Y and 4 bpp each for U and V).

For Windows or Mac, we should instead capture data using PS3EYEDriver, CL-Eye Platform SDK, or another library, and then create an OpenCV `Mat` that references the data. This approach is illustrated in the following partial code sample:

```
int width = 320, height = 240;
int matType = CV_8UC3; // 8 bpp per channel, 3 channels
void *pData;

// Use the camera SDK to capture image data.
someCaptureFunction(&pData);

// Create the matrix. No data are copied; the pointer is copied.
cv::Mat mat(height, width, matType, pData);
```

Indeed, the same approach applies to integrating almost any source of data into OpenCV. Conversely, to use OpenCV as a source of data for another library, we can get a pointer to the data stored in a matrix:

```
void *pData = mat.data;
```

Later in this chapter, in *Supercharging the GS3-U3-23S6M-C and other Point Grey Research cameras*, we cover a nuanced example of integrating OpenCV with other libraries, specifically FlyCapture2 for capture and SDL2 for display. PS3EYEDriver comes with a comparable sample, in which the pointer to captured data is passed to SDL2 for display. As an exercise, you might want to adapt these two examples to build a demo that integrates OpenCV with PS3EYEDriver for capture and SDL2 for display.

Hopefully, after some experimentation, you will conclude that the PlayStation Eye is a more capable camera than its $10 price tag suggests. For fast-moving subjects, its high frame rate is a good tradeoff for its low resolution. Banish motion blur!

If we are willing to invest in hardware modifications, the Eye has even more tricks hidden up its sleeve (or in its socket). The lens and IR blocking filter are relatively easy to replace. An aftermarket lens and filter can allow for NIR capture. Furthermore, an aftermarket lens can yield higher resolution, a different FOV, less distortion, and greater efficiency. Peau Productions sells premodified Eye cameras as well as do-it-yourself (DIY) kits, at http://peauproductions.com/store/index. php?cPath=136_1. The company's modifications support interchangeable lenses with an m12 mount or CS mount (two different standards of screw mounts). The website offers detailed recommendations based on lens characteristics such as distortion and IR transmission. Peau's price for a premodified NIR Eye camera plus a lens starts from approximately $85. More expensive options, including distortion-corrected lenses, range up to $585. However, at these prices, it is advisable to compare lens prices across multiple vendors, as described later in this chapter's *Shopping for glass* section.

Next, we will examine a camera that lacks high-speed modes, but is designed to separately capture visible and NIR light, with active NIR illumination.

Supercharging the ASUS Xtion PRO Live and other OpenNI-compliant depth cameras

ASUS introduced the Xtion PRO Live in 2012 as an input device for motion-controlled games, natural user interfaces (NUIs), and computer vision research. It is one of six similar cameras based on sensors designed by PrimeSense, an Israeli company that Apple acquired and shut down in 2013. For a brief comparison between the Xtion PRO Live and the other devices that use PrimeSense sensors, see the following table:

Name	Price and Availability	Highest Res NIR Mode	Highest Res Color Mode	Highest Res Depth Mode	Depth Range
Microsoft Kinect for Xbox 360	$135 Available	640x480 @ 30 FPS?	640x480 @ 30 FPS	640x480 @ 30 FPS	0.8m to 3.5m?
ASUS Xtion PRO	$200 Discontinued	1280x1024 @ 60 FPS?	None	640x480 @ 30 FPS	0.8m to 3.5m
ASUS Xtion PRO Live	$230 Available	1280x1024 @ 60 FPS	1280x1024 @ 60 FPS	640x480 @ 30 FPS	0.8m to 3.5m
PrimeSense Carmine 1.08	$300 Discontinued	1280x960 @ 60 FPS?	1280x960 @ 60 FPS	640x480 @ 30 FPS	0.8m to 3.5m
PrimeSense Carmine 1.09	$325 Discontinued	1280x960 @ 60 FPS?	1280x960 @ 60 FPS	640x480 @ 30 FPS	0.35m to 1.4m
Structure Sensor	$380 Available	640x480 @ 30 FPS?	None	640x480 @ 30 FPS	0.4m to 3.5m

All of these devices include a NIR camera and a source of NIR illumination. The light source projects a pattern of NIR dots, which might be detectable at a distance of 0.8m to 3.5m, depending on the model. Most of the devices also include an RGB color camera. Based on the appearance of the active NIR image (of the dots) and the passive RGB image, the device can estimate distances and produce a so-called **depth map**, containing distance estimates for 640x480 points. Thus, the device has up to three modes: NIR (a camera image), color (a camera image), and depth (a processed image).

For more information on the types of active illumination or structured light that are useful in depth imaging, see the following paper:

David Fofi, Tadeusz Sliwa, Yvon Voisin, "A comparative survey on invisible structured light", *SPIE Electronic Imaging - Machine Vision Applications in Industrial Inspection XII*, San José, USA, pp. 90-97, January, 2004.

The paper is available online at `http://www.le2i.cnrs.fr/IMG/publications/fofi04a.pdf`.

The Xtion, Carmine, and Structure Sensor devices as well as certain versions of the Kinect are compatible with open source SDKs called OpenNI and OpenNI2. Both OpenNI and OpenNI2 are available under the Apache license. On Windows, OpenNI2 comes with support for many cameras. However, on Linux and Mac, support for the Xtion, Carmine, and Structure Sensor devices is provided through an extra module called PrimeSense Sensor, which is also open source under the Apache license. The Sensor module and OpenNI2 have separate installation procedures and the Sensor module must be installed first. Obtain the Sensor module from one of the following URLs, depending on your operating system:

- **Linux x64**: `http://nummist.com/opencv/Sensor-Bin-Linux-x64-v5.1.6.6.tar.bz2`

- **Linux x86**: `http://nummist.com/opencv/Sensor-Bin-Linux-x86-v5.1.6.6.tar.bz2`

- **Linux ARM**: `http://nummist.com/opencv/Sensor-Bin-Linux-Arm-v5.1.6.6.tar.bz2`

- **Mac**: `http://nummist.com/opencv/Sensor-Bin-MacOSX-v5.1.6.6.tar.bz2`

After downloading this archive, decompress it and run `install.sh` (inside the decompressed folder).

For Kinect compatibility, instead try the SensorKinect fork of the Sensor module. Downloads for SensorKinect are available at `https://github.com/avin2/SensorKinect/downloads`. SensorKinect only supports Kinect for Xbox 360 and it does not support model 1473. (The model number is printed on the bottom of the device.) Moreover, SensorKinect is only compatible with an old development build of OpenNI (and not OpenNI2). For download links to the old build of OpenNI, refer to `http://nummist.com/opencv/`.

Now, on any operating system, we need to build the latest development version of OpenNI2 from source. (Older, stable versions do not work with the Xtion PRO Live, at least on some systems.) The source code can be downloaded as a ZIP archive from `https://github.com/occipital/OpenNI2/archive/develop.zip` or it can be cloned as a Git repository using the following command:

```
$ git clone -b develop https://github.com/occipital/OpenNI2.git
```

Let's refer to the unzipped directory or local repository directory as `<openni2_path>`. This path should contain a Visual Studio project for Windows and a Makefile for Linux or Mac. Build the project (using Visual Studio or the `make` command). Library files are generated in directories such as `<openni2_path>/Bin/x64-Release` and `<openni2_path>/Bin/x64-Release/OpenNI2/Drivers` (or similar names for another architecture besides x64). On Windows, add these two folders to the system's `Path` so that applications can find the `dll` files. On Linux or Mac, edit your `~/.profile` file and add lines such as the following to create environment variables related to OpenNI2:

```
export OPENNI2_INCLUDE="<openni2_path>/Include"
export OPENNI2_REDIST="<openni2_path>/Bin/x64-Release"
```

At this point, we have set up OpenNI2 with support for the Sensor module, so we can create applications for the Xtion PRO Live or other cameras that are based on the PrimeSense hardware. Source code, Visual Studio projects, and Makefiles for several samples can be found in `<openni2_path>/Samples`.

> Optionally, OpenCV's videoio module can be compiled with support for capturing images via OpenNI or OpenNI2. However, we will capture images directly from OpenNI2 and then convert them for use with OpenCV. By using OpenNI2 directly, we gain more control over the selection of camera modes, such as raw NIR capture.

The Xtion devices are designed for USB 2.0 and their standard firmware does not work with USB 3.0 ports. For USB 3.0 compatibility, we need an unofficial firmware update. The firmware updater only runs in Windows, but after the update is applied, the device is USB 3.0-compatible in Linux and Mac, too. To obtain and apply the update, take the following steps:

1. Download the update from `https://github.com/nh2/asus-xtion-fix/blob/master/FW579-RD1081-112v2.zip?raw=true` and unzip it to any destination, which we will refer to as `<xtion_firmware_unzip_path>`.

2. Ensure that the Xtion device is plugged in.

3. Open Command Prompt and run the following commands:

```
> cd <xtion_firmware_unzip_path>\UsbUpdate
> !Update-RD108x!
```

If the firmware updater prints errors, these are not necessarily fatal. Proceed to test the camera using our demo application shown here.

To understand the Xtion PRO Live's capabilities as either an active or passive NIR camera, we will build a simple application that captures and displays images from the device. Let's call this application Infravision.

Infravision's source code and build files are in this book's GitHub repository at https://github.com/OpenCVBlueprints/ OpenCVBlueprints/tree/master/chapter_1/Infravision.

This project needs just one source file, `Infravision.cpp`. From the C standard library, we will use functionality for formatting and printing strings. Thus, our implementation begins with the following import statements:

```
#include <stdio.h>
#include <stdlib.h>
```

Infravision will use OpenNI2 and OpenCV. From OpenCV, we will use the core and imgproc modules for basic image manipulation as well as the highgui module for event handling and display. Here are the relevant import statements:

```
#include <opencv2/core.hpp>
#include <opencv2/highgui.hpp>
#include <opencv2/imgproc.hpp>
#include <OpenNI.h>
```

The documentation for OpenNI2 as well as OpenNI can be found online at http://structure.io/openni.

The only function in Infravision is a `main` function. It begins with definitions of two constants, which we might want to configure. The first of these specifies the kind of sensor data to be captured via OpenNI. This can be `SENSOR_IR` (monochrome output from the IR camera), `SENSOR_COLOR` (RGB output from the color camera), or `SENSOR_DEPTH` (processed, hybrid data reflecting the estimated distance to each point). The second constant is the title of the application window. Here are the relevant definitions:

```
int main(int argc, char *argv[]) {

    const openni::SensorType sensorType = openni::SENSOR_IR;
//   const openni::SensorType sensorType = openni::SENSOR_COLOR;
//   const openni::SensorType sensorType = openni::SENSOR_DEPTH;
    const char windowName[] = "Infravision";
```

Based on the capture mode, we will define the format of the corresponding OpenCV matrix. The IR and depth modes are monochrome with 16 bpp. The color mode has three channels with 8 bpp per channel, as seen in the following code:

```
int srcMatType;
if (sensorType == openni::SENSOR_COLOR) {
  srcMatType = CV_8UC3;
} else {
  srcMatType = CV_16U;
}
```

Let's proceed by taking several steps to initialize OpenNI2, connect to the camera, configure it, and start capturing images. Here is the code for the first step, initializing the library:

```
openni::Status status;

status = openni::OpenNI::initialize();
if (status != openni::STATUS_OK) {
  printf(
      "Failed to initialize OpenNI:\n%s\n",
      openni::OpenNI::getExtendedError());
  return EXIT_FAILURE;
}
```

Next, we will connect to any available OpenNI-compliant camera:

```
openni::Device device;
status = device.open(openni::ANY_DEVICE);
if (status != openni::STATUS_OK) {
  printf(
      "Failed to open device:\n%s\n",
      openni::OpenNI::getExtendedError());
  openni::OpenNI::shutdown();
  return EXIT_FAILURE;
}
```

We will ensure that the device has the appropriate type of sensor by attempting to fetch information about that sensor:

```
const openni::SensorInfo *sensorInfo =
    device.getSensorInfo(sensorType);
if (sensorInfo == NULL) {
  printf("Failed to find sensor of appropriate type\n");
  device.close();
  openni::OpenNI::shutdown();
  return EXIT_FAILURE;
}
```

We will also create a stream but not start it yet:

```
openni::VideoStream stream;
status = stream.create(device, sensorType);
if (status != openni::STATUS_OK) {
  printf(
      "Failed to create stream:\n%s\n",
      openni::OpenNI::getExtendedError());
  device.close();
  openni::OpenNI::shutdown();
  return EXIT_FAILURE;
}
```

We will query the supported video modes and iterate through them to find the one with the highest resolution. Then, we will select this mode:

```
// Select the video mode with the highest resolution.
{
  const openni::Array<openni::VideoMode> *videoModes =
      &sensorInfo->getSupportedVideoModes();
  int maxResolutionX = -1;
```

```
    int maxResolutionIndex = 0;
    for (int i = 0; i < videoModes->getSize(); i++) {
        int resolutionX = (*videoModes)[i].getResolutionX();
        if (resolutionX > maxResolutionX) {
            maxResolutionX = resolutionX;
            maxResolutionIndex = i;
        }
    }
    stream.setVideoMode((*videoModes)[maxResolutionIndex]);
}
```

We will start streaming images from the camera:

```
status = stream.start();
if (status != openni::STATUS_OK) {
    printf(
        "Failed to start stream:\n%s\n",
        openni::OpenNI::getExtendedError());
    stream.destroy();
    device.close();
    openni::OpenNI::shutdown();
    return EXIT_FAILURE;
}
```

To prepare for capturing and displaying images, we will create an OpenNI frame, an OpenCV matrix, and a window:

```
openni::VideoFrameRef frame;
cv::Mat dstMat;
cv::namedWindow(windowName);
```

Next, we will implement the application's main loop. On each iteration, we will capture a frame via OpenNI, convert it to a typical OpenCV format (either grayscale with 8 bpp or BGR with 8 bpp per channel), and display it via the highgui module. The loop ends when the user presses any key. Here is the implementation:

```
// Capture and display frames until any key is pressed.
while (cv::waitKey(1) == -1) {
    status = stream.readFrame(&frame);
    if (frame.isValid()) {
        cv::Mat srcMat(
            frame.getHeight(), frame.getWidth(), srcMatType,
            (void *)frame.getData(), frame.getStrideInBytes());
        if (sensorType == openni::SENSOR_COLOR) {
```

```
      cv::cvtColor(srcMat, dstMat, cv::COLOR_RGB2BGR);
    } else {
      srcMat.convertTo(dstMat, CV_8U);
    }
    cv::imshow(windowName, dstMat);
  }
}
```

OpenCV's highgui module has many shortcomings. It does not allow for handling of a standard quit event, such as the clicking of a window's **X** button. Thus, we quit based on a keystroke instead. Also, highgui imposes a delay of at least 1ms (but possibly more, depending on the operating system's minimum time to switch between threads) when polling events such as keystrokes. This delay should not matter for the purpose of demonstrating a camera with a low frame rate, such as the Xtion PRO Live with its 30 FPS limit. However, in the next section, *Supercharging the GS3-U3-23S6M-C and other Point Gray Research cameras*, we will explore SDL2 as a more efficient alternative to highgui.

After the loop ends (due to the user pressing a key), we will clean up the window and all of OpenNI's resources, as shown in the following code:

```
  cv::destroyWindow(windowName);

  stream.stop();
  stream.destroy();
  device.close();
  openni::OpenNI::shutdown();
}
```

This is the end of the source code. On Windows, Infravision can be built as a Visual C++ Win32 Console Project in Visual Studio. Remember to right-click on the project and edit its **Project Properties** so that **C++ | General | Additional Include Directories** lists the path to OpenCV's and OpenNI's include directories. Also, edit **Linker | Input | Additional Dependencies** so that it lists the paths to opencv_core300.lib and opencv_imgproc300.lib (or similarly named lib files for other OpenCV versions besides 3.0.0) as well as OpenNI2.lib. Finally, ensure that OpenCV's and OpenNI's dll files are in the system's Path.

On Linux or Mac, Infravision can be compiled using a Terminal command such as the following (assuming that the OPENNI2_INCLUDE and OPENNI2_REDIST environment variables are defined as described earlier in this section):

```
$ g++ Infravision.cpp -o Infravision \
  -I include -I $OPENNI2_INCLUDE -L $OPENNI2_REDIST \
  -Wl,-R$OPENNI2_REDIST -Wl,-R$OPENNI2_REDIST/OPENNI2 \
  -lopencv_core -lopencv_highgui -lopencv_imgproc -lOpenNI2
```

> The -Wl, -R flags specify an additional path where the executable should search for library files at runtime.

After building Infravision, run it and observe the pattern of NIR dots that the Xtion PRO Live projects onto nearby objects. When reflected from distant objects, the dots are sparsely spaced, but when reflected from nearby objects, they are densely spaced or even indistinguishable. Thus, the density of dots is a predictor of distance. Here is a screenshot showing the effect in a sunlit room where NIR light is coming from both the Xtion and the windows:

Alternatively, if you want to use the Xtion as a passive NIR camera, simply cover up the camera's NIR emitter. Your fingers will not block all of the emitter's light, but a piece of electrical tape will. Now, point the camera at a scene that has moderately bright NIR illumination. For example, the Xtion should be able to take a good passive NIR image in a sunlit room or beside a campfire at night. However, the camera will not cope well with a sunlit outdoor scene because this is vastly brighter than the conditions for which the device was designed. Here is a screenshot showing the same sunlit room as in the previous example but this time, the Xtion's NIR emitter is covered up:

Note that all the dots have disappeared and the new image looks like a relatively normal black-and-white photo. However, do any objects appear to have a strange glow?

Feel free to modify the code to use SENSOR_DEPTH or SENSOR_COLOR instead of SENSOR_IR. Recompile, rerun the application, and observe the effects. The depth sensor provides a depth map, which appears bright in nearby regions and dark in faraway regions or regions of unknown distance. The color sensor provides a normal-looking image based on the visible spectrum, as seen in the following screenshot of the same sunlit room:

Compare the previous two screenshots. Note that the leaves of the roses are much brighter in the NIR image. Moreover, the printed pattern on the footstool (beneath the roses) is invisible in the NIR image. (When designers choose pigments, they usually do not think about how the object will look in NIR!)

Perhaps you want to use the Xtion as an active NIR imaging device—capable of night vision at short range—but you do not want the pattern of NIR dots. Just cover the illuminator with something to diffuse the NIR light, such as your fingers or a piece of fabric.

As an example of this diffused lighting, look at the following screenshot, showing a woman's wrists in NIR:

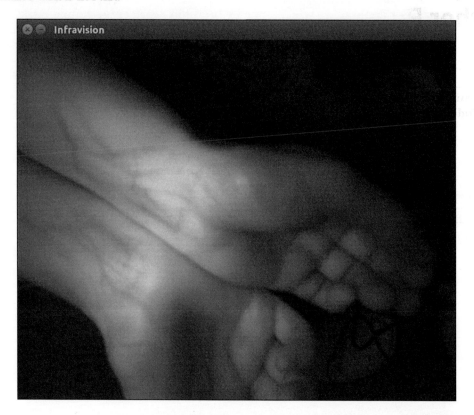

Note that the veins are more distinguishable than they would be in visible light. Similarly, active NIR cameras have a superior ability to capture identifiable details in the iris of a person's eye, as demonstrated in *Chapter 6, Efficient Person Identification Using Biometric Properties*. Can you find other examples of things that look much different in the NIR and visible wavelengths?

By now, we have seen that OpenNI-compatible cameras can be configured (programmatically and physically) to take several kinds of images. However, these cameras are designed for a specific task—depth estimation in indoor scenes—and they do not necessarily cope well with alternative uses such as outdoor NIR imaging. Next, we will look at a more diverse, more configurable, and more expensive family of cameras.

Supercharging the GS3-U3-23S6M-C and other Point Grey Research cameras

Point Grey Research (PGR), a Canadian company, manufactures industrial cameras with a wide variety of features. A few examples are listed in the following table:

Family and Model	Price	Color Sensitivity	Highest Res Mode	Sensor Format and Lens Mount	Interface	Shutter
Firefly MV FMVU-03MTC-CS	$275	Color	752x480 @ 60 FPS	1/3" CS mount	USB 2.0	Global
Firefly MV FMVU-03MTM-CS	$275	Gray from visible light	752x480 @ 60 FPS	1/3" CS mount	USB 2.0	Global
Flea 3 FL3-U3-88S2C-C	$900	Color	4096x2160 @ 21 FPS	1/2.5" C mount	USB 3.0	Rolling with global reset
Grasshopper 3 GS3-U3-23S6C-C	$1,000	Color	1920x1200 @ 162 FPS	1/1.2" C mount	USB 3.0	Global
Grasshopper 3 GS3-U3-23S6M-C	$1,000	Gray from visible light	1920x1200 @ 162 FPS	1/1.2" C mount	USB 3.0	Global
Grasshopper 3 GS3-U3-41C6C-C	$1,300	Color	2048x2048 @ 90 FPS	1" C mount	USB 3.0	Global
Grasshopper 3 GS3-U3-41C6M-C	$1,300	Gray from visible light	2048x2048 @ 90 FPS	1" C mount	USB 3.0	Global
Grasshopper 3 GS3-U3-41C6NIR-C	$1,300	Gray from NIR light	2048x2048 @ 90 FPS	1" C mount	USB 3.0	Global

Family and Model	Price	Color Sensitivity	Highest Res Mode	Sensor Format and Lens Mount	Interface	Shutter
Gazelle GZL-CL-22C5M-C	$1,500	Gray from visible light	2048x1088 @ 280 FPS	2/3" C mount	Camera Link	Global
Gazelle GZL-CL-41C6M-C	$2,200	Gray from visible light	2048x2048 @ 150 FPS	1" C mount	Camera Link	Global

To browse the features of many more PGR cameras, see the company's Camera Selector tool at http://www.ptgrey.com/Camera-selector. For performance statistics about the sensors in PGR cameras, see the company's series of Camera Sensor Review publications such as the ones posted at http://www.ptgrey.com/press-release/10545.

For more information on sensor formats and lens mounts, see the *Shopping for glass* section, later in this chapter.

Some of PGR's recent cameras use the Sony Pregius brand of sensors. This sensor technology is notable for its combination of high resolution, high frame rate, and efficiency, as described in PGR's white paper at http://ptgrey.com/white-paper/id/10795. For example, the GS3-U3-23S6M-C (a monochrome camera) and GS3-U3-23S6C-C (a color camera) use a Pregius sensor called the Sony IMX174 CMOS. Thanks to the sensor and a fast USB 3.0 interface, these cameras are capable of capturing 1920x1200 @ 162 FPS.

The code in this section is tested with the GS3-U3-23S6M-C camera. However, it should work with other PGR cameras, too. Being a monochrome camera, the GS3-U3-23S6M-C allows us to see the full potential of the sensor's resolution and efficiency, without any color filter.

The GS3-U3-23S6M-C, like most PGR cameras, does not come with a lens; rather, it uses a standard C mount for interchangeable lenses. Examples of low-cost lenses for this mount are discussed later in this chapter, in the section *Shopping for glass*.

The GS3-U3-23S6M-C requires a USB 3.0 interface. For a desktop computer, a USB 3.0 interface can be added via a PCIe expansion card, which might cost between $15 and $60. PGR sells PCIe expansion cards that are guaranteed to work with its cameras; however, I have had success with other brands, too.

Once we are armed with the necessary hardware, we need to obtain an application called FlyCapture2 for configuring and testing our PGR camera. Along with this application, we will obtain FlyCapture2 SDK, which is a complete programming interface for all the functionality of our PGR camera. Go to `http://www.ptgrey.com/support/downloads` and download the relevant installer. (You will be prompted to register a user account if you have not already done so.) At the time of writing, the relevant download links have the following names:

- FlyCapture 2.8.3.1 SDK - Windows (64-bit)
- FlyCapture 2.8.3.1 SDK- Windows (32-bit)
- FlyCapture 2.8.3.1 SDK- Linux Ubuntu (64-bit)
- FlyCapture 2.8.3.1 SDK- Linux Ubuntu (32-bit)
- FlyCapture 2.8.3.1 SDK- ARM Hard Float

 PGR does not offer an application or SDK for Mac. However, in principle, third-party applications or SDKs might be able use PGR cameras on Mac, as most PGR cameras are compliant with standards such as IIDC/DCAM.

For Windows, run the installer that you downloaded. If in doubt, choose a **Complete** installation when prompted. A shortcut, **Point Grey FlyCap2**, should appear in your **Start** menu.

For Linux, decompress the downloaded archive. Follow the installation instructions in the README file (inside the decompressed folder). A launcher, **FlyCap2**, should appear in your applications menu.

After installation, plug in your PGR camera and open the application. You should see a window entitled **FlyCapture2 Camera Selection**, as in the following screenshot:

Ensure that your camera is selected and then click the **Configure Selected** button. Another window should appear. Its title includes the camera name, such as **Point Grey Research Grasshopper3 GS3-U3-23S6M**. All the camera's settings can be configured in this window. I find that the **Camera Video Modes** tab is particularly useful. Select it. You should see options relating to the capture mode, pixel format, cropped region (called **region of interest** or **ROI**), and data transfer, as shown in the following screenshot:

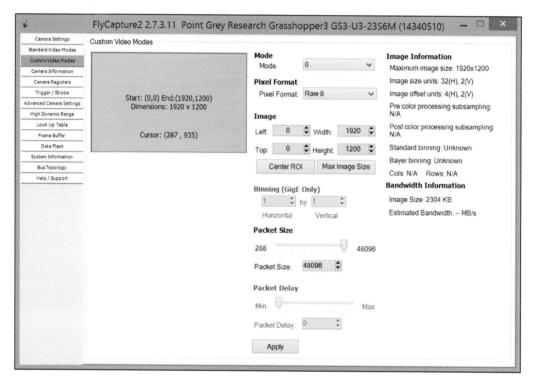

For more information about the available modes and other settings, refer to the camera's Technical Reference Manual, which can be downloaded from http://www. ptgrey.com/support/downloads. Do not worry that you might permanently mess up any settings; they are reset every time you unplug the camera. When you are satisfied with the settings, click **Apply** and close the window. Now, in the **Camera Selection** window, click the **OK** button. On Linux, the FlyCapture2 application exits now. On Windows, we should see a new window, which also has the camera's name in its title bar. This window displays a live video feed and statistics. To ensure that the whole video is visible, select the menu option **View | Stretched To Fit**. Now, you should see the video letterboxed inside the window, as in the following screenshot:

If the video looks corrupted (for example, if you see pieces of multiple frames at one time), the most likely reason is that the host computer is failing to handle the data transfer at a sufficiently high speed. There are two possible approaches to solving this problem:

- We can transfer less data. For example, go back to the **Camera Video Modes** tab of the configuration window and select either a smaller region of interest or a mode with a lower resolution.

- We can configure the operating system and BIOS to give high priority to the task of processing incoming data. For details, see the following Technical Application Note (TAN) by PGR: http://www.ptgrey.com/tan/10367.

Feel free to experiment with other features of the FlyCapture2 application, such as video recording. When you are done, close the application.

Now that we have seen a PGR camera in action, let us write our own application to capture and display frames at high speed. It will support both Windows and Linux. We will call this application LookSpry. ("Spry" means quick, nimble, or lively, and a person who possesses these qualities is said to "look spry". If our high-speed camera application were a person, we might describe it this way.)

LookSpry's source code and build files are in this book's GitHub repository at `https://github.com/OpenCVBlueprints/OpenCVBlueprints/tree/master/chapter_1/LookSpry`.

Like our other demos in this chapter, LookSpry can be implemented in a single source file, `LookSpry.cpp`. To begin the implementation, we need to import some of the C standard library's functionality, including string formatting and timing:

```
#include <stdio.h>
#include <stdlib.h>
#include <string.h>
#include <time.h>
```

LookSpry will use three additional libraries: **FlyCapture2 SDK (FC2)**, OpenCV, and **Simple DirectMedia Layer 2 (SDL2)**. (SDL2 is a cross-platform hardware abstraction layer for writing multimedia applications.) From OpenCV, we will use the core and imgproc modules for basic image manipulation, as well as the objdetect module for face detection. The role of face detection in this demo is simply to show that we can perform a real computer vision task with high-resolution input and a high frame rate. Here are the relevant import statements:

```
#include <flycapture/C/FlyCapture2_C.h>
#include <opencv2/core.hpp>
#include <opencv2/imgproc.hpp>
#include <opencv2/objdetect.hpp>
#include <SDL2/SDL.h>
```

 FC2 is closed-source but owners of PGR cameras receive a license to use it. The library's documentation can be found in the installation directory.

SDL2 is open-source under the zlib license. The library's documentation can be found online at `https://wiki.libsdl.org`.

Throughout LookSpry, we use a string formatting function—either `sprintf_s` in the Microsoft Visual C libraries or `snprintf` in standard C libraries. For our purposes, the two functions are equivalent. We will use the following macro definition so that `snprintf` is mapped to `sprintf_s` on Windows:

```
#ifdef _WIN32
#define snprintf sprintf_s
#endif
```

At several points, the application can potentially encounter an error while calling functions in FlyCapture2 or SDL2. Such an error should be shown in a dialog box. The two following helper functions get and show the relevant error message from FC2 or SDL2:

```
void showFC2Error(fc2Error error) {
  if (error != FC2_ERROR_OK) {
    SDL_ShowSimpleMessage(SDL_MESSAGEBOX_ERROR,
            "FlyCapture2 Error",
            fc2ErrorToDescription(error), NULL);
  }
}

void showSDLError() {
  SDL_ShowSimpleMessageBox(
      SDL_MESSAGEBOX_ERROR, "SDL2 Error", SDL_GetError(), NULL);
}
```

The rest of LookSpry is simply implemented in a `main` function. At the start of the function, we will define several constants that we might want to configure, including the parameters of image capture, face detection, frame rate measurement, and display:

```
int main(int argc, char *argv[]) {

  const unsigned int cameraIndex = 0u;
  const unsigned int numImagesPerFPSMeasurement = 240u;
  const int windowWidth = 1440;
  const int windowHeight = 900;
  const char cascadeFilename[] = "haarcascade_frontalface_alt.xml";
  const double detectionScaleFactor = 1.25;
  const int detectionMinNeighbours = 4;
  const int detectionFlags = CV_HAAR_SCALE_IMAGE;
  const cv::Size detectionMinSize(120, 120);
  const cv::Size detectionMaxSize;
  const cv::Scalar detectionDrawColor(255.0, 0.0, 255.0);
  char strBuffer[256u];
  const size_t strBufferSize = 256u;
```

We will declare an image format, which will help OpenCV interpret captured image data. (A value will be assigned to this variable later, when we start capturing images.) We will also declare an OpenCV matrix that will store an equalized, grayscale version of the captured image. The declarations are as follows:

```
  int matType;
  cv::Mat equalizedGrayMat;
```

Equalization is a kind of contrast adjustment that makes all levels of brightness equally common in the output image. This adjustment makes a subject's appearance more stable with respect to variations in lighting. Thus, it is common practice to equalize an image before attempting to detect or recognize subjects (such as faces) in it.

For face detection, we will create a `CascadeClassifier` object (from OpenCV's objdetect module). The classifier loads a cascade file, for which we must specify an absolute path on Windows or a relative path on Unix. The following code constructs the path, the classifier, and a vector in which face detection results will be stored:

```
#ifdef _WIN32
  snprintf(strBuffer, strBufferSize, "%s/../%s", argv[0],
cascadeFilename);
  cv::CascadeClassifier detector(strBuffer);
#else
  cv::CascadeClassifier detector(cascadeFilename);
#endif
  if (detector.empty()) {
    snprintf(strBuffer, strBufferSize, "%s could not be loaded.",
             cascadeFilename);
    SDL_ShowSimpleMessageBox(
      SDL_MESSAGEBOX_ERROR, "Failed to Load Cascade File", strBuffer,
      NULL);
    return EXIT_FAILURE;
  }
  std::vector<cv::Rect> detectionRects;
```

Now, we must set up several things related to FlyCapture2. First, the following code creates an image header that will receive captured data and metadata:

```
  fc2Error error;

  fc2Image image;
  error = fc2CreateImage(&image);
  if (error != FC2_ERROR_OK) {
    showFC2Error(error);
    return EXIT_FAILURE;
  }
```

The following code creates an FC2 context, which is responsible for querying, connecting to, and capturing from available cameras:

```
fc2Context context;
error = fc2CreateContext(&context);
if (error != FC2_ERROR_OK) {
  showFC2Error(error);
  return EXIT_FAILURE;
}
```

The following lines use the context to fetch the identifier of the camera with the specified index:

```
fc2PGRGuid cameraGUID;
error = fc2GetCameraFromIndex(context, cameraIndex, &cameraGUID);
if (error != FC2_ERROR_OK) {
  showFC2Error(error);
  return EXIT_FAILURE;
}
```

We connect to the camera:

```
error = fc2Connect(context, &cameraGUID);
if (error != FC2_ERROR_OK) {
  showFC2Error(error);
  return EXIT_FAILURE;
}
```

We finish our initialization of FC2 variables by starting the capture session:

```
error = fc2StartCapture(context);
if (error != FC2_ERROR_OK) {
  fc2Disconnect(context);
  showFC2Error(error);
  return EXIT_FAILURE;
}
```

Our use of SDL2 also requires several initialization steps. First, we must load the library's main module and video module, as seen in the following code:

```
if (SDL_Init(SDL_INIT_VIDEO) < 0) {
  fc2StopCapture(context);
  fc2Disconnect(context);
  showSDLError();
  return EXIT_FAILURE;
}
```

Next, in the following code, we create a window with a specified title and size:

```
SDL_Window *window = SDL_CreateWindow(
    "LookSpry", SDL_WINDOWPOS_UNDEFINED, SDL_WINDOWPOS_UNDEFINED,
    windowWidth, windowHeight, 0u);
if (window == NULL) {
  fc2StopCapture(context);
  fc2Disconnect(context);
  showSDLError();
  return EXIT_FAILURE;
}
```

We will create a renderer that is capable of drawing textures (image data) to the window's surface. The parameters in the following code permit SDL2 to select any rendering device and any optimizations:

```
SDL_Renderer *renderer = SDL_CreateRenderer(window, -1, 0u);
if (renderer == NULL) {
  fc2StopCapture(context);
  fc2Disconnect(context);
  SDL_DestroyWindow(window);
  showSDLError();
  return EXIT_FAILURE;
}
```

Next, we will query the renderer to see which rendering backend was selected by SDL2. The possibilities include Direct3D, OpenGL, and software rendering. Depending on the back-end, we might request a high-quality scaling mode so that the video does not appear pixelated when we scale it. Here is the code for querying and configuring the renderer:

```
SDL_RendererInfo rendererInfo;
SDL_GetRendererInfo(renderer, &rendererInfo);

if (strcmp(rendererInfo.name, "direct3d") == 0) {
  SDL_SetHint(SDL_HINT_RENDER_SCALE_QUALITY, "best");
} else if (strcmp(rendererInfo.name, "opengl") == 0) {
  SDL_SetHint(SDL_HINT_RENDER_SCALE_QUALITY, "linear");
}
```

To provide feedback to the user, we will display the name of the rendering backend in the window's title bar:

```
snprintf(strBuffer, strBufferSize, "LookSpry | %s",
    rendererInfo.name);
SDL_SetWindowTitle(window, strBuffer);
```

We will declare variables relating to the image data rendered each frame. SDL2 uses a texture as an interface to these data:

```
SDL_Texture *videoTex = NULL;
void *videoTexPixels;
int pitch;
```

We will also declare variables relating to frame rate measurements:

```
clock_t startTicks = clock();
clock_t endTicks;
unsigned int numImagesCaptured = 0u;
```

Three more variables will track the application's state—whether it should continue running, whether it should be detecting faces, and whether it should be mirroring the image (flipping it horizontally) for display. Here are the relevant declarations:

```
bool running = true;
bool detecting = true;
bool mirroring = true;
```

Now, we are ready to enter the application's main loop. On each iteration, we poll the SDL2 event queue for any and all events. A quit event (which arises, for example, when the window's close button is clicked) causes the running flag to be cleared and the main loop to exit at the iteration's end. When the user presses *D* or *M*, respectively, the detecting or mirroring flag is negated. The following code implements the event handling logic:

```
SDL_Event event;
while (running) {
  while (SDL_PollEvent(&event)) {
    if (event.type == SDL_QUIT) {
      running = false;
      break;
    } else if (event.type == SDL_KEYUP) {
      switch(event.key.keysym.sym) {
      // When 'd' is pressed, start or stop [d]etection.
      case SDLK_d:
        detecting = !detecting;
        break;
      // When 'm' is pressed, [m]irror or un-mirror the video.
      case SDLK_m:
        mirroring = !mirroring;
        break;
```

```
        default:
          break;
        }
      }
    }
```

Still in the main loop, we attempt to retrieve the next image from the camera. The following code does this synchronously:

```
    error = fc2RetrieveBuffer(context, &image);
    if (error != FC2_ERROR_OK) {
        fc2Disconnect(context);
        SDL_DestroyTexture(videoTex);
        SDL_DestroyRenderer(renderer);
        SDL_DestroyWindow(window);
        showFC2Error(error);
        return EXIT_FAILURE;
    }
```

 Given the high throughput of the GS3-U3-23S6M-C and many other Point Grey cameras, synchronous capture is justifiable here. Images are coming in so quickly that we can expect zero or negligible wait time until a buffered frame is available. Thus, the user will not experience any perceptible lag in the processing of events. However, FC2 also offers asynchronous capture, with a callback, via the `fc2SetCallbck` function. The asynchronous option might be better for low-throughput cameras and, in this case, capture and rendering would not occur in the same loop as event polling.

If we have just captured the first frame in this run of the application, we still need to initialize several variables; for example, the texture is NULL. Based on the captured image's dimensions, we can set the size of the equalized matrix and of the renderer's (pre-scaling) buffer, as seen in the following code:

```
    if (videoTex == NULL) {
        equalizedGrayMat.create(image.rows, image.cols, CV_8UC1);
        SDL_RenderSetLogicalSize(renderer, image.cols, image.rows);
```

Based on the captured image's pixel format, we can select closely matching formats for OpenCV matrices and for the SDL2 texture. For monochrome capture—and raw capture, which we assume to be monochrome—we will use single-channel matrices and a YUV texture (specifically, the Y channel). The following code handles the relevant cases:

```
        Uint32 videoTexPixelFormat;
        switch (image.format) {
```

```
// For monochrome capture modes, plan to render captured data
// to the Y plane of a planar YUV texture.
case FC2_PIXEL_FORMAT_RAW8:
case FC2_PIXEL_FORMAT_MONO8:
  videoTexPixelFormat = SDL_PIXELFORMAT_YV12;
  matType = CV_8UC1;
  break;
```

For color capture in YUV, RGB, or BGR format, we select a matching texture format and a number of matrix channels based on the format's bytes per pixel:

```
// For color capture modes, plan to render captured data
// to the entire space of a texture in a matching color
// format.
case FC2_PIXEL_FORMAT_422YUV8:
  videoTexPixelFormat = SDL_PIXELFORMAT_UYVY;
  matType = CV_8UC2;
  break;
case FC2_PIXEL_FORMAT_RGB:
  videoTexPixelFormat = SDL_PIXELFORMAT_RGB24;
  matType = CV_8UC3;
  break;
case FC2_PIXEL_FORMAT_BGR:
  videoTexPixelFormat = SDL_PIXELFORMAT_BGR24;
  matType = CV_8UC3;
  break;
```

Some capture formats, including those with 16 bpp per channel, are not currently supported in LookSpry and are considered failure cases, as seen in the following code:

```
default:
  fc2StopCapture(context);
  fc2Disconnect(context);
  SDL_DestroyTexture(videoTex);
  SDL_DestroyRenderer(renderer);
  SDL_DestroyWindow(window);
      SDL_ShowSimpleMessageBox(
  SDL_MESSAGEBOX_ERROR,
  "Unsupported FlyCapture2 Pixel Format",
  "LookSpry supports RAW8, MONO8, 422YUV8, RGB, and BGR.",
  NULL);
  return EXIT_FAILURE;
}
```

We will create a texture with the given format and the same size as the captured image:

```
videoTex = SDL_CreateTexture(
    renderer, videoTexPixelFormat, SDL_TEXTUREACCESS_STREAMING,
    image.cols, image.rows);
if (videoTex == NULL) {
  fc2StopCapture(context);
  fc2Disconnect(context);
  SDL_DestroyRenderer(renderer);
  SDL_DestroyWindow(window);
  showSDLError();
  return EXIT_FAILURE;
}
```

Using the following code, let's update the window's title bar to show the pixel dimensions of the captured image and the rendered image, in pixels:

```
snprintf(
    strBuffer, strBufferSize, "LookSpry | %s | %dx%d --> %dx%d",
    rendererInfo.name, image.cols, image.rows, windowWidth,
    windowHeight);
  SDL_SetWindowTitle(window, strBuffer);
}
```

Next, if the application is in its face detection mode, we will convert the image to an equalized, grayscale version, as seen in the following code:

```
cv::Mat srcMat(image.rows, image.cols, matType, image.pData,
        image.stride);
if (detecting) {
  switch (image.format) {
    // For monochrome capture modes, just equalize.
    case FC2_PIXEL_FORMAT_RAW8:
    case FC2_PIXEL_FORMAT_MONO8:
      cv::equalizeHist(srcMat, equalizedGrayMat);
      break;
    // For color capture modes, convert to gray and equalize.
    cv::cvtColor(srcMat, equalizedGrayMat,
        cv::COLOR_YUV2GRAY_UYVY);
    cv::equalizeHist(equalizedGrayMat, equalizedGrayMat);
      break;
    case FC2_PIXEL_FORMAT_RGB:
```

```
        cv::cvtColor(srcMat, equalizedGrayMat, cv::COLOR_RGB2GRAY);
        cv::equalizeHist(equalizedGrayMat, equalizedGrayMat);
        break;
    case FC2_PIXEL_FORMAT_BGR:
        cv::cvtColor(srcMat, equalizedGrayMat, cv::COLOR_BGR2GRAY);
        cv::equalizeHist(equalizedGrayMat, equalizedGrayMat);
        break;
    default:
        break;
}
```

We will perform face detection on the equalized image. Then, in the original image, we will draw rectangles around any detected faces:

```
// Run the detector on the equalized image.
detector.detectMultiScale(
    equalizedGrayMat, detectionRects, detectionScaleFactor,
    detectionMinNeighbours, detectionFlags, detectionMinSize,
    detectionMaxSize);
// Draw the resulting detection rectangles on the original
image.
for (cv::Rect detectionRect : detectionRects) {
    cv::rectangle(srcMat, detectionRect, detectionDrawColor);
}
}
```

At this stage, we have finished our computer vision task for this frame and we need to consider our output task. The image data are destined to be copied to the texture and then rendered. First, we will lock the texture, meaning that we will obtain write access to its memory. This is accomplished in the following SDL2 function call:

```
SDL_LockTexture(videoTex, NULL, &videoTexPixels, &pitch);
```

Remember, if the camera is in a monochrome capture mode (or a raw mode, which we assume to be monochrome), we are using a YUV texture. We need to fill the U and V channels with the mid-range value, 128, to ensure that the texture is gray. The following code accomplishes this efficiently by using the `memset` function from the C standard library:

```
switch (image.format) {
case FC2_PIXEL_FORMAT_RAW8:
case FC2_PIXEL_FORMAT_MONO8:
    // Make the planar YUV video gray by setting all bytes in its U
```

```
     // and V planes to 128 (the middle of the range).
     memset(((unsigned char *)videoTexPixels + image.dataSize), 128,
             image.dataSize / 2u);
   break;
 default:
   break;
 }
```

Now, we are ready to copy the image data to the texture. If the `mirroring` flag is set, we will copy and mirror the data at the same time. To accomplish this efficiently, we will wrap the destination array in an OpenCV `Mat` and then use OpenCV's `flip` function to flip and copy the data simultaneously. Alternatively, if the `mirroring` flag is not set, we will simply copy the data using the standard C `memcpy` function. The following code implements these two alternatives:

```
if (mirroring) {
    // Flip the image data while copying it to the texture.
    cv::Mat dstMat(image.rows, image.cols, matType, videoTexPixels,
                   image.stride);
    cv::flip(srcMat, dstMat, 1);
} else {
    // Copy the image data, as-is, to the texture.
    // Note that the PointGrey image and srcMat have pointers to the
    // same data, so the following code does reference the data that
    // we modified earlier via srcMat.
    memcpy(videoTexPixels, image.pData, image.dataSize);
}
```

Typically, the `memcpy` function (from the C standard library) compiles to block transfer instructions, meaning that it provides the best possible hardware acceleration for copying large arrays. However, it does not support any modification or reordering of data while copying. An article by David Nadeau benchmarks `memcpy` against four other copying techniques, using four compilers for each technique , and can be found at: `http://nadeausoftware.com/articles/2012/05/c_c_tip_how_copy_memory_quickly`.

Now that we have written the frame's data to the texture, we will unlock the texture (potentially causing data to be uploaded to the GPU) and we will tell the renderer to render it:

```
SDL_UnlockTexture(videoTex);
SDL_RenderCopy(renderer, videoTex, NULL, NULL);
SDL_RenderPresent(renderer);
```

After a specified number of frames, we will update our FPS measurement and display it in the window's title bar, as seen in the following code:

```
numImagesCaptured++;
if (numImagesCaptured >= numImagesPerFPSMeasurement) {
  endTicks = clock();
  snprintf(
    strBuffer, strBufferSize,
    "LookSpry | %s | %dx%d --> %dx%d | %ld FPS",
    rendererInfo.name, image.cols, image.rows, windowWidth,
    windowHeight,
    numImagesCaptured * CLOCKS_PER_SEC /
      (endTicks - startTicks));
  SDL_SetWindowTitle(window, strBuffer);
  startTicks = endTicks;
  numImagesCaptured = 0u;
  }
}
```

There is nothing more in the application's main loop. Once the loop ends (as a result of the user closing the window), we will clean up FC2 and SDL2 resources and exit:

```
fc2StopCapture(context);
fc2Disconnect(context);
SDL_DestroyTexture(videoTex);
SDL_DestroyRenderer(renderer);
SDL_DestroyWindow(window);
return EXIT_SUCCESS;
}
```

On Windows, LookSpry can be built as a Visual C++ Win32 Console Project in Visual Studio. Remember to right-click on the project and edit its **Project Properties** so that **C++ | General | Additional Include Directories** lists the paths to OpenCV's, FlyCapture 2's, and SDL 2's `include` directories. Similarly, edit **Linker | Input | Additional Dependencies** so that it lists the paths to `opencv_core300.lib`, `opencv_imgproc300.lib`, and `opencv_objdetect300.lib` (or similarly named `lib` files for other OpenCV versions besides 3.0.0) as well as `FlyCapture2_C.lib`, `SDL2.lib`, and `SDL2main.lib`. Finally, ensure that OpenCV's `dll` files are in the system's `Path`.

On Linux, a Terminal command such as the following should succeed in building LookSpry:

```
$ g++ LookSpry.cpp -o LookSpry `sdl2-config --cflags --libs` \
  -lflycapture-c -lopencv_core -lopencv_imgproc -lopencv_objdetect
```

Ensure that the GS3-U3-23S6M-C camera (or another PGR camera) is plugged in and that it is properly configured using the FlyCap2 GUI application. Remember that the configuration is reset whenever the camera is unplugged.

 All the camera settings in the FlyCap2 GUI application can also be set programmatically via the FlyCapture2 SDK. Refer to the official documentation and samples that come with the SDK.

When you are satisfied with the camera's configuration, close the FlyCap2 GUI application and run LookSpry. Try different image processing modes by pressing *M* to un-mirror or mirror the video and *D* to stop or restart detection. How many frames per second are processed in each mode? How is the frame rate in detection mode affected by the number of faces?

Hopefully, you have observed that in some or all modes, LookSpry processes frames at a much faster rate than a typical monitor's 60Hz refresh rate. The real-time video would look even smoother if we viewed it on a high-quality 144Hz gaming monitor. However, even if the refresh rate is a bottleneck, we can still appreciate the low latency or responsiveness of this real-time video.

Since the GS3-U3-23S6M-C and other PGR cameras take interchangeable, C-mount lenses, we should now educate ourselves about the big responsibility of buying a lens!

Shopping for glass

There is nothing quite like a well-crafted piece of glass that has survived many years and continued to sparkle because someone cared for it. On the mantle at home, my parents have a few keepsakes like this. One of them—a little, colorful glass flower—comes from a Parisian shopping mall where my brother and I ate many cheap but good meals during our first trip away from home and family. Other pieces go back earlier than I remember.

Some of the secondhand lenses that I use are 30 or 40 years old; their country of manufacture no longer exists; yet their glass and coatings are in perfect condition. I like to think that these lenses earned such good care by taking many fine pictures for previous owners and that they might still be taking fine pictures for somebody else 40 years from now.

Glass lasts. So do lens designs. For example, the Zeiss Planar T* lenses, one of the most respected names in the trade, are based on optical designs from the 1890s and coating processes from the 1930s. Lenses have gained electronic and motorized components to support autoexposure, autofocus, and image stabilization. However, the evolution of optics and coatings has been relatively slow. Mechanically, many old lenses are excellent.

> **Chromatic and spherical aberrations**
>
>
>
> An ideal lens causes all incoming rays of light to converge at one focal point. However, real lenses suffer from aberrations, such that the rays do not converge at precisely the same point. If different colors or wavelengths converge at different points, the lens suffers from **chromatic aberrations**, which are visible in the image as colorful haloes around high-contrast edges. If rays from the center and edge of the lens converge at different points, the lens suffers from **spherical aberrations**, which appear in the image as bright haloes around high-contrast edges in out-of-focus regions.
>
> Starting in the 1970s, new manufacturing techniques have allowed for better correction of chromatic and spherical aberrations in high-end lenses. Apochromatic or "APO" lenses use highly refractive materials (often, rare earth elements) to correct chromatic aberrations. Aspherical or "ASPH" lenses use complex curves to correct spherical aberrations. These corrected lenses tend to be more expensive, but you should keep an eye out for them as they may sometimes appear at bargain prices.
>
> Due to shallow depth of field, wide apertures produce the most visible aberrations. Even with non-APO and non-ASPH lenses, aberrations may be insignificant at most aperture settings, and in most scenes.

With a few bargain-hunting skills, we can find half a dozen good lenses from the 1960s to 1980s for the price of one good, new lens. Moreover, even recent lens models might sell at a 50 percent discount on the secondhand market. Before discussing specific examples of bargains, let's consider five steps we might follow when shopping for any secondhand lens:

1. Understand the requirements. As we discussed earlier in the *Capturing the subject in the moment* section, many parameters of the lens and camera interact to determine whether we can take a clear and timely picture. At minimum, we should consider the appropriate focal length, f-number or T-number, and nearest focusing distance for a given application and given camera. We should also attempt to gauge the importance of high resolution and low distortion to the given application. Wavelengths of light matter, too. For example, if a lens is optimized for visible light (as most are), it is not necessarily efficient at transmitting NIR.

2. Study the supply. If you live in a large city, perhaps local merchants have a good stock of used lenses at low prices. Otherwise, the lowest prices can typically be found on auction sites such as eBay. Search based on the requirements that we defined in step 1, such as "100 2.8 lens" if we are looking for a focal length of 100mm and an f-number or T-number of 2.8. Some of the lenses you find will not have the same type of mount as your camera. Check whether adapters are available. Adapting a lens is often an economical option, especially in the case of long lenses, which tend not to be mass-produced for cameras with a small sensor. Create a shortlist of the available lens models that seem to meet the requirements at an attractive price.

3. Study the lens models. Online, have users published detailed specifications, sample images, test data, comparisons, and opinions? MFlenses (`http://www.mflenses.com/`) is an excellent source of information on old, manual focus lenses. It offers numerous reviews and an active forum. Image and video hosting sites such as Flickr (`https://www.flickr.com/`) are also good places to search for reviews and sample output of old and unusual lenses, including cine (video) lenses, nightvision scopes, and more! Find out about variations in each lens model over the years of its manufacture. For example, early versions of a given lens might be single-coated, while newer versions would be multicoated for better transmittance, contrast, and durability.

4. Pick an item in good condition. The lens should have no fungus or haze. Preferably, it should have no scratches or cleaning marks (smudges in the coatings), though the effect on image quality might be small if the damage is to the front lens element (the element farthest from the camera).

A little dust inside the lens should not affect image quality. The aperture and focusing mechanism should move smoothly and, preferably, there should be no oil on the aperture blades.

5. Bid, make an offer, or buy at the seller's price. If you think the bidding or negotiation is reaching too high a price, save your money for another deal. Remember, despite what sellers might tell you, most bargain items are not rare and most bargain prices will occur again. Keep looking!

Some brands enjoy an enduring reputation for excellence. Between the 1860s and 1930s, German manufacturers such as Carl Zeiss, Leica, and Schneider Kreuznach solidified their fame as creators of premium optics. (Schneider Kreuznach is best known for cine lenses.) Other, venerable European brands include Alpa (of Switzerland) and Angéniuex (of France), which are both best known for cine lenses. By the 1950s, Nikon began to gain recognition as the first Japanese manufacturer to rival the quality of German lenses. Subsequently, Fuji and Canon became regarded as makers of high-end lenses for both cine and photo cameras.

Although Willy Loman (from Arthur Miller's play *Death of a Salesman*) might advise us to buy "a well-advertised machine", this is not necessarily the best bargain. Assuming we are buying lenses for their practical value and not their collectible value, we would be delighted if we found excellent quality in a mass-produced, no-name lens. Some lenses come reasonably close to this ideal.

East Germany and the Soviet Union mass-produced good lenses for photo cameras, cine cameras, projectors, microscopes, night vision scopes, and other devices. Optics were also important in major projects ranging from submarines to spacecraft! East German manufacturers included Carl Zeiss Jena, Meyer, and Pentacon. Soviet (later Russian, Ukrainian, and Belarusian) manufacturers included KMZ, BelOMO, KOMZ, Vologda, LOMO, Arsenal, and many others. Often, lens designs and manufacturing processes were copied and modified by multiple manufacturers in the Eastern Bloc, giving a recognizable character to lenses of this region and era.

Many lenses from the Eastern Bloc were no-name goods insofar as they did not bear a manufacturer's name. Some models, for export, were simply labeled "MADE IN USSR" or "aus JENA" (from Jena, East Germany). However, most Soviet lenses bear a symbol and serial number that encode the location and date of manufacture. For a catalogue of these markings and a description of their historical significance, see Nathan Dayton's article, "An Attempt to Clear the FOG", at `http://www.commiecameras.com/sov/`.

Some of the lesser-known Japanese brands tend to be bargains, too. For example, Pentax makes good lenses but it has never commanded quite the same premium as its competitors do. The company's older photo lenses come in an M42 mount, and these are especially plentiful at low prices. Also, search for the company's C-mount cine lenses, which were formerly branded Cosmicar.

Let's see how we can couple some bargain lenses with the GS3-U3-23S6M-C to produce fine images. Remember that the GS3-U3-23S6M-C has a C mount and a sensor whose format is 1/1.2". For C-mount and CS-mount cameras, the name of the sensor format does not refer to any actual dimension of the sensor! Rather, for historical reasons, the measurement such as 1/1.2" refers to the diameter that a vacuum tube would have if video cameras still used vacuum tubes! The following table lists the conversions between common sensors formats and the actual dimensions of the sensor:

Format Name	Typical Lens Mounts	Typical Uses	Diagonal (mm)	Width (mm)	Height (mm)	Aspect Ratio
1/4"	CS	Machine vision	4.0	3.2	2.4	4:3
1/3"	CS	Machine vision	6.0	4.8	3.6	4:3
1/2.5"	C	Machine vision	6.4	5.1	3.8	4:3
1/2"	C	Machine vision	8.0	6.4	4.8	4:3
1/1.8"	C	Machine vision	9.0	7.2	5.4	4:3
2/3"	C	Machine vision	11.0	8.8	6.6	4:3
16mm	C	Cine	12.7	10.3	7.5	4:3
1/1.2"	C	Machine vision	13.3	10.7	8.0	4:3
Super 16	C	Cine	14.6	12.5	7.4	5:3
1"	C	Machine vision	16.0	12.8	9.6	4:3
Four Thirds	Four Thirds Micro Four Thirds	Photography Cine	21.6	17.3	13.0	4:3
APS-C	Various proprietary such as Nikon F	Photography	27.3	22.7	15.1	3:2
35mm ("Full Frame")	M42 Various proprietary such as Nikon F	Photography Machine vision	43.3	36.0	24.0	3:2

For more information about typical sensor sizes in machine vision cameras, see the following article from Vision-Doctor.co.uk: `http://www.vision-doctor.co.uk/camera-technology-basics/sensor-and-pixel-sizes.html`.

A lens casts a circular image, which needs to have a large enough diameter to cover the diagonal of the sensor. Otherwise, the captured image will suffer from **vignetting**, meaning that the corners will be blurry and dark. For example, vignetting is obvious in the following image of a painting, *Snow Monkeys*, by Janet Howse. The image was captured using a 1/1.2" sensor, but the lens was designed for a 1/2" sensor, and therefore the image is blurry and dark, except for a circular region in the center:

A lens designed for one format can cover any format that is approximately the same size or smaller, without vignetting; however, we might need an adapter to mount the lens. The system's diagonal field of view, in degrees, depends on the sensor's diagonal size and the lens's focal length, according to the following formula:

```
diagonalFOVDegrees =
    2 * atan(0.5 * sensorDiagonal / focalLength) * 180/pi
```

For example, if a lens has the same focal length as the sensor's diagonal, the diagonal FOV is 53.1 degrees. Such a lens is called a **normal lens** (with respect to the given sensor format) and a FOV of 53.1 degrees is considered neither wide nor narrow.

Consulting the table above, we see that the 1/1.2" format is similar to the 16mm and Super 16 formats. Thus, the GS3-U3-23S6M-C (and similar cameras) should be able to use most C-mount cine lenses without vignetting, without an adapter, and with approximately the same FOV as the lens designers intended.

Suppose we want a narrow FOV to capture a subject at a distance. We might need a long focal length that is not commonly available in C-mount. Comparing diagonal sizes, note that the 35mm format is larger than the 1/1.2" format by a factor of 3.25. A normal lens for 35mm format becomes a long lens with a 17.5 degree FOV when mounted for 1/1.2" format! An M42 to C mount adapter might cost $30 and lets us use a huge selection of lenses!

Suppose we want to take close-up pictures of a subject but none of our lenses can focus close enough. This problem has a low-tech solution—an **extension tube**, which increases the distance between the lens and camera. For C-mount, a set of several extension tubes, of various lengths, might cost $30. When the lens's total extension (from tubes plus its built-in focusing mechanism) is equal to the focal length, the subject is projected onto the sensor at 1:1 magnification. For example, a 13.3mm subject would fill the 13.3mm diagonal of a 1/1.2" sensor. The following formula holds true:

```
magnificationRatio = totalExtension / focalLength
```

However, for a high magnification ratio, the subject must be very close to the front lens element in order to come into focus. Sometimes, the use of extension tubes creates an impractical optical system that cannot even focus as far as its front lens element! Other times, parts of the subject and lens housing (such as a built-in lens shade) might bump into each other. Some experimentation might be required in order to determine the practical limits of extending the lens.

The following table lists some of the lenses and lens accessories that I have recently purchased for use with the GS3-U3-23S6M-C:

Name	Price	Origin	Mount and Intended Format	Focal Length (mm)	FOV for 1/1.2" Sensor (degrees)	Max f-number or T-number
Cosmicar TV Lens 12.5mm 1:1.8	$41	Japan 1980s?	C Super 16	12.5	56.1	T/1.8

Name	Price	Origin	Mount and Intended Format	Focal Length (mm)	FOV for 1/1.2" Sensor (degrees)	Max f-number or T-number
Vega-73	$35	LZOS factory Lytkarino, USSR 1984	C Super 16	20.0	36.9	T/2.0
Jupiter-11A	$50	KOMZ factory Kazan, USSR 1975	M42 35mm	135.0	5.7	f/4.0
C-mount extension tubes: 10mm, 20mm, and 40mm	$30	Japan New	C	-	-	-
Fotodiox M42 to C adapter	$30	USA New	M42 to C	-	-	-

For comparison, consider the following table, which gives examples of new lenses that are specifically intended for the machine vision:

Name	Price	Origin	Mount and Intended Format	Focal Length (mm)	FOV for 1/1.2" Sensor (degrees)	Max f-number or T-number
Fujinon CF12.5HA-1	$268	Japan New	C 1"	12.5	56.1	T/1.4
Fujinon CF25HA-1	$270	Japan New	C 1"	25.0	29.9	T/1.4
Fujinon CF50HA-1	$325	Japan New	C 1"	50.0	15.2	T/1.8
Fujinon CF75HA-1	$320	Japan New	C 1"	75.0	10.2	T/1.4

Prices in the preceding table are from B&H (`http://www.bhphotovideo.com`), a major photo and video supplier in the United States. It offers a good selection of machine vision lenses, often at lower prices than listed by industrial suppliers.

These new, machine vision lenses are probably excellent. I have not tested them. However, let's look at a few sample shots from our selection of old, used, photo and cine lenses that are cheaper by a factor of six or more. All the images are captured at a resolution of 1920x1200 using FlyCapture2, but they are resized for inclusion in this book.

First, let's try the Cosmicar 12.5mm lens. For a wide-angle lens such as this, a scene with many straight lines can help us judge the amount of distortion. The following sample shot shows a reading room with many bookshelves:

To better see the detail, such as the text on books' spines, look at the following crop of 480x480 pixels (25 percent of the original width) from the center of the image:

The following image is a close-up of blood vessels in my eye, captured with the Vega-73 lens and a 10mm extension tube:

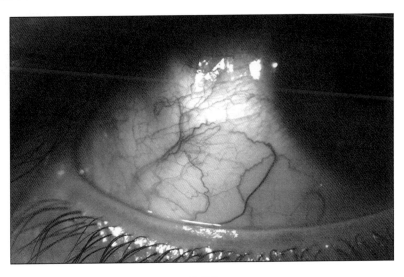

Again, the detail can be better appreciated in a 480x480 crop from the center, as shown here:

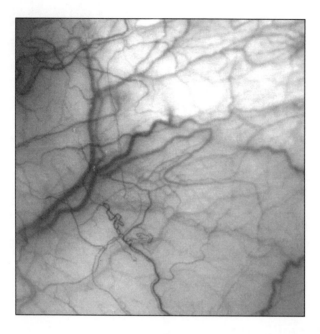

Finally, let's capture a distant subject with the Jupiter-11A. Here is the Moon on a clear night:

Once more, let's examine a 480x480 crop from the image's center in order to see the level of detail captured by the lens:

By now, our discussion of bargain lenses has spanned many decades and the distance from here to the Moon! I encourage you to explore even further on your own. What are the most interesting and capable optical systems that you can assemble within a given budget?

Summary

This chapter has been an opportunity to consider the inputs of a computer vision system at the hardware and software levels. Also, we have addressed the need to efficiently marshal image data from the input stage to the processing and output stages. Our specific accomplishments have included the following:

- Understanding differences among various wavelengths of light and radiation
- Understanding various properties of sensors, lenses, and images
- Capturing and recording slow-motion video with the PlayStation Eye camera and OpenCV's videoio module

- Comparing subjects' appearance in visible and NIR light using the ASUS Xtion PRO Live camera with OpenNI2 and OpenCV's highgui module
- Capturing and rendering HD video at high speed while detecting faces, using FlyCapture2, OpenCV, SDL2, and the GS3-U3-23S6M-C camera
- Shopping for cheap, old, used lenses that are surprisingly good!

Next, in *Chapter 2, Photographing Nature and Wildlife with an Automated Camera,* we will deepen our appreciation of high-quality images as we build a smart camera that captures and edits documentary footage of a natural environment!

2

Photographing Nature and Wildlife with an Automated Camera

National Geographic is famous for its intimate photos of wild animals. Often, in the magazine's pages, the animals seem larger than life, as if they belong to the same "geographic" scale as the landscapes behind them. This enlargement effect can be achieved by capturing the subject at a very close distance with a wide-angle lens. For example, one memorable photograph by Steve Winter shows a snarling tiger reaching out to strike the lens!

Let's consider the possible methods behind such a photo. The photographer could try to stalk a wild tiger in person, but for safety, this approach would require some distance and a long lens. A close encounter is likely to endanger the human, the tiger, or both. Alternatively, the photographer could use a remote-controlled rover or drone to approach and photograph the tiger. This would be safer but like the first technique it is laborious, only covers one site at a time, and may spoil opportunities for candid or natural photos because it attracts the animal's attention. Finally, the photographer could deploy concealed and automated cameras, called **camera traps**, in multiple locations that the tiger is likely to visit.

This chapter will explore techniques for programming a camera trap. Maybe we will not capture any tigers, but something will wander into our trap!

Despite the name, a camera trap does not physically "trap" anything. It just captures photos when a trigger is tripped. Different camera traps may use different triggers but in our case, the trigger will be a computer vision system that is sensitive to motion, color, or certain classes of objects. Our system's software components will include OpenCV 3, Python scripts, shell scripts, and a camera control tool called gPhoto2. While building our system, we will address the following questions:

- How can we configure and trigger a photo camera from a host computer?

- How can we detect the presence of a photogenic subject?

- How can we capture and process multiple photos of a subject to create an effective composite image or video?

 All the scripts and data for this chapter's project can be found in the book's GitHub repository at `https://github.com/OpenCVBlueprints/OpenCVBlueprints/tree/master/chapter_2/CameraTrap`.

This chapter will focus on techniques for Unix-like systems, including Linux and Mac. We assume that users will ultimately deploy our camera trap on low-cost, low-powered, single-board computers (SBCs), which will typically run Linux. A good example is the Raspberry Pi 2 hardware, which typically runs the Raspbian distribution of Linux.

Let's begin with an outline of a few simple tasks that our software will perform before, during, and after image capture.

Planning the camera trap

Our camera trap will use a computer with two attached cameras. One camera will continuously capture low-resolution images. For example, this first camera may be an ordinary webcam. Our software will analyze the low-resolution images to detect the presence of a subject. We will explore three basic detection techniques based on motion, color, and object classification. When a subject is detected, the second camera will activate to capture and save a finite series of high-resolution images. This second camera will be a dedicated photo camera, with its own battery and storage. We will not necessarily analyze and record images at the fastest possible rate; rather, we will take care to conserve the host computer's resources as well as the photo camera's battery power and storage so that our photo trap can function for a long time.

Optionally, our software will configure the photo camera for **exposure bracketing**. This means that some photos in a series will be deliberately underexposed while others will be overexposed. Later, we will upload photos from the camera to the host computer, and merge the exposures to produce **high dynamic range (HDR)** images. This means that the merged photo will exhibit fine details and saturated colors throughout a broader range of shadows, midtones, and highlights than any one exposure could capture. For example, the following lineup illustrates underexposure (left), overexposure (right), and a merged HDR photo (center):

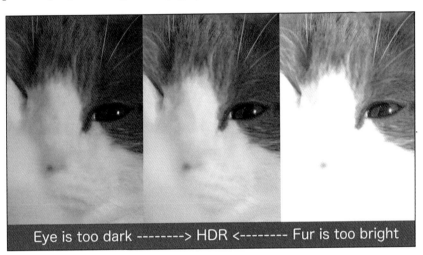

Eye is too dark --------> HDR <-------- Fur is too bright

HDR imaging is especially important in landscape photography. Typically, the sky is much brighter than the land, yet we want to tame this contrast in order to obtain saturated midtone colors in both these regions, rather than white, featureless sky or black, featureless land. We will also explore techniques for turning a series of images into a time-lapse video.

Note that the two cameras in this project fulfill different requirements. The webcam provides a stream of images for real-time processing, and the photo camera stores images for high-quality processing later. Consider the following comparison table:

Feature	Typical webcam	Typical photo camera	High-end industrial camera
Price	Low	Medium	High
Power consumption	Low	High (but has its own battery)	Medium
Configuration options	Few	Many	Many

Feature	Typical webcam	Typical photo camera	High-end industrial camera
Latency	Low	High	Low
Resolution	Low	Very high	High
Ruggedness	Poor	Good	Fair

Potentially, a high-end industrial camera could serve both purposes—real-time imaging and high-quality imaging. However, the combination of a webcam and a photo camera is likely to be cheaper. Consider the following examples:

Name	Purpose	Sensor Format	Highest Res Mode	Interface	Price
Point Grey Research Grasshopper 3 GS3-U3-120S6M-C	Industrial camera	1"	4242x2830 @ 7 FPS	USB 3.0	$3,700 (new)
Carl Zeiss Jena DDR Tevidon 10mm f/2 lens	Lens for industrial camera	Covers 1"	Sharp, suitable for high res		$300 (used)
Nikon 1 J5 with 10-30mm PD-ZOOM lens	Photo camera and lens	1"	5568x3712 @ 20 FPS	USB 2.0	$500 (new)
Odroid USB-Cam 720p	Webcam	1/4"	1280x720 @ 30 FPS	USB 2.0	$20 (new)

Here, the industrial camera and lens cost eight times as much as the photo camera, lens, and webcam, yet the photo camera should offer the best image quality. Although the photo camera has a *capture mode* of 5568x3712 @ 20 FPS, note that its USB 2.0 interface is much too slow to support this as a *transfer mode*. At the listed resolution and rate, the photo camera can just record the images to its local storage.

For our purposes, a photo camera's main weakness is its high latency. The latency pertains to not only the electronics, but also the moving mechanical parts. To mitigate the problem, we can take the following steps:

- Use a webcam with a slightly wider angle of view than the photo camera. This way, the camera trap may detect the subject early, and provide the photo camera with more lead time to take the first shot.

- Put the photo camera in the manual focus mode, and set the focus to the distance where you plan to photograph a subject. Manual focus is quicker and quieter because the autofocus motor does not run.

- If you are using a **digital single-lens reflex (DSLR)** camera, put it in **mirror lock-up (MLU)** mode (if it supports MLU). Without MLU, the reflex mirror (which deflects light into the optical viewfinder) must move out of the optical path before each shot. With MLU, the mirror is already out of the way (but the optical viewfinder is disabled). MLU is quicker, quieter, and has less vibration because the mirror does not move. On some cameras, MLU is called **live view** because the digital ("live") viewfinder may be activated when the optical viewfinder is disabled.

Controlling a photo camera is a big part of this project. Once you learn to write scripts of photographic commands, perhaps you will begin to think about photography in new ways—for it is a process, not just a final moment when the shutter falls. Let's turn our attention to this scripting topic now.

Controlling a photo camera with gPhoto2

gPhoto2 is an open source, vendor-neutral camera control tool for Unix-like systems, such as Linux and Mac. It supports photo cameras of multiple brands, including Canon, Nikon, Olympus, Pentax, Sony, and Fuji. The supported features vary by model. The following table lists gPhoto2's major features, alongside the official count of supported cameras for each feature:

Feature	Number of Supported Devices	Description
File transfer	2105	files to and from the device
Image capture	489	Make the device capture an image to its local storage
Configuration	428	Change the device's settings, such as shutter speed
Liveview	309	Continuously grab frames of live video from the device

These numbers are current as of version 2.5.8, and are conservative. For example, some configuration features are supported on the Nikon D80, even though the gPhoto2 documentation does not list this camera as configurable. For our purposes, image capture and configuration are required features, so gPhoto2 adequately supports at least 428 cameras, and perhaps many more. This number includes all manner of cameras, from point-and-shoot compacts to professional DSLRs.

To check whether the latest version of gPhoto2 officially supports a feature on a specific camera, see the official list at http://www.gphoto.org/proj/libgphoto2/support.php.

Typically, gPhoto2 communicates with a camera via USB using a protocol called **Picture Transfer Protocol (PTP)**. Before proceeding, check whether your camera has any instructions regarding PTP mode. You might need to change a setting on the camera to ensure that the host computer will see it as a PTP device and not a USB mass storage device. For example, on many Nikon cameras, it is necessary to select **SETUP MENU | USB | PTP**, as seen in the following image:

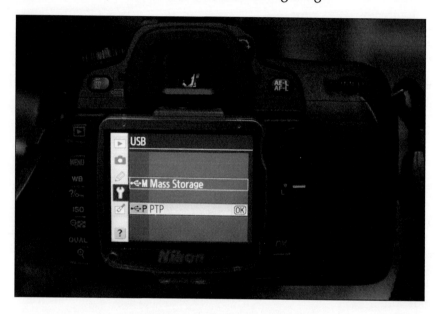

Moreover, if a camera is mounted as a disk drive, gPhoto2 cannot communicate with it. This is slightly problematic because most operating systems automatically mount a camera as a disk drive, regardless of whether the camera is in the PTP mode. Thus, before we proceed to install and use gPhoto2, let's look at ways to programmatically unmount a camera drive.

Writing a shell script to unmount camera drives

On Mac, a process called PTPCamera is responsible for mounting and controlling cameras on behalf of applications such as iPhoto. After connecting a camera, we can kill PTPCamera by running the following command in Terminal:

```
$ killall PTPCamera
```

Then, the camera will be available to receive commands from gPhoto2. However, keep reading because we want to write code that will support Linux too!

On most desktop Linux systems, when the camera is connected, it will be mounted as a **Gnome Virtual File System** (**GVFS**) volume. We can list the mounted GVFS volumes by running the following command in Terminal:

```
$ gvfs-mount -l
```

For example, this command produces the following output in Ubuntu, on a MacBook Pro laptop with a Nikon D80 camera attached via USB:

```
Drive(0): APPLE SSD SM1024F
  Type: GProxyDrive (GProxyVolumeMonitorUDisks2)
  Volume(0): Recovery HD
    Type: GProxyVolume (GProxyVolumeMonitorUDisks2)
  Volume(1): Macintosh HD
    Type: GProxyVolume (GProxyVolumeMonitorUDisks2)
Drive(1): APPLE SD Card Reader
  Type: GProxyDrive (GProxyVolumeMonitorUDisks2)
Volume(0): NIKON DSC D80
  Type: GProxyVolume (GProxyVolumeMonitorGPhoto2)
  Mount(0): NIKON DSC D80 -> gphoto2://[usb:001,007]/
    Type: GProxyShadowMount (GProxyVolumeMonitorGPhoto2)
Mount(1): NIKON DSC D80 -> gphoto2://[usb:001,007]/
  Type: GDaemonMount
```

Note that the output includes the camera's mount point, in this case, gphoto2://[usb:001,007]/. For a camera drive, the GVFS mount point will always start with gphoto2://. We can unmount the camera drive by running a command such as the following:

```
$ gvfs-mount -u gphoto2://[usb:001,007]/
```

Now, if we run `gvfs-mount -l` again, we should see that the camera is no longer listed. Thus, it is unmounted and should be available to receive commands from gPhoto2.

 Alternatively, a file browser such as Nautilus will show mounted camera drives, and will provide GUI controls to unmount them. However, as programmers, we prefer shell commands because they are easier to automate.

We will need to unmount the camera every time it is plugged in. To simplify this, let's write a Bash shell script that supports multiple operating systems (Mac or any Linux system with GVFS) and multiple cameras. Create a file named `unmount_cameras.sh` and fill it with the following Bash code:

```
#!/usr/bin/env bash

if [ "$(uname)" == "Darwin" ]; then
  killall PTPCamera
else
  mounted_cameras=`gvfs-mount -l | grep -Po 'gphoto2://.*/' | uniq`
  for mounted_camera in $mounted_cameras; do
    gvfs-mount -u $mounted_camera
  done
fi
```

Note that this script checks the operating system's family (where `"Darwin"` is the family of Mac). On Mac, it runs `killall PTPCamera`. On other systems, it uses a combination of the `gvfs-mount`, `grep`, and `uniq` commands to find each unique `gphoto2://` mount point and then unmount all the cameras.

Let's give the script "executable" permissions by running the following command:

```
$ chmod +x unmount_cameras.sh
```

Anytime we want to ensure that the camera drives are unmounted, we can execute the script like this:

```
$ ./unmount_cameras.sh
```

Now, we have a standard way to make a camera available, so we are ready to install and use gPhoto2.

Setting up and testing gPhoto2

gPhoto2 and related libraries are widely available in open source software repositories for Unix-like systems. No wonder—connecting to a photo camera is a common task in desktop computing today!

For Mac, Apple does not provide a package manager but third parties do. The MacPorts package manager has the most extensive repository.

 To set up MacPorts and its dependencies, follow the official guide at `https://www.macports.org/install.php`.

To install gPhoto2 via MacPorts, run the following command in Terminal:

```
$ sudo port install gphoto2
```

On Debian and its derivatives, including Ubuntu, Linux Mint, and Raspbian, we can install gPhoto2 by running the following command:

```
$ sudo apt-get install gphoto2
```

On Fedora and its derivatives, including Red Hat Enterprise Linux (RHEL) and CentOS, we can use the following installation command:

```
$ sudo yum install gphoto2
```

OpenSUSE has a one-click installer for gPhoto2 at `https://software.opensuse.org/package/gphoto.`

After installing gPhoto2, let's connect a camera. Ensure that the camera is turned on and in PTP mode. Then, run the following commands to unmount the camera drive and take a photo:

```
$ ./unmount_cameras.sh
$ gphoto2 --capture-image
```

If the camera is in autofocus mode, you might see or hear the lens move. (Ensure that the camera has a subject in view so that autofocus will succeed. Otherwise, no photo will be captured.) Then, you might hear the shutter open and close. Disconnect the camera and use its review menu to browse the captured photos. If a new photo is there, gPhoto2 is working!

To upload all images from the camera to the current working directory, we could reconnect the camera and run the following commands:

```
$ ./unmount_cameras.sh
$ gphoto2 --get-all-files
```

To read about all the flags that gphoto2 supports, we can open its manual by running the following command:

```
$ man gphoto2
```

Next, let's try a more advanced task, involving configuration as well as image capture. We will take a series of photos with exposure bracketing.

Writing a shell script for exposure bracketing

gPhoto2 provides a flag, `--set-config`, which allows us to reconfigure many camera parameters, including **exposure compensation**. For example, suppose we want to overexpose an image by the equivalent of one full f-stop (doubling the aperture's area or increasing its radius by a factor of sqrt(2)). This bias is called an exposure compensation (or exposure adjustment) of +1.0 **exposure value (EV)**. The following command configures the camera to use +1.0 EV and then takes a photo:

```
$ gphoto2 --set-config exposurecompensation=1000 --capture-image
```

Note that the value of `exposurecompensation` is denominated in thousandths of an EV, so `1000` is +1.0 EV. To underexpose, we would use a negative value. A series of these commands, each with a different EV, would achieve exposure bracketing.

We can use the `--set-config` flag to control many photographic properties, not just exposure compensation. For example, the following command captures a photo with an exposure time of one second, while firing the flash in slow sync mode:

```
$ gphoto2 --set-config shutterspeed=1s flashmode=2 --capture-image
```

The following command lists all the supported properties and values for the given camera:

```
$ gphoto2 --list-all-config
```

 For further discussion of f-stops, exposure, and other photographic properties, refer back to *Chapter 1*, *Getting the Most out of Your Camera System*, especially the *Capturing the subject in the moment* section.

Before taking a series of exposure bracketed photos, dial your camera to the **aperture priority (A)** mode. This means that the aperture will be held constant while the shutter speed will vary based on lighting and EV. A constant aperture will help ensure that the same region is in focus in all images.

Let's automate the exposure bracketing commands with another shell script, which we will call `capture_exposure_bracket.sh`. It will accept a flag, `-s`, to specify the exposure step size between frames (in thousandths of an EV), and another flag `-f`, to specify the number of frames. The defaults will be 3 frames spaced at an interval of 1.0 EV. Here is the script's implementation:

```bash
#!/usr/bin/env bash

ev_step=1000
frames=3
while getopts s:f: flag; do
  case $flag in
    s)
       ev_step="$OPTARG"

       ;;
    f)
       frames="$OPTARG"

       ;;
    ?)
       exit

       ;;
  esac
done

min_ev=$((-ev_step * (frames - 1) / 2))
for ((i=0; i<frames; i++)); do
  ev=$((min_ev + i * ev_step))
  gphoto2 --set-config exposurecompensation=$ev \
    --capture-image
done
gphoto2 --set-config exposurecompensation=0
```

All the commands in this script are cross-platform for Linux and Mac. Note that we are using the `getopts` command to parse arguments, and Bash arithmetic to compute the EV of each photo.

Remember to give the script "executable" permissions by running the following command:

```
$ chmod +x capture_exposure_bracket.sh
```

To unmount the camera and capture 5 photos at an interval of 1.5 EV, we could run the following commands:

```
$ ./unmount_cameras.sh
$ ./capture_exposure_bracket.sh -s 1500 -f 5
```

Now that we have a clear idea of how to control a camera from the command line, let's consider how to wrap this functionality in a general-purpose programming language that can also interface with OpenCV.

Writing a Python script to wrap gPhoto2

Python is a high-level, dynamic programming language with great third-party libraries for mathematics and science. OpenCV's Python bindings are efficient and quite mature, wrapping all the C++ library's major functionality except GPU optimizations. Python is also a convenient scripting language, as its standard libraries provide cross-platform interfaces to access much of the system's functionality. For example, it is easy to write Python code to spawn a subprocess (also called a child process), which may run any executable, even another interpreter such as a Bash shell.

 For more information on spawning and communicating with a child process from Python, see the `subprocess` module's documentation at `https://docs.python.org/2/library/subprocess.html`. For the special case where the child process is an additional Python interpreter, see the documentation of the `multiprocessing` module at `https://docs.python.org/2/library/multiprocessing.html`.

We will use Python's standard subprocessing functionality to wrap gPhoto2 and our own shell scripts. By sending camera commands from a child process, we will enable the caller (in Python) to treat these as "fire and forget" commands. That is to say, functions in the Python process return immediately so that the caller is not obliged to wait for the camera to handle the commands. This is a good thing because a camera might typically require several seconds to autofocus and capture a series of photos.

Let's create a new file, `CameraCommander.py`, and begin its implementation with the following import statements:

```
import os
import subprocess
```

We will write a class, `CameraCommander`. As member variables, it will have a current capture process (which may be `None`) and a log file. By default, the log file will be `/dev/null`, which means that the log output will be discarded. After setting member variables, the initialization method will call a helper method to unmount the camera drive so that the camera is ready to receive commands. Here are the class's declaration and initializer:

```python
class CameraCommander(object):

    def __init__(self, logPath=os.devnull):
        self._logFile = open(logPath, 'w')
        self._capProc = None
        self.unmount_cameras()
```

When an instance of `CameraCommander` is deleted, it should close the log file, as seen in the following code:

```python
    def __del__(self):
        self._logFile.close()
```

Every time `CameraCommander` opens a subprocess, the command should be interpreted by the shell (Bash), and the command's print output and errors should be redirected to the log file. Let's standardize this configuration of a subprocess in the following helper method:

```python
    def _open_proc(self, command):
        return subprocess.Popen(
            command, shell=True, stdout=self._logFile,
            stderr=self._logFile)
```

Now, as our first wrapper around a shell command, let's write a method to run `unmount_cameras.sh` in a subprocess. Unmounting the camera drives is a short process, and it must finish before other camera commands can run. Thus, we will implement our wrapper method so that it does not return until `unmount_cameras.sh` returns. That is to say, the subprocess will run synchronously in this case. Here is the wrapper's implementation:

```python
    def unmount_cameras(self):
        proc = self._open_proc('./unmount_cameras.sh')
        proc.wait()
```

Next, let's consider how to capture a single image. We will start by calling a helper method to stop any previous, conflicting command. Then, we will invoke the gphoto2 command with the usual --capture-image flag. Here is the implementation of the wrapper method:

```
def capture_image(self):
  self.stop_capture()
  self._capProc = self._open_proc(
    'gphoto2 --capture-image')
```

As another capture mode, we can invoke gphoto2 to record a time-lapse series. The -I or --interval flag, with an integer value, specifies the delay between frames, in seconds. The -F or --frames flag also takes an integer value, specifying the number of frames in the series. If the -I flag is used but -F is omitted, the process continues to capture frames indefinitely until forced to terminate. Let's provide the following wrapper for time-lapse functionality:

```
def capture_time_lapse(self, interval, frames=0):
  self.stop_capture()
  if frames <= 0:
    # Capture an indefinite number of images.
    command = 'gphoto2 --capture-image -I %d' % interval
  else:
    command = 'gphoto2 --capture-image -I %d -F %d' %\
      (interval, frames)
  self._capProc = self._open_proc(command)
```

Before taking a series of time-lapse photos, you might want to dial your camera to the **manual exposure (M)** mode. This means that the aperture and shutter speed will be held constant at manually specified values. Assuming that the scene's light level is approximately constant, a constant exposure will help prevent unpleasant flickering in the time-lapse video. On the other hand, if we do expect lighting conditions to vary a lot over the course of the time-lapse series, the M mode may be inappropriate because in these circumstances, it will cause some frames to be noticeably underexposed and others overexposed.

To allow for exposure bracketing, we can simply wrap our capture_exposure_bracket.sh script, as seen in the following code:

```
def capture_exposure_bracket(self, ev_step=1.0, frames=3):
  self.stop_capture()
  self._capProc = self._open_proc(
```

```
'./capture_exposure_bracket.sh -s %d -f %d' %\
   (int(ev_step * 1000), frames))
```

As we have seen in the previous three methods, it is sensible to terminate any ongoing capture process before trying to start another. (After all, a camera can only process one command at a time). Moreover, a caller might have other reasons to terminate a capture process. For example, the subject might have gone away. We will provide the following method to force the termination of any ongoing capture process:

```python
def stop_capture(self):
    if self._capProc is not None:
        if self._capProc.poll() is None:
            # The process is currently running but might finish
            # before the next function call.
            try:
                self._capProc.terminate()
            except:
                # The process already finished.
                pass
        self._capProc = None
```

Similarly, we will provide the following method to await the completion of any currently running capture process:

```python
def wait_capture(self):
    if self._capProc is not None:
        self._capProc.wait()
        self._capProc = None
```

Finally, we will provide the following property getter to enable a caller to check whether a capture process is currently running:

```python
@property
def capturing(self):
    if self._capProc is None:
        return False
    elif self._capProc.poll() is None:
        return True
    else:
        self._capProc = None
        return False
```

This concludes the `CameraCommander` module. To test our work, let's write another script, `test_camera_commands.py`, with the following implementation:

```python
#!/usr/bin/env python

import CameraCommander

def main():

    cc = CameraCommander.CameraCommander('test_camera_commands.log')

    cc.capture_image()
    print('Capturing image...')
    cc.wait_capture()
    print('Done')

    cc.capture_time_lapse(3, 2)
    print('Capturing 2 images at time interval of 3 seconds...')
    cc.wait_capture()
    print('Done')

    cc.capture_exposure_bracket(1.0, 3)
    print('Capturing 3 images at exposure interval of 1.0 EV...')
    cc.wait_capture()
    print('Done')

if __name__ == '__main__':
    main()
```

Ensure that your camera is on, is in the PTP mode, and is connected. Then, make the test script executable and run it, like this:

```
$ chmod +x test_camera_commands.py
$ ./test_camera_commands.py
```

Wait for all the commands to finish, and then disconnect the camera to review the images. Check the timestamp and EV number of each photo. Ideally, a total of six photos should have been captured. However, the actual number could vary depending on factors such as the success or failure of autofocus, and the time spent capturing and saving each image. In case of any doubts, review the log file, `test_camera_commands.log`, in a text editor.

Finding libgphoto2 and wrappers

As an alternative to using the gPhoto2 command line tool, we could use the underlying C library, libgphoto2 (https://github.com/gphoto/libgphoto2). The library has several third-party wrappers, including a set of up-to-date Python bindings called python-gphoto2 (https://github.com/gphoto/libgphoto2-python).

OpenCV 3's videoio module has optional support for libgphoto2. To enable this feature, we could configure and build OpenCV from source using the `WITH_GPHOTO2` CMake definition. Of course, for this option to work, the system must already have an installation of libgphoto2 and its header files. For example, these can be installed by the following command on Debian, Ubuntu, Linux Mint, Raspbian, and similar systems:

```
$ sudo apt-get install libgphoto2-dev
```

For our purposes, controlling the photo camera via libgphoto2 or OpenCV's videoio module is overkill. We do not want to grab frames for real-time processing. We simply want our Python scripts to initiate additional processes to unmount and configure the camera, and make it capture photos to its local storage. The gPhoto2 command-line tool and our own shell scripts are perfectly convenient to use as subprocesses, so we will continue to rely on them throughout the rest of this chapter.

 One of OpenCV's official samples demonstrates the use of a gPhoto2-compatible camera via the videoio module. Specifically, the sample deals with focus control. See the source code in OpenCV's GitHub repository at https://github.com/Itseez/opencv/blob/master/samples/cpp/autofocus.cpp.

Detecting the presence of a photogenic subject

Chapter 1, Getting the Most out of Your Camera System, proposed that a photograph ought to capture a subject in a moment. Let's explore this notion further as we search for ways to detect a desirable or "photogenic" subject and moment.

As a medium, photography uses light, an aperture, a photosensitive surface, and time to draw an image of a scene. The earliest photographic technology, in the 1820s, lacked the resolution and speed to convey a detailed subject in a precise moment, but it was able to capture a grainy scene on a sunny day. Later, with better lenses, flashes, and photosensitive surfaces, photography became capable of capturing a sharp scene, a formal portrait, a faster and more natural portrait, and finally a moment of action, frozen in time.

Consider the following series of famous photographs, ranging from 1826 to 1942:

For general interest, here are some details about the preceding photographs:

- Upper left: *View from the Window at Le Gras* is history's earliest surviving photograph, taken by Nicéphore Niépce in 1826 or 1827 at Saint-Loup-de-Varennes, France. The scene includes parts of the rooftops and countryside at Niépce's estate.

- Middle left: *Boulevard du Temple,* taken by Louis Daguerre in 1838, is believed to be the first photograph to include people. The scene is a busy street in Paris, but most of the passersby are invisible because of the photograph's slow speed. Near the street corner, one man is polishing another man's boots, so these two people were in one place long enough to be recorded.

- Upper right: Jean-Baptiste Sabatier-Blot captured this formal portrait of Louis Daguerre in 1844.

- Lower left: Sergei Prokudin-Gorsky, a pioneer of color photography, captured this relatively informal portrait of factory workers in Kasli, Russia, in 1910. The men in the photograph are creating casts at the Kasli Iron Works, which produced sculptures and luxury furniture in the 19th and early 20th centuries.

- Lower right: Max Alpert took this combat photograph on July 12, 1942, near Luhansk (today in Ukraine). The subject is Aleksey Gordeyevich Yeremenko, a 23-year-old junior political officer in the Red Army. At the moment of the photograph, Yeremenko is rallying his regiment to attack. A few seconds later, he was shot dead.

Even from these few examples, we can infer a historical trend toward more dynamic images, which capture an atmosphere of activity, change, or even violence. Let's contemplate this trend in the context of nature and wildlife photography. Color photography began to reach the public eye around 1907, and after several more decades of technological improvements, it prevailed as a more popular format than black and white. Color is dynamic. Landscapes, plants, and even animals change color depending on the season, weather, time of day, and their age. Today, it would seem strange to see a nature documentary shot in black and white.

Changes in lens technology have also had a profound influence on nature and wildlife photography. With longer, faster, and sharper lenses, photographers have been able to peer into the lives of wild animals from a distance. For example, today, documentaries are filled with scenes of predatory animals chasing their prey. To shoot these scenes would have been difficult, or impossible, with lenses of the 1920s. Similarly, the quality of macro (close-up) lenses has improved a lot, and has been a boon to documentary work on insects and other small creatures.

Finally, as we discussed in the opening of this chapter, advances in automation have enabled photographers to deploy cameras in remote wilderness, in the midst of the action. With digital technology, a remote camera can store a huge number of photos, and these photos can be combined easily to produce effects, such as time-lapse (which accentuates motion) or HDR (which accentuates color). Today, these techniques are in widespread use, so documentary fans may be familiar with the sight of time-lapse flowers rocketing up from the ground, or time-lapse clouds racing across saturated HDR skies. Whether small or large, everything is portrayed as dynamic.

We can design a few simple rules to help distinguish between a dynamic scene and a static scene. Here are some useful cues:

- **Motion**: We may assume that any movement in a scene represents a chance to capture a subject in a moment of action or change. Without needing to know what the subject is, we can detect its motion and capture a photograph.

- **Color**: We may assume that certain color patterns are unusual in a given environment, and that they arise in a dynamic situation. Without needing to know exactly what the colorful subject is, we can detect its presence and photograph it. For example, a big new splash of color could be a sunset as the clouds part, or a flower as it opens.

- **Classification**: We may assume that certain kinds of subjects are alive and will interact with their environment, creating opportunities for dynamic photos. When we detect a given class of subject, we can respond by photographing it. As an example, we will detect and photograph the faces of mammals.

Regardless of the approach to detecting a subject, we must ensure that our webcam and photo camera have a similar view of the scene. They should point at the same target. The webcam's angle of view should be as wide as the photo camera's, and perhaps a little wider to allow the webcam to detect a subject just before it enters the photo camera's view. Both cameras should be fixed firmly in place so that they do not become misaligned due to vibrations, wind, or other typical disturbances. For example, the photo camera could be mounted on a sturdy tripod, and the webcam could be taped to the photo camera's hotshoe (the slot that is typically reserved for an external flash or external viewfinder). The following image shows an example of this setup:

For context, the following image is a slightly more distant view of the same setup. Observe that the webcam and photo camera point at the same subject:

We will implement each type of camera trap as a separate script, which will accept command-line arguments to adjust the trap's sensitivity. To begin, let's develop a motion-sensitive trap.

Detecting a moving subject

Our motion-activated camera trap will rely on the `CameraCommander` module that we implemented earlier, in the section *Writing a Python script to wrap gPhoto2*. Also, we will use OpenCV and NumPy to capture and analyze webcam images. Finally, from Python's standard library, we will import the `argparse` module, which will help parse command-line arguments, and the `time` module, which we will use to control the time delay between detection attempts. Let's create a file, `set_motion_trap.py`, and begin its implementation with the following imports:

```
#!/usr/bin/env python

import argparse
import time

import numpy
import cv2

import CameraCommander
```

This script will have a simple structure, with just a `main()` function that reads command-line arguments and performs motion detection in a loop. Several arguments pertain to the use of the webcam, which we will call the detection camera. Other arguments concern the motion detection algorithm and the use of the photo camera. The `main()` function begins with the following definitions of the command-line arguments:

```
def main():

    parser = argparse.ArgumentParser(
        description='This script detects motion using an '
                    'attached webcam. When it detects '
                    'motion, it captures photos on an '
                    'attached gPhoto2-compatible photo '
                    'camera.')

    parser.add_argument(
        '--debug', type=bool, default=False,
```

```
    help='print debugging information')

parser.add_argument(
    '--cam-index', type=int, default=-1,
    help='device index for detection camera '
        '(default=0)')
parser.add_argument(
    '--width', type=int, default=320,
    help='capture width for detection camera '
        '(default=320)')
parser.add_argument(
    '--height', type=int, default=240,
    help='capture height for detection camera '
        '(default=240)')
parser.add_argument(
    '--detection-interval', type=float, default=0.25,
    help='interval between detection frames, in seconds '
        '(default=0.25)')

parser.add_argument(
    '--learning-rate', type=float, default=0.008,
    help='learning rate for background subtractor, which '
        'is used in motion detection (default=0.008)')
parser.add_argument(
    '--min-motion', type=float, default=0.15,
    help='proportion of frame that must be classified as '
        'foreground to trigger motion event '
        '(default=0.15, valid_range=[0.0, 1.0])')

parser.add_argument(
    '--photo-count', type=int, default=1,
    help='number of photo frames per motion event '
        '(default=1)')
parser.add_argument(
    '--photo-interval', type=float, default=3.0,
    help='interval between photo frames, in seconds '
        '(default=3.0)')
parser.add_argument(
    '--photo-ev-step', type=float, default=None,
    help='exposure step between photo frames, in EV. If '
        'this is specified, --photo-interval is ignored '
        'and --photo-count refers to the length of an '
```

```
'exposure bracketing sequence, not a time-lapse '
'sequence.')
```

 The arguments' `help` text will appear when we run our script with the -h or --help flag, like this:

```
$ ./set_motion_trap.py -h
```

At this point, we have only declared the arguments. Next, we need to parse them and access their values, as shown in the following code:

```
args = parser.parse_args()

debug = args.debug

cam_index = args.cam_index
w, h = args.width, args.height
detection_interval = args.detection_interval

learning_rate = args.learning_rate
min_motion = args.min_motion

photo_count = args.photo_count
photo_interval = args.photo_interval
photo_ev_step = args.photo_ev_step
```

Besides the arguments, we will use several variables. A `VideoCapture` object will enable us to configure and capture from the webcam. Matrices (which are actually NumPy arrays in OpenCV's Python wrapper) will enable us to store BGR and grayscale versions of each webcam frame as well as a **foreground mask**. The foreground mask will be output from a motion detection algorithm, and it will be a grayscale image that is white in foreground (moving) areas, gray in shadow areas, and black in background areas. Specifically, in our case, the motion detector will be an instance of OpenCV's `BackgroundSubtractorMOG2` class. Last, we need an instance of our `CameraCommander` class to control the photo camera. Here are the declarations of the relevant variables:

```
cap = cv2.VideoCapture(cam_index)
cap.set(cv2.CAP_PROP_FRAME_WIDTH, w)
cap.set(cv2.CAP_PROP_FRAME_HEIGHT, h)

bgr = None
```

```
gray = None
fg_mask = None

bg_sub = cv2.createBackgroundSubtractorMOG2()

cc = CameraCommander.CameraCommander()
```

The remainder of the `main()` function's implementation is a loop. On each iteration, we will put the thread to sleep for a specified interval (by default, 0.25 seconds) because this will conserve system resources. As a result, we will skip some of the webcam's frames, but we probably do not need the full frame rate to detect the subject. If we did not impose a sleep period, the camera trap could utilize 100% of a CPU core all the time, particularly on a slow CPU in a low-powered SBC. Here is this first part of the loop's implementation:

```
while True:
    time.sleep(detection_interval)
```

When we do read a frame, we will convert it to grayscale and equalize it:

```
success, bgr = cap.read(bgr)
if success:
    gray = cv2.cvtColor(bgr, cv2.COLOR_BGR2GRAY, gray)
    gray = cv2.equalizeHist(gray, gray)
```

We will pass the equalized frame and the foreground mask to the `BackgroundSubtractorMOG2`'s `apply` method. This method accumulates a history of frames, and estimates whether each pixel is part of a foreground region, shadow, or background region based on differences between frames in the history. As a third argument, we will pass a **learning rate**, which is a value in the range [0.0, 1.0]. A low value means that more weight will be given to old frames, and thus the estimates will change slowly. See how we call the method in this line of code:

```
fg_mask = bg_sub.apply(gray, fg_mask, learning_rate)
```

> Note that in background subtraction algorithms such as MOG2, the foreground is defined as a region whose pixel values have changed in recent history. Conversely, the background is a region whose pixel values have not changed. The shadow refers to the foreground's shadow. For details about MOG2 and the other background subtraction algorithms supported in OpenCV, see the official documentation at http://docs.opencv.org/3.0-beta/modules/video/doc/motion_analysis_and_object_tracking.html#backgroundsubtractormog2.

As an example of the background subtractor's input and output, consider the following pair of images. The top image is an RGB frame from a video, while the bottom image is a foreground mask based on the video. Note that the scene is a rocky seacoast with waves breaking in the foreground and boats going past in the distance:

By counting the white (foreground) values in the foreground mask, we can get a rough measurement of the amount of movement that the webcam has captured in recent history. We should normalize this figure based on the number of pixels in the frame. Here is the relevant code:

```
h, w = fg_mask.shape
motion = numpy.sum(numpy.where(fg_mask == 255, 1, 0))
motion /= float(h * w)
```

If the script is running with the --debug flag, we will print the measurement of motion:

```
if debug:
  print('motion=%f' % motion)
```

If the motion exceeds a specified threshold, and if we are not already capturing photos, we will start to capture photos now. Depending on the command-line arguments, we may capture either an exposure-bracketed series or a time-lapse series, as seen in the next block of code:

```
if motion >= min_motion and not cc.capturing:
    if photo_ev_step is not None:
        cc.capture_exposure_bracket(photo_ev_step, photo_count)
    else:
        cc.capture_time_lapse(photo_interval, photo_count)
```

Here, the loop and the `main()` function end. To ensure that `main()` runs when the script is executed, we must add the following code to the script:

```
if __name__ == '__main__':
    main()
```

We can give this Python script "executable" permissions and then run it like any other shell script, as seen in following example:

```
$ chmod +x set_motion_trap.py
$ ./set_motion_trap.py --debug True
```

Consider the pair of images below. The left-hand image shows the physical setup of the motion-activated camera trap, which happens to be running `set_motion_trap.py` with default parameters. The right-hand image is one of the resulting photos:

These images were taken with two different cameras, and for this reason they differ in color and contrast. However, they represent the same scene.

Experiment with the optional arguments to see which settings work best for a given camera and a particular kind of moving subject. Once you have gained an understanding of this camera trap's sensitivities, let's proceed to another design, using a set of color values as the trigger.

Detecting a colorful subject

OpenCV provides a set of functions to measure and compare the color distribution in images. This field is called histogram analysis. A histogram is just an array of pixel counts for various colors or ranges of colors. Thus, for a BGR image with 256 possible values per channel, a histogram can have as many as 256 ^ 3 = 16.8 million elements. To create such a histogram, we can use the following code:

```
images = [myImage]  # One or more input images
channels = [0, 1, 2]  # The channel indices
mask = None  # The image region, or None for everything
histSize = [256, 256, 256]  # The channel depths
ranges = [0, 255, 0, 255, 0, 255]  # The color bin boundaries
hist = cv2.calcHist(images, channels, mask, histSize, ranges)
```

The sum of the histogram's values equals the total number of pixels in the input images. To facilitate comparisons, we should normalize the histogram so that the sum of its values is 1.0 or, in other words, each value represents the *proportion* of pixels belonging to the given color bin. We can use the following code to perform this type of normalization:

```
normalizedHist = cv2.normalize(hist, norm_type=cv2.NORM_L1)
```

Then, to obtain a similarity measurement for two normalized histograms, we can use code such as the following:

```
method = cv2.HISTCMP_INTERSECT  # A method of comparison
similarity = cv2.compareHist(
   normalizedHist, otherNormalizedHist, method)
```

For the HISTCMP_INTERSECT method, the similarity is the sum of the per-element minimums of the two histograms. If we consider the histograms as two curves, this value measures the intersecting area beneath the curves.

 For a list of all the supported methods of histogram comparison and their mathematical definitions, see the official documentation at http://docs.opencv.org/3.0-beta/modules/imgproc/doc/histograms.html#comparehist.

We will build a camera trap that uses histogram similarity as a trigger. When the histogram of the webcam's image is sufficiently similar to the histogram of a reference image, we will activate the photo camera. The reference image could be a colorful landscape (if we are interested in all the colors of the landscape), or it could be a tightly cropped photo of a colorful object (if we are interested in just the object's colors, regardless of the surroundings). Consider the following examples of tightly cropped photos:

The first image (left) shows an orange jacket, which is a common piece of outdoor clothing during hunting season. (The intense, warm color makes the wearer more visible, reducing the risk of hunting accidents.) This is potentially a good reference image if we want to detect people in the woods. The second image (right) shows an alpine poppy with red petals and yellow stamen. This may be a good reference image if we want to detect a flower when it opens.

These and other colorful images can be found in the book's GitHub repository at https://github.com/OpenCVBlueprints/ OpenCVBlueprints/tree/master/chapter_2/CameraTrap/ media.

Let's implement the color-based camera trap in a new script called
`set_color_trap.py`. Much of the code will be similar to `set_motion_trap.py`,
but we will cover the differences here.

Under some circumstances, `set_color_trap.py` will print error messages to `stderr`.
For this functionality, Python 2 and Python 3 have different syntax. We will add
the following import statement for compatibility, to make Python 3's `print` syntax
available even if we are running Python 2:

```
from __future__ import print_function
```

Our script's command-line arguments will include the path to the reference image,
and a similarity threshold, which will determine the trap's sensitivity. Here are the
definitions of the arguments:

```python
def main():

    parser = argparse.ArgumentParser(
      description='This script detects colors using an '
                  'attached webcam. When it detects colors '
                  'that match the histogram of a reference '
                  'image, it captures photos on an '
                  'attached gPhoto2-compatible photo '
                  'camera.')

    # ...

    parser.add_argument(
      '--reference-image', type=str, required=True,
      help='path to reference image, whose colors will be '
           'detected in scene')
    parser.add_argument(
      '--min-similarity', type=float, default=0.02,
      help='similarity score that histogram comparator '
           'must find in order to trigger similarity event '
           '(default=0.02, valid_range=[0.0, 1.0])')

    # ...
```

To read the omitted sections of this script, go to the book's GitHub repository at `https://github.com/OpenCVBlueprints/OpenCVBlueprints/chapter_2/CameraTrap/set_color_trap.py`.

We will parse the arguments and try to load the reference image from file. If the image cannot be loaded, the script will print an error message and exit prematurely, as the following code shows:

```
args = parser.parse_args()

# ...

reference_image = cv2.imread(args.reference_image,
                             cv2.IMREAD_COLOR)
if reference_image is None:
  print('Failed to read reference image: %s' %
        args.reference_image, file=sys.stderr)
  return

min_similarity = args.min_similarity

# ...
```

We will create a normalized histogram of the reference image, and later, we will also create a normalized histogram of each frame from the webcam. To help with the creation of a normalized histogram, we will define another function locally. (Python allows nested function definitions.) Here is the relevant code:

```
# ...

channels = range(3)
hist_size = [256] * 3
ranges = [0, 255] * 3

def create_normalized_hist(image, hist=None):
  hist = cv2.calcHist(
    [image], channels, None, hist_size, ranges, hist)
```

```
    return cv2.normalize(hist, hist, norm_type=cv2.NORM_L1)

reference_hist = create_normalized_hist(reference_image)
query_hist = None

# ...
```

To reiterate, every time we capture a frame from the webcam, we will find its normalized histogram. Then, we will measure the similarity of the reference histogram and the current scene's histogram based on the `HISTCMP_INTERSECT` method of comparison, meaning that we simply want to calculate the histograms' intersection or overlapping area. If the similarity is equal to or greater than the threshold, we will begin to capture photos.

Here is the main loop's implementation:

```
while True:
    time.sleep(detection_interval)
    success, bgr = cap.read(bgr)
    if success:
        query_hist = create_normalized_hist(
            bgr, query_hist)
        similarity = cv2.compareHist(
            reference_hist, query_hist, cv2.HISTCMP_INTERSECT)
        if debug:
            print('similarity=%f' % similarity)
        if similarity >= min_similarity and not cc.capturing:
            if photo_ev_step is not None:
                cc.capture_exposure_bracket(photo_ev_step, photo_count)
            else:
                cc.capture_time_lapse(photo_interval, photo_count)
```

This concludes the `main()` function. Again, to ensure that `main()` is called when the script is executed, we will add the following code:

```
if __name__ == '__main__':
    main()
```

Make the script executable. Then, for example, we can run it like this:

```
$ ./set_color_trap.py --reference-image media/OrangeCoat.jpg --min-similarity 0.13 --width 640 --height 480 --debug True
```

See the pair of the following images. The left-hand image shows the physical setup of the camera trap, which is running `set_color_trap.py` with the custom parameters that we just noted. The right-hand image is one of the resulting photos:

Again, these images come from different cameras, which give different renditions of the scene's color and contrast.

You may wish to experiment with `set_color_trap`'s arguments, especially the reference image and similarity threshold. Note that the `HISTCMP_INTERSECT` method of comparison tends to produce low similarities, so the default threshold is just 0.02, or a 2% overlap of the histograms. If you modify the code to use a different method of comparison, you may need a much higher threshold, and the maximum similarity may exceed 1.0.

Once you finish testing the color-based camera trap, let's proceed to use face detection as our final kind of trigger.

Detecting the face of a mammal

As you probably know, OpenCV's `CascadeClassifier` class is useful for face detection and other kinds of object detection, using a model of the object's features called a cascade, which is loaded from an XML file. We used `CascadeClassifier` and `haarcascade_frontalface_alt.xml` for human face detection in the section *Supercharging the GS3-U3-23S6M-C and other Point Grey Research cameras* of *Chapter 1, Getting the Most out of Your Camera System*. Later in this book, in *Chapter 5, Generic Object Detection for Industrial Applications*, we will examine all of `CascadeClassifier`'s functionality, along with a set of tools to create a cascade for any kind of object. For now, we will continue to use pretrained cascades that come with OpenCV. Notably, OpenCV offers the following cascade files for human and cat face detection:

- For human frontal faces:
  - `data/haarcascades/haarcascade_frontalface_default.xml`
  - `data/haarcascades/haarcascade_frontalface_alt.xml`
  - `data/haarcascades/haarcascade_frontalface_alt2.xml`
  - `data/lbpcascades/lbpcascade_frontalface.xml`

- For human profile faces:
  - `data/haarcascades/haarcascade_profileface.xml`
  - `data/lbpcascades/lbpcascade_profileface.xml`

- For cat frontal faces:
  - `data/haarcascades/haarcascade_frontalcatface.xml`
  - `data/haarcascades/haarcascade_frontalcatface_extended.xml`
  - `data/lbpcascades/lbpcascade_frontalcatface.xml`

LBP cascades are faster but slightly less accurate than Haar cascades. The extended version of Haar cascades (as used in `haarcascade_frontalcatface_extended.xml`) is sensitive to both horizontal and diagonal features, whereas standard Haar cascades are only sensitive to horizontal features. For example, a cat's whiskers could register as diagonal features.

> *Chapter 5, Generic Object Detection for Industrial Applications*, in this book, will discuss types of cascades in detail. Also, for a complete tutorial on how OpenCV's cat cascades were trained, see *Chapter 3, Training a Smart Alarm to Recognize the Villain and His Cat*, in the book *OpenCV for Secret Agents*, by Joseph Howse (Packt Publishing, 2015).

Incidentally, the cat face detection cascades may also detect other mammal faces. The following images are visualizations of the detection results using `haarcascade_frontalcatface_extended.xml` on photos of a cat (left), a red panda (upper right), and a lynx (lower right):

 The photos of the red panda and lynx are by Mathias Appel, who has generously released these and many other images into the public domain. See his Flickr page at `https://www.flickr.com/photos/mathiasappel/`.

Let's implement the classification-based camera trap in a new script called
`set_classifier_trap.py`. The necessary imports are the same as for
`set_color_trap.py`. The command-line arguments for `set_classifier_trap.py`
include the path to the cascade file as well as other parameters that affect the use
of `CascadeClassifer`. Here is the relevant code:

```python
def main():

    parser = argparse.ArgumentParser(
        description='This script detects objects using an '
                    'attached webcam. When it detects '
                    'objects that match a given cascade '
                    'file, it captures photos on an attached '
                    'gPhoto2-compatible photo camera.')

    # ...

    parser.add_argument(
        '--cascade-file', type=str, required=True,
        help='path to cascade file that classifier will use '
             'to detect objects in scene')
    parser.add_argument(
        '--scale-factor', type=float, default=1.05,
        help='relative difference in scale between '
             'iterations of multi-scale classification '
             '(default=1.05)')
    parser.add_argument(
        '--min-neighbors', type=int, default=8,
        help='minimum number of overlapping objects that '
             'classifier must detect in order to trigger '
             'classification event (default=8)')
    parser.add_argument(
        '--min-object-width', type=int, default=40,
        help='minimum width of each detected object'
             '(default=40)')
    parser.add_argument(
```

```
    '--min-object-height', type=int, default=40,
  help='minimum height of each detected object'
       '(default=40)')

# ...
```

 To read the omitted sections of this script, go to the book's GitHub repository at `https://github.com/OpenCVBlueprints/ OpenCVBlueprints/chapter_2/CameraTrap/set_ classifier_trap.py`.

After parsing the arguments as usual, we will initialize an instance of `CascadeClassifier` with the specified cascade file. If the file failed to load, we will print an error message and exit the script prematurely. See the following code:

```
args = parser.parse_args()

# ...

classifier = cv2.CascadeClassifier(args.cascade_file)
if classifier.empty():
  print('Failed to read cascade file: %s' %
         args.cascade_file, file=sys.stderr)
  return

scale_factor = args.scale_factor
min_neighbors = args.min_neighbors
min_size = (args.min_object_width, args.min_object_height)

# ...
```

On each iteration of the script's main loop, we will convert the webcam image to an equalized black and white version, which we will pass to the `CascadeClassifier`'s `detectMultiScale` method. We will use some of the command-line arguments as additional parameters to control the sensitivity of `detectMultiScale`. If at least one face (or other relevant object) is detected, we will start to capture photos, as usual. Here is the loop's implementation:

```
while True:
  time.sleep(detection_interval)
  success, bgr = cap.read(bgr)
  if success:
    gray = cv2.cvtColor(bgr, cv2.COLOR_BGR2GRAY, gray)
    gray = cv2.equalizeHist(gray, gray)
```

```
objects = classifier.detectMultiScale(
  gray, scaleFactor=scale_factor,
  minNeighbors=min_neighbors, minSize=min_size)
num_objects = len(objects)
if debug:
  print('num_objects=%d' % num_objects)
if num_objects > 0 and not cc.capturing:
  if photo_ev_step is not None:
    cc.capture_exposure_bracket(photo_ev_step, photo_count)
  else:
    cc.capture_time_lapse(photo_interval, photo_count)
```

This completes the `main()` function, and all that remains is to call `main()` when the script executes, as usual:

```
if __name__ == '__main__':
  main()
```

Make the script executable. Then, for example, we can run it like this:

```
$ ./set_classifier_trap.py --cascade-file cascades/haarcascade_
frontalcatface_extended.xml --min-neighbors 16 --scale-factor 1.2 --width
640 --height 480 --debug True
```

Refer to the following set of images. The left-hand image shows the physical setup of the camera trap, which is running `set_classifier_trap.py` with the custom parameters that we just noted. The right-hand images are two of the resulting photos:

The left-hand image and right-hand images come from two different cameras, so the color and contrast differ. Also, the two right-hand images come from separate runs of `set_classifier_trap.py`, and the lighting conditions and camera position have changed very slightly.

Feel free to experiment with the arguments of `set_classifier_trap.py`. You might even want to create your own cascade files to detect different kinds of faces or objects. *Chapter 5, Generic Object Detection for Industrial Applications*, will provide a wealth of information to help you do more with `CascadeClassifier` and cascade files.

Next, we will consider ways to process the photos that we may capture with any of our scripts, or with simple gPhoto2 commands.

Processing images to show subtle colors and motion

By now, you have probably captured some exposure-bracketed photos and time-lapse photos. Upload them onto your computer using a photo management application, a file browser, or the following gPhoto2 command:

```
$ gphoto2 --get-all-files
```

The latter command will upload the files to the current working directory.

We will merge exposure-bracketed photos to create HDR images, which will improve color rendition in shadows and highlights. Similarly, we will merge time-lapse photos to create time-lapse videos, which will show gradual motion on an accelerated scale. We will start by processing some of the sample photos from the book's GitHub repository at https://github.com/OpenCVBlueprints/OpenCVBlueprints/tree/master/chapter_2/CameraTrap/media, and then you will be able to adapt the code to use your photos instead.

Creating HDR images

OpenCV 3 has a new module called "photo". Two of its classes, `MergeDebevec` and `MergeMertens`, create an HDR image by merging exposure-bracketed photos. Regardless of which class is used, the resulting HDR image has channel values in the range [0.0, 1.0]. `MergeDebevec` produces an HDR image that requires gamma correction before it can be displayed or printed. The photo module provides several **tone mapping** functions that are capable of performing the correction.

On the other hand, the HDR image from `MergeMertens` does not require gamma correction. Its channel values just need to be scaled up to the range [0, 255]. We will use `MergeMertens` because it is simpler and tends to be better at preserving color saturation.

> For more information about HDR imaging and tone mapping in OpenCV 3, see the official documentation at `http://docs.opencv.org/3.0-beta/modules/photo/doc/hdr_imaging.html`. Also, see the official tutorial at `http://docs.opencv.org/3.0-beta/doc/tutorials/photo/hdr_imaging/hdr_imaging.html`.
>
> The `MergeDebevec` and `MergeMertens` classes are based on the following papers, respectively:
>
> P. Debevec, and J. Malik, *Recovering High Dynamic Range Radiance Maps from Photographs*, Proceedings OF ACM SIGGRAPH, 1997, 369 - 378.
>
> T. Mertens, J. Kautz, and F. Van Reeth, *Exposure Fusion*, Proceedings of the 15th Pacific Conference on Computer Graphics and Applications, 2007, 382 - 390.

For demonstration purposes, the GitHub repository contains a pair of exposure-bracketed photos of a cat named Plasma. (Her photos and the HDR merged version appear earlier in this chapter, in the section *Planning the camera trap*.) Let's create a script, `test_hdr_merge.py`, to merge the unprocessed photos, `media/PlasmaWink_0.jpg` and `media/PlasmaWink_1.jpg`. Here is the implementation:

```python
#!/usr/bin/env python

import cv2

def main():

    ldr_images = [
      cv2.imread('media/PlasmaWink_0.jpg'),
      cv2.imread('media/PlasmaWink_1.jpg')]

    hdr_processor = cv2.createMergeMertens()
    hdr_image = hdr_processor.process(ldr_images) * 255
    cv2.imwrite('media/PlasmaWink_HDR.jpg', hdr_image)

if __name__ == '__main__':
    main()
```

Obtain the script and media from the repository, run the script, and view the resulting HDR image. Then, adapt the script to process your own exposure-bracketed photos. HDR can produce dramatic results for any scene that has intense light and deep shadows. Landscapes and sunlit rooms are good examples.

With HDR imaging, we have compressed differences in exposure. Next, with time-lapse videography, we will compress differences in time.

Creating time-lapse videos

Previously, in the section *Supercharging the PlayStation Eye* in *Chapter 1, Getting the Most out of Your Camera System*, we created a slow-motion video. Remember that we simply captured images at a high speed (187 FPS) and put them in a video that was configured to play at a normal speed (60 FPS). Similarly, to create a time-lapse video, we will read image files that were captured at a low speed (less than 1 FPS) and put them in a video that is configured to play at a normal speed (60 FPS).

For demonstration purposes, the book's GitHub repository contains a set of time-lapse photographs of a cat named Josephine. When we make a time-lapse video of Josephine, we will see that she is very dynamic, even when she is sitting in a chair! As a preview, here are three consecutive frames of the time lapse:

The series spans 56 photos with names ranging from `media/JosephineChair_00.jpg` to `media/JosephineChair_55.jpg`. The following script, which we will call `test_time_lapse_merge.py`, will read the photos and produce a one-second time-lapse video named `media/JosephineChair_TimeLapse.avi`:

```python
#!/usr/bin/env python

import cv2

def main():

    num_input_files = 56
    input_filename_pattern = 'media/JosephineChair_%02d.jpg'
```

```
    output_filename = 'media/JosephineChair_TimeLapse.avi'
    fourcc = cv2.VideoWriter_fourcc('M', 'J', 'P', 'G')
    fps = 60.0
    writer = None

    for i in range(num_input_files):
      input_filename = input_filename_pattern % i
      image = cv2.imread(input_filename)
      if writer is None:
        is_color = (len(image.shape) > 2)
        h, w = image.shape[:2]
        writer = cv2.VideoWriter(
          output_filename, fourcc, fps, (w, h), is_color)
      writer.write(image)

  if __name__ == '__main__':
      main()
```

Obtain the script and media from the repository, run the script, and view the resulting video of Josephine watching the world from her chair. Then, adapt the script to process some of your own images. Perhaps you will capture the motion of other slow animals, flowers as they bloom, or sunlight and clouds as they cross a landscape.

As a further project, you may wish to create HDR time-lapse videos. You could start by modifying our `capture_exposure_bracket.sh` script to capture multiple batches of exposure-bracketed images, with a time delay between each batch. (For example, the command `sleep 3` could be used to delay for 3 seconds.) After uploading the captured images onto your computer, you can merge each batch into an HDR image, and then merge the HDR images into a time-lapse video.

Explore other photographic techniques, and then try to automate them!

Further study

Computational photography is a diverse and popular field, which combines the work of artists, technicians, and scientists. Thus, there are many types of authors, instructors, and mentors who can help you become a better "computational photographer". Here are just a few examples of helpful guides:

- *Learning Image Processing with OpenCV*, by Gloria Bueno García et al (Packt Publishing, 2015), covers a wide range of OpenCV 3's capabilities with respect to image capture, image editing, and computational photography. The book uses C++, and is suitable for beginners in computer vision.

- The *National Geographic Masters of Photography* video lectures (The Great Courses, 2015) provide great insight into the goals and techniques of master photographers. Several of the lecturers are wildlife photographers, whose use of camera traps was an inspiration for this chapter.

- *OpenSource Astrophotography*, by Karl Sarnow (CreateSpace Independent Publishing Platform, 2013), covers the use of gPhoto2 and other open source software, along with photographic hardware, to capture and process detailed images of the night sky.

- *Science for the Curious Photographer*, by Charles S. Johnson, Jr. (CRC Press, 2010), explains the scientific history and principles of light, lenses, and photography. Moreover, it provides practical solutions to common photographic problems, such as selecting and setting up good equipment for macro photography.

Whether as a hobby or a profession, computational photography is a great way to explore and chronicle the world from a particular viewpoint. It requires observation, experimentation, and patience, so slow down! Take time to learn from other people's explorations, and to share yours.

Summary

This chapter has demonstrated a set of surprisingly flexible commands and classes, which enable us to conduct experiments in computational photography, with short and simple code. We have written scripts to control a photo camera. Along the way, we have acquainted ourselves with gPhoto2, the Bash shell, PTP communication, GVFS mount points, and Python's support for subprocesses. We have also scripted several variations of a photo trap to take pictures when a subject comes into view. For this, OpenCV has provided us with the capability to detect motion, measure color similarities, and classify objects. Finally, we have used OpenCV to combine a set of photos into a time-lapse video or HDR image.

So far, this book has provided a fairly broad survey of ways to capture light as data, control a camera, detect a subject, and process a photo. The remaining chapters will focus on a selection of advanced techniques, which will enable us to perform much finer classification and identification of an image's subject, and to process photos and videos in ways that account for camera motion and perspective.

3
Recognizing Facial Expressions with Machine Learning

Automatic facial expression recognition has attracted much attention since the early nineties, especially in human-computer interaction. As computers start becoming a part of our life, they need to become more and more intelligent. Expression recognition systems will enhance this intelligent interaction between the human and the computer.

Although humans can recognize facial expressions easily, a reliable expression recognition system is still a challenge. In this chapter, we will introduce a basic implementation of facial expression using various algorithms from the OpenCV library, including feature extraction and classification using the ml module.

In this chapter, we will be going through the following topics in brief:

- A simple architecture to recognize human facial expressions
- Feature extraction algorithms in the OpenCV library
- The learning and testing stage, with various machine learning algorithms

Introducing facial expression recognition

Automatic facial expression recognition is an interesting and challenging problem and has several important applications in many areas such as human-computer interaction, human behavior understanding, and data-driven animation. Unlike face recognition, facial expression recognition needs to discriminate between the same expression in different individuals. The problem becomes more difficult as a person may show the same expression in different ways.

The current existing approaches for measuring facial expressions can be categorized into two types: static image and image sequence. In the static image approach, the system analyzes the facial expression in each image frame separately. In the image sequence approach, the system tries to capture the temporal pattern of the motion and changes seen on the face in the sequence of image frames. Recently, attention has been shifted toward the image sequence approach. However, this approach is more difficult and requires more computation than the static approach. In this chapter, we will follow the static image approach and compare several algorithms using the OpenCV 3 library.

The problem of automatic facial expression recognition includes three sub-problems:

- **Finding the face region in the image**: The precise position of the face is very important for facial analysis. In this problem, we want to find the face region in the image. This problem can be viewed as a detection problem. In our implementation, we will use the cascade classifier in OpenCV's objdetect module to detect the faces. However, the cascade classifier is prone to alignment error. Therefore, we apply the flandmark library to extract the facial landmarks from the face region and use these landmarks to extract the precise face region.

> Flandmark is an open source C library implementing a facial landmark detector. You can get more information about flandmark in the following sections. Basically, you can use whatever library you want to extract the landmarks. In our implementation, we will use this library to reduce complexity while integrating the library into our project.

- **Extracting features from the face region**: Given the face region, the system will extract facial expression information as a feature vector. The feature vector encodes the relevant information from the input data. In our implementation, the feature vector is obtained by using the combination of the feature detector from the feature2d module and the kmeans algorithm from the core module.

- **Classifying the features into emotion categories**: This is a classification problem. The system uses classification algorithms to map the extracted feature from the previous step to an emotion category (such as happy, neutral, or sad). This is the main subject of the chapter. We will evaluate machine learning algorithms from the ml module, including neural networks, the support vector machine, and K-Nearest-Neighbor.

In the following sections, we will show you a complete process for implementing a facial expression system. In the next section, you will find several approaches to improve system performance to suit your needs.

Facial expression dataset

In order to simplify the chapter, we will use a dataset to demonstrate the process instead of a live camera. We will use a standard dataset, **Japanese Female Facial Expression (JAFFE)**. There are 214 images of 10 people in the dataset. Each person has three images of each expression. The dataset includes seven expressions (happy, sad, angry, disgust, fear, surprise, and neutral) as shown in the following figure:

 You need to download the dataset from the following link:
http://www.kasrl.org/jaffe.html

ANGRY   DISGUST   FEAR   HAPPY   SAD   SURPRISE   NEURAL

Sample image from the JAFFE dataset.

Finding the face region in the image

In this section, we will show you a basic approach to detect faces in an image. We will use the cascade classifier in OpenCV to detect the face location. This approach may have alignment errors. In order to obtain a precise location, we will also provide another advanced approach to find the face region using facial landmarks. In our implementation, we will only use the face region. However, many researchers use facial landmarks to extract facial components, such as eyes and mouths, and operate on these components separately.

 If you want to find out more, you should check the *Facial landmarks* section in this chapter.

Extracting the face region using a face detection algorithm

In our implementation, we will use the Haar Feature-based cascade classifier in the objdetect module. In OpenCV, you can also extract the the face region with LBP-based cascade. LBP-based cascade is faster than Haar-based cascade. With the pre-trained model, the performance of LBP-based is lower than Haar-based cascade. However, it is possible to train an LBP-based cascade to attain the same performance as the Haar-based cascade.

 If you want to understand object detection in detail, you should check *Chapter 5, Generic Object Detection for Industrial Applications*.

The code for detecting faces is very simple. First, you need to load the pre-trained cascade classifier for faces into your OpenCV installation folder:

```
CascadeClassifier face_cascade;
face_cascade.load("haarcascade_frontalface_default.xml");
```

Then, load the input image in color mode, convert the image to grayscale, and apply histogram equalization to enhance the contrast:

```
Mat img, img_gray;
img = imread(imgPath[i], CV_LOAD_IMAGE_COLOR);
cvtColor(img, img_gray, CV_RGB2GRAY);
equalizeHist(img_gray, img_gray);
```

Now, we can find faces in the image. The detectMultiScale function stores all the detected faces in the vector as Rect(x, y, w, h):

```
vector<Rect> faces;
face_cascade.detectMultiScale( img_gray, faces, 1.1, 3 );
```

In this code, the third parameter 1.1 is the scale factor, which specifies how much the image size will be resized at each scale. The following figure shows the scale pyramid using the scale factor. In our case, the scale factor is 1.1. This means that the image size is reduced by 10%. The lower this factor is, the better chance we have of finding the faces. The scaling process starts with the original image and ends when the image resolution reaches the model dimension in the X or Y direction. However, the computation cost is high if we have too many scales. Therefore, if you want to reduce the number of scales, increase the scale factor to 1.2 (20%), 1.3 (30%) ,or more. If you want to increase the number of scales, reduce the scale factor to 1.05 (5%) or more. The fourth parameter 3 is the minimum number of neighbors that each candidate position should have to become a face position.

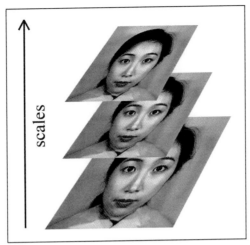

Pyramid of image scales

The following figure is the result of face detection if we set the number of neighbors to zero:

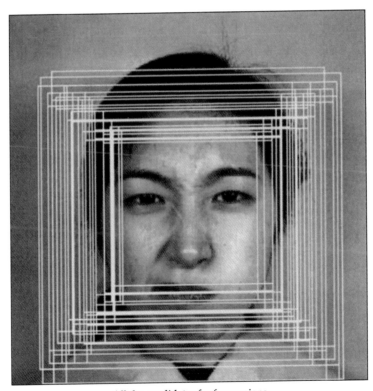

All the candidates for face regions

Finally, the position of the face region can be obtained as follows:

```
int bbox[4] = { faces[i].x, faces[i].y, faces[i].x + faces[i].width,
faces[i].y + faces[i].height };
```

Each element of the faces vector is a `Rect` object. Therefore, we can get the position of the top-left corner with `faces[i].x` and `faces[i].y`. The position of the bottom-right corner is `faces[i].x + faces[i].width` and `faces[i].y + faces[i].height`. This information will be used as the initial position for the facial landmarks process, as described in the following section.

Extracting facial landmarks from the face region

One disadvantage of the face detector is that the results may have misalignment. The misalignment may happen in scaling or translation. Therefore, the extracted face regions in all images will not align with each other. This misalignment can lead to poor recognition performance, especially with DENSE features. With the help of facial landmarks, we can align all the extracted faces so that each facial component is in the same area over the datasets.

Many researchers make use of facial landmarks for classification with other emotion recognition approaches.

We will use the flandmark library to find the location of the eyes, nose and mouth. Then, we will use these facial landmarks to extract the precise facial bounding box.

Introducing the flandmark library

Flandmark is an open source C library implementing a facial landmark detector.

You can access the flandmark library main page at: `http://cmp.felk.cvut.cz/~uricamic/flandmark/`.

Given a face image, the goal of the flandmark library is to estimate an S shape that represents the location of the facial component. A facial shape in an S is an array of (x, y) positions shown as: $S = [x_0 y_0 x_1 y_1 .... x_n y_n]$.

The pre-trained model in flandmark contains eight points, as shown in the following figure:

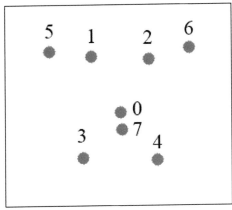

The 8 landmarks model and the corresponding index for each landmark.

In our implementation, we use flandmark because it is easy to integrate it into an OpenCV project. Besides, the flandmark library is really robust in many scenarios, even when the person is wearing glasses. In the following figure, we show the result of using the flandmark library on an image where the person is wearing dark glasses. The red dots indicate the facial landmarks.

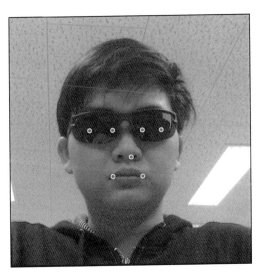

In the next section, we will show you the steps to download and use flandmark in our project.

Downloading and compiling the flandmark library

Flandmark is implemented in C and can be integrated into our project easily. However, we need to modify some headers in the library source to use it with OpenCV 3. The following are the steps to download and compile the library:

1. Go to the main page of the flandmark library and follow the GitHub link:
   `http://github.com/uricamic/flandmark`

2. Clone the library to your local machine with the following command:
   ```
   git clone http://github.com/uricamic/flandmark
   ```

3. Copy the `libflandmark` folder to your project folder.

4. Copy `flandmark_model.dat`, which is in the data folder, to your project folder.

5. Edit the `liblbp.h` file in `libflandmark` and change:
   ```
   #include "msvc-compat.h"
   ```

   to

   ```
   #include <stdint.h>
   ```

6. Edit the `flandmark_detector.h` file in `libflandmark` and change:
   ```
   #include "msvc-compat.h"
   #include <cv.h>
   #include <cvaux.h>
   ```

   to

   ```
   #include <stdint.h>
   #include "opencv2/opencv.hpp"
   #include "opencv2/objdetect/objdetect.hpp"
   #include "opencv2/highgui/highgui.hpp"
   #include "opencv2/imgproc/imgproc.hpp"
   #include <iostream>
   #include <stdio.h>
   using namespace std;
   using namespace cv;
   ```

7. Edit `CMakeLists.txt` in your project folder to add the flandmark library:
   ```
   add_subdirectory(libflandmark)
   include_directories("${PROJECT_SOURCE_DIR}/libflandmark")
   ```

8. Link the executable file with the flandmark static library.

9. Add the flandmark header to your source code:

```
#include "flandmark_detector.h"
```

Detecting facial landmarks with flandmark

Once you have finished the above steps, the process to extract facial components is very straightforward.

First, we create a `FLANDMARK_Model` variable to load the pre-trained model:

```
FLANDMARK_Model * model = flandmark_init("flandmark_model.dat");
```

Then, we save the number of landmarks into the `num_of_landmark` variable and create an array to store the output result:

```
int num_of_landmark = model->data.options.M;
double *points = new double[2 * num_of_landmark];
```

Finally, for each face region, we create an integer array to store the face location and use the `flandmark_detect` function to obtain the final result in the `points` array:

```
int bbox[4] = { faces[i].x, faces[i].y, faces[i].x + faces[i].width,
faces[i].y + faces[i].height };
flandmark_detect(new IplImage(img_gray), bbox, model, points);
```

The first parameter in the `flandmark_detect` function is `IplImage` so we need to pass our gray image into the `IplImage` constructor.

Visualizing the landmarks in an image

This step is optional. You don't need to implement the code in this section. However, we recommend that you try and understand the results. The following code draws a circle on the image at the location of the landmarks:

```
for(int j = 0 ; j < num_of_landmark; j++){
  Point landmark = Point((int)points[2 * j], (int)points[2* j + 1]);
  circle(img, landmark, 4, Scalar(255, 255, 255), -1);
}
```

The following figure shows multiple examples of the results using the above code:

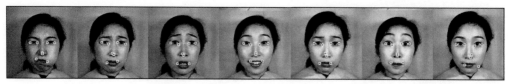

Some examples of flandmark results on JAFFE images

Extracting the face region

We now have the location of the eyes, nose, and mouth. It is very easy to extract the face region.

First, we compute the center of the left eye as the middle of point 2 and point 6:

```
Point centerLeft = Point( (int) (points[2 * 6] + points[2 * 2]) / 2,
(int) (points[2 * 6 + 1] + points[2 * 2 + 1]) / 2 );
```

Second, the width of the eye region is the difference between x coordinates of point 2 and point 6:

```
int widthLeft = abs(points[2 * 6] - points[2 * 2]);
```

Then, we find the center and the width of the right eye:

```
Point centerRight = Point( (int) (points[2 * 1] + points[2 * 5]) / 2,
(int) (points[2 * 1 + 1] + points[2 * 5 + 1]) / 2 );
int widthRight = abs(points[2 * 1] - points[2 * 5]);
```

We can assume that the width of the face is a bit larger than the distance between the eyes, and the height of the face is larger than the width of the face, so we can get the eyebrows. We can obtain a good face position with the following code:

```
int widthFace = (centerLeft.x + widthLeft) - (centerRight.x -
widthRight);

int heightFace = widthFace * 1.2;
```

Finally, the face region can be extracted with the following code:

```
Mat face = img(Rect( centerRight.x - widthFace/4   , centerRight.y -
heightFace/4, widthFace, heightFace ));
```

The following figure shows some extracted images from our implementation:

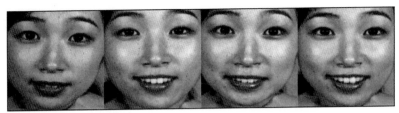

Some examples of extracted face regions from JAFFE images

Software usage guide

We have implemented the software to extract facial components from the JAFFE dataset. You can use the code as follows:

1. Download the source code. Open the terminal and change directory to the source code folder.

2. Build the software with cmake using the following command:

   ```
   mkdir build && cd build && cmake .. && make
   ```

3. You can use the facial_components tool, as follows:

   ```
   ./facial_components -src <input_folder> -dest <out_folder>
   ```

> The software for this chapter based on OpenCV 3 can be found at:
> https://github.com/OpenCVBlueprints/OpenCVBlueprints/

In order to simplify the process, we save the image paths in a .yaml file, list.yml. The structure of this .yaml file is simple. First, we save the number of images in the num_of_image variable. After that, we save the paths of all the images, as shown in the following screenshot:

```
1  %YAML:1.0
2  num_of_image: 213
3  img_0_face: "/Volumes/Data/Dataset/JAFFE/output/KA.AN1.39.face.tiff"
4  img_1_face: "/Volumes/Data/Dataset/JAFFE/output/KA.AN2.40.face.tiff"
5  img_2_face: "/Volumes/Data/Dataset/JAFFE/output/KA.AN3.41.face.tiff"
6  img_3_face: "/Volumes/Data/Dataset/JAFFE/output/KA.DI1.42.face.tiff"
7  img_4_face: "/Volumes/Data/Dataset/JAFFE/output/KA.DI2.43.face.tiff"
```

An image of the list.yml file

Feature extraction

Given a dataset of face regions, we can use feature extraction to obtain the feature vector, which gives us the most important information from the expression. The following figure shows the process that we use in our implementation to extract features vectors:

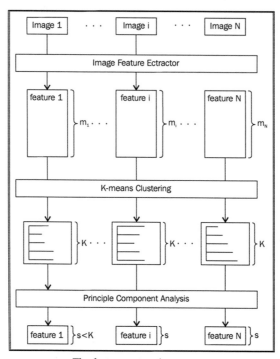

The feature extraction process

In order to understand this chapter, you need to understand that the feature representation of the expression image is the distribution of image features over k clusters (k = 1000 in our implementation). We have implemented a few common types of features that are supported in OpenCV, such as SIFT, SURF, and some advanced features, such as DENSE-SIFT, KAZE, DAISY. Since these image features are computed at image key points such as corners, except for DENSE cases, the number of image features can vary between images. However, we want to have a fixed feature size for every image to perform classification, since we will apply machine learning classification techniques later. It is important that the feature size of the images is the same so that we can compare them to obtain the final result. Therefore, we apply a clustering technique (kmeans in our case) to separate the image feature space into a k cluster. The final feature representation for each image is the histogram of the image features over k bins. Moreover, in order to reduce the dimension of the final feature, we apply principle component analysis as a last step.

In the following sections, we will explain the process step by step. At the end of this section, we will show you how to use our implementation to obtain the final feature representation of the dataset.

Extracting image features from facial component regions

At this point, we will assume that you have the face region for each image in the dataset. The next step is to extract the image features from these face regions. OpenCV provides good implementations of many well-known key point detection and feature description algorithms.

 Detailed explanations for each algorithm are out of the scope of this chapter.

In this section, we will show you how to use some of these algorithms in our implementation.

We will use a function that takes current regions, a feature type, and returns a matrix with image features as rows:

```
Mat extractFeature(Mat face, string feature_name);
```

In this extractFeature function, we will extract image features from each Mat and return the descriptors. The implementation of extractFeature is simple, and shown here:

```
Mat extractFeature(Mat img, string feature_name){
    Mat descriptors;
    if(feature_name.compare("brisk") == 0){
        descriptors = extractBrisk(img);
    } else if(feature_name.compare("kaze") == 0){
        descriptors = extractKaze(img);
    } else if(feature_name.compare("sift") == 0){
        descriptors = extractSift(img);
    } else if(feature_name.compare("dense-sift") == 0){
        descriptors = extractDenseSift(img);
    } else if(feature_name.compare("daisy") == 0){
        descriptors = extractDaisy(img);
    }
    return descriptors;
}
```

In the above code, we call the corresponding function for each feature. For simplicity, we only use one feature each time. In this chapter, we will discuss two types of features:

- **Contributed features**: SIFT, DAISY, and DENSE SIFT. In OpenCV 3, the implementation of SIFT and SURF have been moved to the opencv_contrib module.

 These features are patented and you should pay for them if you want to use them in commercial applications.

In this chapter, we will use SIFT features and the SIFT variant, DENSE SIFT.

 If you want to use the opencv_contrib module, we suggest that you go to the *Further reading* section and take a look at the *Compiling the opencv_contrib module* section.

- **Advanced features**: BRISK and KAZE. These features are a good alternative to SIFT and SURF in both performance and computation time. DAISY and KAZE are only available in OpenCV 3. DAISY is in opencv_contrib. KAZE is in the main OpenCV repository.

Contributed features

Let's take a look at SIFT features first.

In order to use SIFT features in OpenCV 3, you need to compile the opencv_contrib module with OpenCV.

 We will assume that you have followed the instructions in the *Further reading* section.

The code to extract SIFT features is very simple:

```
Mat extractSift(Mat img){
    Mat descriptors;
    vector<KeyPoint> keypoints;

    Ptr<Feature2D> sift = xfeatures2d::SIFT::create();
    sift->detect(img, keypoints, Mat());
```

```
    sift->compute(img, keypoints, descriptors);

    return descriptors;
}
```

First, we create the `Feature2D` variable with `xfeatures2d::SIFT::create()` and use the `detect` function to obtain key points. The first parameter for the detection function is the image that we want to process. The second parameter is a vector to store detected key points. The third parameter is a mask specifying where to look for key points. We want to find key points in every position of the images so we just pass an empty Mat here.

Finally, we use the `compute` function to extract features descriptors at these key points. The computed descriptors are stored in the descriptors variable.

Next, let's take a look at the SURF features.

The code to obtain SURF features is more or less the same as that for SIFT features. We only change the namespace from SIFT to SURF:

```
Mat extractSurf(Mat img){
    Mat descriptors;
    vector<KeyPoint> keypoints;

    Ptr<Feature2D> surf = xfeatures2d::SURF::create();
    surf->detect(img, keypoints, Mat());
    surf->compute(img, keypoints, descriptors);

    return descriptors;
}
```

Let's now move on to DAISY.

DAISY is an improved version of the rotation-invariant BRISK descriptor and the LATCH binary descriptor that is comparable to the heavier and slower SURF. DAISY is only available in OpenCV 3 in the opencv_contrib module. The code to implement DAISY features is fairly similar to the Sift function. However, the DAISY class doesn't have a `detect` function so we will use SURF to detect key points and use DAISY to extract descriptors:

```
Mat extractDaisy(Mat img){
    Mat descriptors;
    vector<KeyPoint> keypoints;

    Ptr<FeatureDetector> surf = xfeatures2d::SURF::create();
```

```
    surf->detect(img, keypoints, Mat());
    Ptr<DescriptorExtractor> daisy = xfeatures2d::DAISY::create();
    daisy->compute(img, keypoints, descriptors);

    return descriptors;
}
```

It is now time to take a look at dense SIFT features.

Dense collects features at every location and scale in an image. There are plenty of applications where dense features are used. However, in OpenCV 3, the interface for extracting dense features has been removed. In this section, we show a simple approach to extracting dense features using the function in the OpenCV 2.4 source code to extract the vector of key points.

The function to extract dense Sift is similar to the Sift function:

```
Mat extractDenseSift(Mat img){
    Mat descriptors;
    vector<KeyPoint> keypoints;

    Ptr<Feature2D> sift = xfeatures2d::SIFT::create();
    createDenseKeyPoints(keypoints, img);
    sift->compute(img, keypoints, descriptors);

    return descriptors;
}
```

Instead of using the detect function, we can use the createDenseKeyPoints function to obtain key points. After that, we pass this dense key points vector to compute the function. The code for createDenseKeyPoints is obtained from the OpenCV 2.4 source code. You can find this code at modules/features2d/src/detectors.cpp in the OpenCV 2.4 repository:

```
void createDenseFeature(vector<KeyPoint> &keypoints, Mat image, float
initFeatureScale=1.f, int featureScaleLevels=1,
                                    float featureScaleMul=0.1f,
                                    int initXyStep=6, int
initImgBound=0,

                                    bool varyXyStepWithScale=true,
                                    bool varyImgBoundWithScale=false){
    float curScale = static_cast<float>(initFeatureScale);
    int curStep = initXyStep;
    int curBound = initImgBound;
```

```
        for( int curLevel = 0; curLevel < featureScaleLevels; curLevel++ )
        {
            for( int x = curBound; x < image.cols - curBound; x += curStep
)
            {
                for( int y = curBound; y < image.rows - curBound; y +=
curStep )
                {
                    keypoints.push_back( KeyPoint(static_cast<float>(x),
static_cast<float>(y), curScale) );
                }
            }
            curScale = static_cast<float>(curScale * featureScaleMul);
            if( varyXyStepWithScale ) curStep = static_cast<int>( curStep
* featureScaleMul + 0.5f );
            if( varyImgBoundWithScale ) curBound = static_cast<int>(
curBound * featureScaleMul + 0.5f );
        }
    }
```

Advanced features

OpenCV 3 comes bundled with many new and advanced features. In our implementation, we will only use the BRISK and KAZE features. However, there are many other features in OpenCV.

Let us familiarize ourselves with the BRISK features.

BRISK is a new feature and a good alternative to SURF. It has been added to OpenCV since the 2.4.2 version. BRISK is under a BSD license so you don't have to worry about the patent problem, as with SIFT or SURF.

```
Mat extractBrisk(Mat img){
    Mat descriptors;
    vector<KeyPoint> keypoints;

    Ptr<DescriptorExtractor> brisk = BRISK::create();
    brisk->detect(img, keypoints, Mat());
    brisk->compute(img, keypoints, descriptors);

    return descriptors;
}
```

There is an interesting article about all this, *A battle of three descriptors: SURF, FREAK and BRISK,* available at `http://computer-vision-talks.com/articles/2012-08-18-a-battle-of-three-descriptors-surf-freak-and-brisk/`.

Let's now move on and have a look at the KAZE features.

KAZE is a new feature in OpenCV 3. It produces the best results in many scenarios, especially with image matching problems, and it is comparable to SIFT. KAZE is in the OpenCV repository so you don't need opencv_contrib to use it. Apart from the high performance, one reason to use KAZE is that it is open source and you can use it freely in any commercial applications. The code to use this feature is very straightforward:

```
Mat extractKaze(Mat img){
    Mat descriptors;
    vector<KeyPoint> keypoints;

    Ptr<DescriptorExtractor> kaze = KAZE::create();
    kaze->detect(img, keypoints, Mat());
    kaze->compute(img, keypoints, descriptors);

    return descriptors;
}
```

 The image matching comparison between KAZE, SIFT, and SURF is available at the author repository: `https://github.com/pablofdezalc/kaze`

Visualizing key points for each feature type

In the following figure, we visualize the position of key points for each feature type. We draw a circle at each key point; the radius of the circle specifies the scale of the image where the key point is extracted. You can see that the key points and the corresponding descriptors differ between these features. Therefore, the performance of the system will vary, based on the quality of the feature.

 We recommend that you refer to the *Evaluation* section for more details.

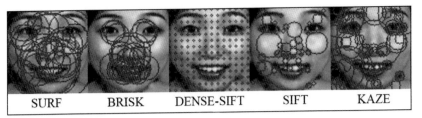

The feature extraction process

Computing the distribution of feature representation over k clusters

If you have followed the previous pseudo-code, you should now have a vector of descriptors. You can see that the size of descriptors varies between images. Since we want a fixed size of feature representation for each image, we will compute the distribution of feature representation over k clusters. In our implementation, we will use the kmeans clustering algorithm in the core module.

Clustering image features space into k clusters

First, we assume that the descriptors of all the images are added to a vector, called `features_vector`. Then, we need to create a Mat `rawFeatureData` that will contain all of the image features as a row. In this case, `num_of_feature` is the total number of features in every image and `image_feature_size` is the size of each image feature. We choose the number of clusters based on experiment. We start with 100 and increase the number for a few iterations. It depends on the type of features and data, so you should try to change this variable to suit your situation. One downside of a large number of clusters is that the cost for computation with kmeans will be high. Moreover, if the number of clusters is too large, the feature vector will be too sparse and it may not be good for classification.

```
Mat rawFeatureData = Mat::zeros(num_of_feature, image_feature_size,
CV_32FC1);
```

We need to copy the data from the vector of descriptors (`features_vector` in the code) to `imageFeatureData`:

```
int cur_idx = 0;
for(int i = 0 ; i < features_vector.size(); i++){
    features_vector[i].copyTo(rawFeatureData.rowRange(cur_idx, cur_idx
+ features_vector[i].rows));
    cur_idx += features_vector[i].rows;
}
```

Finally, we use the `kmeans` function to perform clustering on the data, as follows:

```
Mat labels, centers;
kmeans(rawFeatureData, k, labels, TermCriteria( TermCriteria::EPS+Term
Criteria::COUNT, 100, 1.0), 3, KMEANS_PP_CENTERS, centers);
```

Let's discuss the parameters of the `kmeans` function:

```
double kmeans(InputArray data, int K, InputOutputArray bestLabels,
TermCriteria criteria, int attempts, int flags, OutputArray
centers=noArray())
```

- **InputArray data**: It contains all the samples as a row.
- **int K**: The number of clusters to split the samples (k = 1000 in our implementation).
- **InputOutputArray bestLabels**: Integer array that contains the cluster indices for each sample.
- **TermCriteria criteria**: The algorithm termination criteria. This contains three parameters (`type`, `maxCount`, `epsilon`).
- **Type**: Type of termination criteria. There are three types:
    - **COUNT**: Stop the algorithm after a number of iterations (`maxCount`).
    - **EPS**: Stop the algorithm if the specified accuracy (epsilon) is reached.
    - **EPS+COUNT**: Stop the algorithm if the COUNT and EPS conditions are fulfilled.
- **maxCount**: It is the maximum number of iterations.
- **epsilon**: It is the required accuracy needed to stop the algorithm.
- **int attemtps**: It is the number of times the algorithm is executed with different initial centroids. The algorithm returns the labels that have the best compactness.
- **int flags**: This flag specifies how initial centroids are random. There are three types of flags. Normally, `KMEANS_RANDOM_CENTERS` and `KMEANS_PP_CENTERS` are used. If you want to provide your own initial labels, you should use `KMEANS_USE_INITIAL_LABELS`. In this case, the algorithm will use your initial labels on the first attempt. For further attempts, `KMEANS_*_CENTERS` flags are applied.
- **OutputArray centers**: It contains all cluster centroids, one row per each centroid.
- **double compactness**: It is the returned value of the function. This is the sum of the squared distance between each sample to the corresponding centroid.

Computing a final feature for each image

We now have labels for every image feature in the dataset. The next step is to compute a fixed size feature for each image. With this in mind, we iterate through each image and create a feature vector of k elements, where k is the number of clusters.

Then, we iterate through the image features in the current image and increase the ith element of the feature vector where i is the label of the image features.

Imagine that we are trying to make a histogram representation of the features based on the k centroids. This method looks like a bag of words approach. For example, image X has 100 features and image Y has 10 features. We cannot compare them because they do not have the same size. However, if we make a histogram of 1,000 dimensions for each of them, they are then the same size and we can compare them easily.

Dimensionality reduction

In this section, we will use **Principle Component Analysis (PCA)** to reduce the dimension of the feature space. In the previous step, we have 1,000 dimensional feature vectors for each image. In our dataset, we only have 213 samples. Hence, the further classifiers tend to overfit the training data in high dimensional space. Therefore, we want to use PCA to obtain the most important dimension, which has the largest variance.

Next, we will show you how to use PCA in our system.

First, we assume that you can store all the features in a Mat named `featureDataOverBins`. The number of rows of this Mat should equal to the number of images in the dataset and the number of columns of this Mat should be 1,000. Each row in `featureDataOverBins` is a feature of an image.

Second, we create a PCA variable:

```
PCA pca(featureDataOverBins, cv::Mat(), CV_PCA_DATA_AS_ROW, 0.90);
```

The first parameter is the data that contains all the features. We don't have a pre-computed mean vector so the second parameter should be an empty Mat. The third parameter indicates that the feature vectors are stored as matrix rows. The final parameter specifies the percentage of variance that PCA should retain.

Finally, we need to project all the features from 1,000 dimensional feature spaces to a lower space. After the projection, we can save these features for further processes.

```
for(int i = 0 ; i < num_of_image; i++){
    Mat feature = pca.project(featureDataOverBins.row(i));
    // save the feature in FileStorage
```

```
}
```

The number of dimensions of the new features can be obtained by:

```
int feature_size = pca.eigenvectors.rows;
```

Software usage guide

We have implemented the previous process to extract the fixed size feature for the dataset. Using the software is quite easy:

1. Download the source code. Open the terminal and change directory to the source code folder.

2. Build the software with cmake using the following command:

    ```
    mkdir build && cd build && cmake .. && make
    ```

3. You can use the feature_extraction tool as follows:

    ```
    ./feature_extraction  -feature <feature_name> -src <input_folder>
    -dest <output_folder>
    ```

The feature_extraction tool creates a YAML file in the output folder which contains the features and labels of every image in the dataset. The available parameters are:

*   feature_name: This can be sift, surf, opponent-sift, or opponent-surf. This is the name of the feature type which is used in the feature extraction process.

*   input_folder: This has the absolute path to the location of facial components.

*   output_folder: This has the absolute path to the folder where you want to keep the output file.

The structure of the output file is fairly simple.

We store the size of the feature, cluster centers, the number of images, the number of train and test images, the number of labels, and the corresponding label names. We also store PCA means, eigenvectors, and eigenvalues. The following figure shows a part of the YAML file:

```
feature_size: 140
num_of_image: 213
num_of_label: 7
label_0: Angry
label_1: Disgusted
label_2: Fear
label_3: Happy
label_4: Neural
label_5: Sad
label_6: Surprised
num_of_train: 169
num_of_test: 44
pca_mean: !!opencv-matrix
   rows: 1
   cols: 1000
   dt: f
   data: ...
pca_eigenvalues: !!opencv-matrix
   rows: 140
   cols: 1
   dt: f
   data: ...
centers: !!opencv-matrix
   rows: 1000
   cols: 128
   dt: f
```

A part of the features.yml file

For each image, we store three variables, as follows:

- `image_feature_<idx>`: It is a Mat that contains features of image idx
- `image_label_<idx>`: It is a label of the image idx
- `image_is_train_<idx>`: It is a Boolean specifying whether the image is used for training or not.

Classification

Once you have extracted the features for all the samples in the dataset, it is time to start the classification process. The target of this classification process is to learn how to make accurate predictions automatically based on the training examples. There are many approaches to this problem. In this section, we will talk about machine learning algorithms in OpenCV, including neural networks, support vector machines, and k-nearest neighbors.

Classification process

Classification is considered supervised learning. In a classification problem, a correctly labelled training set is necessary. A model is produced during the training stage which makes predictions and is corrected when predictions are wrong. Then, the model is used for predicting in other applications. The model needs to be trained every time you have more training data. The following figure shows an overview of the classification process:

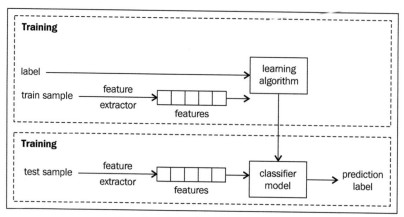

Overview of the classification process

The choice of learning algorithm to use is a critical step. There are a lot of solutions to the classification problem. In this section, we list some of the popular machine learning algorithms in OpenCV. The performance of each algorithm can vary between classification problems. You should make some evaluations and select the one that is the most appropriate for your problem to get the best results. It is essential as feature selection may affect the performance of the learning algorithm. Therefore, we also need to evaluate each learning algorithm with each different feature selection.

Splitting the dataset into a training set and testing set

It is important that the dataset is separated into two parts, the training set and the testing set. We will use the training set for the learning stage and the testing set for the testing stage. In the testing stage, we want to test how the trained model predicts unseen samples. In other words, we want to test the *generalization capability* of the trained model. Therefore, it is important that the test samples are different from the trained samples. In our implementation, we will simply split the dataset into two parts. However, it is better if you use k-fold cross validation as mentioned in the *Further reading* section.

There is no accurate way to split the dataset into two parts. Common ratios are 80:20 and 70:30. Both the training set and the testing set should be selected randomly. If they have the same data, the evaluation is misleading. Basically, even if you achieve 99 percent accuracy on your testing set, the model can't work in the real world, where the data is different from the training data.

In our implementation of feature extraction, we have already randomly split the dataset and saved the selection in the YAML file.

> The k-fold cross validation is explained in more detail at the end of the *Further reading* section.

Support vector machines

A **Support Vector Machine (SVM)** is a supervised learning technique applicable to both classification and regression. Given labelled training data, the goal of SVM is to produce an optimal hyper plane which predicts the target value of a test sample with only test sample attributes. In other words, SVM generates a function to map between input and output based on labelled training data.

For example, let's assume that we want to find a line to separate two sets of 2D points. The following figure shows that there are several solutions to the problem:

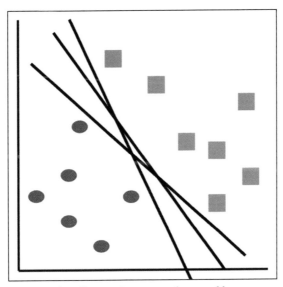

A lot of hyper planes can solve a problem

The goal of SVM is to find a hyper plane that maximizes the distances to the training samples. The distances are calculated to only support those vectors that are closest to the hyper plane. The following figure shows an optimal hyper plane to separate two sets of 2D points:

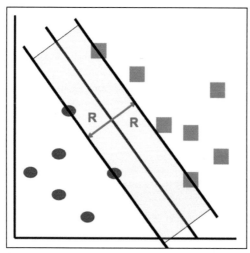

An optimal hyper plane that maximizes the distances to the training samples. R is the maximal margin

In the following sections, we will show you how to use SVM to train and test facial expression data.

Training stage

One of the most difficult parts about training an SVM is parameters selection. It is not possible to explain everything without some deep understanding of how SVM works. Luckily, OpenCV implements a trainAuto method for automatic parameter estimation. If you have enough knowledge of SVM, you should try to use your own parameters. In this section, we will introduce the trainAuto method to give you an overview of SVM.

SVM is inherently a technique for building an optimal hyper plane in binary (2-class) classification. In our facial expression problem, we want to classify seven expressions. One-versus-all and one-versus-one are two common approaches that we can follow to use SVM in this problem. One-versus-all trains one SVM for each class. There are seven SVMs in our case. For class i, every sample with the label i is considered as positive and the rest of the samples are negative. This approach is prone to error when the dataset samples are imbalanced between classes. The one-versus-one approach trains an SVM for each different pairs of classes. The number of SVMs in total is $N*(N-1)/2$ SVMs. This means 21 SVMs in our case.

In OpenCV, you don't have to follow these approaches. OpenCV supports the training of one multiclass SVM. However, you should follow the above methods for better results. We will still use one multiclass SVM. The training and testing process will be simpler.

Next, we will demonstrate our implementation to solve the facial expression problem.

First, we create an instance of SVM:

```
Ptr<ml::SVM> svm = ml::SVM::create();
```

If you want to change parameters, you can call the `set` function in the `svm` variable, as shown:

```
svm->setType(SVM::C_SVC);
svm->setKernel(SVM::RBF);
```

- **Type**: It is the type of SVM formulation. There are five possible values: `C_SVC`, `NU_SVC`, `ONE_CLASS`, `EPS_SVR`, and `NU_SVR`. However, in our multiclass classification, only `C_SVC` and `NU_SVC` are suitable. The difference between these two lies in the mathematical optimization problem. For now, we can just use `C_SVC`.

- **Kernel**: It is the type of SVM kernel. There are four possible values: `LINEAR`, `POLY`, `RBF`, and `SIGMOID`. The kernel is a function to map the training data to a higher dimensional space that makes data linearly separable. This is also known as *Kernel Trick*. Therefore, we can use SVM in non-linear cases with the support of the kernel. In our case, we choose the most commonly-used kernel, RBF. You can switch between these kernels and choose the best.

You can also set other parameters such as TermCriteria, Degree, Gamma. We are just using the default parameters.

Second, we create a variable of `ml::TrainData` to store all the training set data:

```
Ptr<ml::TrainData> trainData = ml::TrainData::create(train_features,
ml::SampleTypes::ROW_SAMPLE, labels);
```

- `train_features`: It is a Mat that contains each features vector as a row. The number of rows of `train_features` is the number of training samples, and the number of columns is the size of one features vector.

- `SampleTypes::ROW_SAMPLE`: It specifies that each features vector is in a row. If your features vectors are in columns, you should use COL_SAMPLE.

- `train_labels`: It is a Mat that contains labels for each training feature. In SVM, `train_labels` will be a Nx1 matrix, N is the number of training samples. The value of each row is the truth label of the corresponding sample. At the time of writing, the type of `train_labels` should be `CV_32S`. Otherwise, you may encounter an error. The following code is what we use to create the `train_labels` variable:

```
Mat train_labels = Mat::zeros( labels.rows, 1, CV_32S);
for(int i = 0 ; i < labels.rows; i ++){
    train_labels.at<unsigned int>(i, 0) = labels.at<int>(i, 0);
}
```

Finally, we pass `trainData` to the `trainAuto` function so that OpenCV can select the best parameters automatically. The interface of the `trainAuto` function contains many other parameters. In order to keep things simple, we will use the default parameters:

```
svm->trainAuto(trainData);
```

Testing stage

After we've trained the SVM, we can pass a test sample to the predict function of the `svm` model and receive a label prediction, as follows:

```
float predict = svm->predict(sample);
```

In this case, the sample is a feature vector just like the feature vector in the training features. The response is the label of the sample.

Multi-layer perceptron

OpenCV implements the most common type of artificial neural network, the multi-layer perceptron (MLP). A typical MLP consists of an input layer, an output layer, and one or more hidden layers. It is known as a supervised learning method because it needs a desired output to train. With enough data, MLP, given enough hidden layers, can approximate any function to any desired accuracy.

An MLP with a single hidden layer can be represented as it is in the following figure:

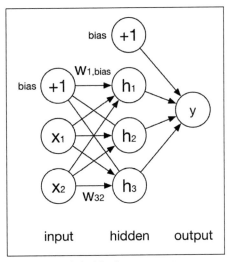

A single hidden layer perceptron

A detailed explanation and proof of how the MLP learns are out of the scope of this chapter. The idea is that the output of each neuron is a function of neurons from previous layers.

In the above single hidden layer MLP, we use the following notation:

Input layer: $x_1 x_2$

Hidden layer: $h_1 h_2 h_3$

Output layer: y

Each connection between each neuron has a weight. The weight shown in the above figure is between neuron i (that is i = 3) in the current layer and neuron j (that is j = 2) in the previous layer is w_{ij}. Each neuron has a bias value 1 with a weight, $w_{i,bias}$.

The output at neuron i is the result of an activation function f:

$$f\left(\sum w_{ij} * x_j\right) + w_{i,bias}$$

There are many types of activation functions. In OpenCV, there are three types of activation functions: Identity, Sigmoid, and Gaussian. However, the Gaussian function is not completely supported at the time of writing and the Identity function is not commonly used. We recommend that you use the default activation, Sigmoid.

In the following sections, we will show you how to train and test a multi-layer perceptron.

Training stage

In the training stage, we first define the network and then train the network.

Define the network

We will use a simple four layer neural network in our facial expression problem. The network has one input layer, two hidden layers, and one output layer.

First, we need to create a matrix to hold the layers definition. This matrix has four rows and one column:

```
Mat layers = Mat(3, 1, CV_32S);
```

Then, we assign the number of neurons for each layer, as follows:

```
layers.row(0) = Scalar(feature_size);
layers.row(1) = Scalar(20);
layers.row(2) = Scalar(num_of_labels);
```

In this network, the number of neurons for the input layer has to be equal to the number of elements of each feature vector, and number of neurons for the output layer is the number of facial expression labels (`feature_size` equals `train_features.cols` where `train_features` is the Mat that contains all features and `num_of_labels` equals 7 in our implementation).

The above parameters in our implementation are not optimal. You can try different values for different numbers of hidden layers and numbers of neurons. Remember that the number of hidden neurons should not be larger than the number of training samples. It is very difficult to choose the number of neurons in a hidden layer and the number of layers in your network. If you do some research, you can find several rules of thumb and diagnostic techniques. The best way to choose these parameters is experimentation. Basically, the more layers and hidden neurons there are, the more capacity you have in the network. However, more capacity may lead to overfitting. One of the most important rules is that the number of examples in the training set should be larger than the number of weights in the network. Based on our experience, you should start with one hidden layer with a small number of neurons and calculate the generalization error and training error. Then, you should modify the number of neurons and repeat the process.

Remember to make a graph to visualize the error when you change parameters. Keep in mind that the number of neurons is usually between the input layer size and the output layer size. After a few iterations, you can decide whether to add an additional layer or not.

However, in this case, we don't have much data. This makes the network hard to train. We may not add neurons and layers to improve the performance.

Train the network

First, we create a network variable, ANN_MLP, and add the layers definition to the network:

```
Ptr<ml::ANN_MLP> mlp = ml::ANN_MLP::create();
mlp->setLayerSizes(layers);
```

Then, we need to prepare some parameters for training algorithms. There are two algorithms for training MLP: the back-propagation algorithm and the RPROP algorithm. RPROP is the default algorithm for training. There are many parameters for RPROP so we will use the back-propagation algorithm for simplicity.

Below is our code for setting parameters for the back-propagation algorithm:

```
mlp->setTrainMethod(ml::ANN_MLP::BACKPROP);
mlp->setActivationFunction(ml::ANN_MLP::SIGMOID_SYM, 0, 0);
mlp->setTermCriteria(TermCriteria(TermCriteria::EPS+TermCriteria::COU
NT, 100000, 0.00001f));
```

We set the `TrainMethod` to `BACKPROP` to use the back-propagation algorithm. Select Sigmoid as the activation function There are three types of activation in OpenCV: `IDENTITY`, `GAUSSIAN`, and `SIGMOID`. You can go to the overview of this section for more details.

The final parameter is `TermCriteria`. This is the algorithm termination criteria. You can see an explanation of this parameter in the kmeans algorithm in the previous section.

Next, we create a `TrainData` variable to store all the training sets. The interface is the same as in the SVM section.

```
Ptr<ml::TrainData> trainData = ml::TrainData::create(train_features,
ml::SampleTypes::ROW_SAMPLE, train_labels);
```

train_features is the Mat which stores all training samples as in the SVM section. However, train_labels is different:

- train_features: This is a Mat that contains each features vector as a row as we did in the SVM. The number of rows of train_features is the number of training samples and the number of columns is the size of one features vector.

- train_labels: This is a Mat that contains labels for each training feature. Instead of the Nx1 matrix in SVM, train_labels in MLP should be a NxM matrix, N is the number of training samples and M is the number of labels. If the feature at row i is classified as label j, the position (i, j) of train_labels will be 1. Otherwise, the value will be zero. The code to create the train_labels variable is as follows:

```
Mat train_labels = Mat::zeros( labels.rows, num_of_label,
CV_32FC1);
for(int i = 0 ; i < labels.rows; i ++){
    int idx = labels.at<int>(i, 0);
    train_labels.at<float>(i, idx) = 1.0f;
}
```

Finally, we train the network with the following code:

```
mlp->train(trainData);
```

The training process takes a few minutes to complete. If you have a lot of training data, it may take a few hours.

Testing stage

Once we have trained our MLP, the testing stage is very simple.

First, we create a Mat to store the response of the network. The response is an array, whose length is the number of labels.

```
Mat response(1, num_of_labels, CV_32FC1);
```

Then, we assume that we have a Mat, called sample, which contains a feature vector. In our facial expression case, its size should be 1x1000.

We can call the predict function of the mlp model to obtain the response, as follows:

```
mlp->predict(sample, response);
```

The predicted label of the input sample is the index of the maximum value in the response array. You can find the label by simply iterating through the array. The disadvantage of this type of response is that you have to apply a `softmax` function if you want a probability for each response. In other neural network frameworks, there is usually a softmax layer for this reason. However, the advantage of this type of response is that the magnitude of each response is retained.

K-Nearest Neighbors (KNN)

K-Nearest Neighbors (KNN) is a very simple algorithm for machine learning but works very well in many practical problems. The idea of KNN is to classify an unknown example with the most common class among k-nearest known examples. KNN is also known as a non-parametric lazy learning algorithm. It means that KNN doesn't make any assumptions about the data distribution. The training process is very fast since it only caches all training examples. However, the testing process requires a lot of computation. The following figure demonstrates how KNN works in a 2D points case. The green dot is an unknown sample. KNN will find k-nearest known samples in space, (k = 5 in this example). There are three samples of red labels and two samples of blue labels. Therefore, the label for the prediction is red.

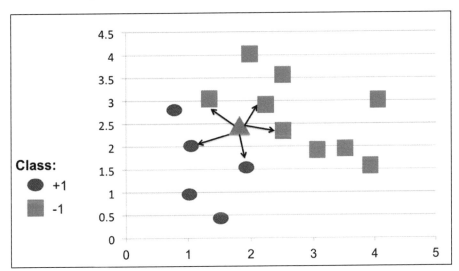

An explanation of how KNN predicts labels for unknown samples

Training stage

The implementation of KNN algorithms is very simple. We only need three lines of code to train a KNN model:

```
Ptr<ml::KNearest> knn = ml::KNearest::create();
Ptr<ml::TrainData> trainData = ml::TrainData::create(train_features,
ml::SampleTypes::ROW_SAMPLE, labels);
knn->train(trainData);
```

The preceding code is the same as with SVM:

- `train_features`: This is a Mat that contains each features vector as a row. The number of rows in `train_features` is the number of training samples and the number of columns is the size of one features vector.

- `train_labels`: This is a Mat that contains labels for each training feature. In KNN, `train_labels` is a Nx1 matrix, N is the number of training samples. The value of each row is the truth label of the corresponding sample. The type of this Mat should be `CV_32S`.

The testing stage

The testing stage is very straightforward. We can just pass a feature vector to the `findNearest` method of the `knn` model and obtain the label:

```
Mat predictedLabels;
knn->findNearest(sample, K, predictedLabels);
```

The second parameter is the most important parameter. It is the number of maximum neighbors that may be used for classification. In theory, if there are an infinite number of samples available, a larger K always means a better classification. However, in our facial expression problem, we only have 213 samples in total and about 170 samples in the training set. Therefore, if we use a large K, KNN may end up looking for samples that are not neighbors. In our implementation, K equals 2.

The predicted labels are stored in the `predictedLabels` variable and can be obtained as follows:

```
float prediction = bestLabels.at<float>(0,0);
```

Normal Bayes classifier

The Normal Bayes classifier is one of the simplest classifiers in OpenCV. The Normal Bayes classifier assumes that features vectors from each class are normally distributed, although not necessarily independently. This classifier is an effective classifier that can handle multiple classes. In the training step, the classifier estimates the mean and co-variance of the distribution for each class. In the testing step, the classifier computes the probability of the features to each class. In practice, we then test to see if the maximum probability is over a threshold. If it is, the label of the sample will be the class that has the maximum probability. Otherwise, we say that we can't recognize the sample.

OpenCV has already implemented this classifier in the ml module. In this section, we will show you the code to use the Normal Bayes classifier in our facial expression problem.

Training stage

The code to implement the Normal Bayes classifier is the same as with SVM and KNN. We only need to call the `create` function to obtain the classifier and start the training process. All the other parameters are the same as with SVM and KNN.

```
Ptr<ml::NormalBayesClassifier> bayes = ml::NormalBayesClassifier::cre
ate();
Ptr<ml::TrainData> trainData = ml::TrainData::create(train_features,
ml::SampleTypes::ROW_SAMPLE, labels);
bayes->train(trainData);
```

Testing stage

The code to test a sample with the Normal Bayes classifier is a little different from previous methods:

1. First, we need to create two Mats to store the output class and probability:

    ```
    Mat output, outputProb;
    ```

2. Then, we call the `predictProb` function of the model:

    ```
    bayes->predictProb(sample, output, outputProb);
    ```

3. The computed probability is stored in `outputProb` and the corresponding label can be retrieved as:

    ```
    unsigned int label = output.at<unsigned int>(0, 0);
    ```

Software usage guide

We have implemented the above process to perform classification with a training set. Using the software is quite easy:

1. Download the source code. Open the terminal and change directory to the source code folder.

2. Build the software with `cmake` using the follow command:

   ```
   mkdir build && cd build && cmake .. && make
   ```

3. You can use the `train` tool as follows:

   ```
   ./train -algo <algorithm_name> -src <input_features> -dest
   <output_folder>
   ```

The `train` tool performs the training process and outputs the accuracy on the console. The learned model will be saved to the output folder for further use as `model.yml`. Furthermore, kmeans centers and pca information from features extraction are also saved in `features_extraction.yml`. The available parameters are:

- `algorithm_name`: This can be `mlp`, `svm`, `knn`, `bayes`. This is the name of the learning algorithm.

- `input_features`: This is the absolute path to the location of the YAML features file from the `prepare_dataset` tool.

- `output_folder`: This is the absolute path to the folder where you want to keep the output model.

Evaluation

In this section, we will show the performance of our facial expression recognition system. In our test, we will keep the parameters of each learning algorithm the same and only change the feature extraction. We will evaluate the feature extraction with the number of clusters equaling 200, 500, 1,000, 1,500, 2,000, and 3,000.

The following table shows the accuracy of the system with the number of clusters equaling 200, 500, 1,000, 1,500, 2,000, and 3,000.

Table 1: The accuracy (%) of the system with 1,000 clusters

K = 1000	MLP	SVM	KNN	Normal Bayes
SIFT	72.7273	93.1818	81.8182	88.6364
SURF	61.3636	79.5455	72.7273	79.5455

K = 1000	MLP	SVM	KNN	Normal Bayes
BRISK	61.3636	65.9091	59.0909	68.1818
KAZE	50	79.5455	61.3636	77.2727
DAISY	59.0909	77.2727	65.9091	81.8182
DENSE-SIFT	20.4545	45.4545	43.1818	40.9091

Table 2: The accuracy (%) of the system with 500 clusters

K = 500	MLP	SVM	KNN	Normal Bayes
SIFT	56.8182	70.4545	75	77.2727
SURF	54.5455	63.6364	68.1818	79.5455
BRISK	36.3636	59.0909	52.2727	52.2727
KAZE	47.7273	56.8182	63.6364	65.9091
DAISY	54.5455	75	63.6364	75
DENSE-SIFT	27.2727	43.1818	38.6364	43.1818

Table 3: The accuracy (%) of the system with 200 clusters

K = 200	MLP	SVM	KNN	Normal Bayes
SIFT	50	68.1818	65.9091	75
SURF	43.1818	54.5455	52.2727	63.6364
BRISK	29.5455	47.7273	50	54.5455
KAZE	50	59.0909	72.7273	59.0909
DAISY	45.4545	68.1818	65.9091	70.4545
DENSE-SIFT	29.5455	43.1818	40.9091	31.8182

Table 4: The accuracy (%) of the system with 1,500 clusters

K = 1500	MLP	SVM	KNN	Normal Bayes
SIFT	45.4545	84.0909	75	79.5455
SURF	72.7273	88.6364	79.5455	86.3636
BRISK	54.5455	72.7273	56.8182	68.1818
KAZE	45.4545	79.5455	72.7273	77.2727
DAISY	61.3636	88.6364	65.9091	81.8182
DENSE-SIFT	34.0909	47.7273	38.6364	38.6364

Table 5: The accuracy (%) of the system with 2,000 clusters

K = 2000	MLP	SVM	KNN	Normal Bayes
SIFT	63.6364	88.6364	81.8182	88.6364
SURF	65.9091	84.0909	68.1818	81.8182
BRISK	47.7273	68.1818	47.7273	61.3636
KAZE	47.7273	77.2727	72.7273	75
DAISY	77.2727	81.8182	72.7273	84.0909
DENSE-SIFT	38.6364	45.4545	36.3636	43.1818

Table 6: The accuracy (%) of the system with 3,000 clusters

K = 3000	MLP	SVM	KNN	Normal Bayes
SIFT	52.2727	88.6364	77.2727	86.3636
SURF	59.0909	79.5455	65.9091	77.2727
BRISK	52.2727	65.9091	43.1818	59.0909
KAZE	61.3636	81.8182	70.4545	84.0909
DAISY	72.7273	79.5455	70.4545	68.1818
DENSE-SIFT	27.2727	47.7273	38.6364	45.4545

Evaluation with different learning algorithms

We can create graphs with the above results to compare the performance between features and learning algorithms in the following figure. We can see that SVM and Normal Bayes have better results than the others in most cases. The best result is 93.1818% for SVM and SIFT in 1,000 clusters. MLP has the lowest result in almost every case. One reason is that MLP requires lots of data to prevent over fitting. We only have around 160 training images. However, the feature size for each sample is between 100 and 150. Even with two hidden neurons, the number of weights is larger than the number of samples. KNN seems to work better than MLP but can't beat SVM and Normal Bayes.

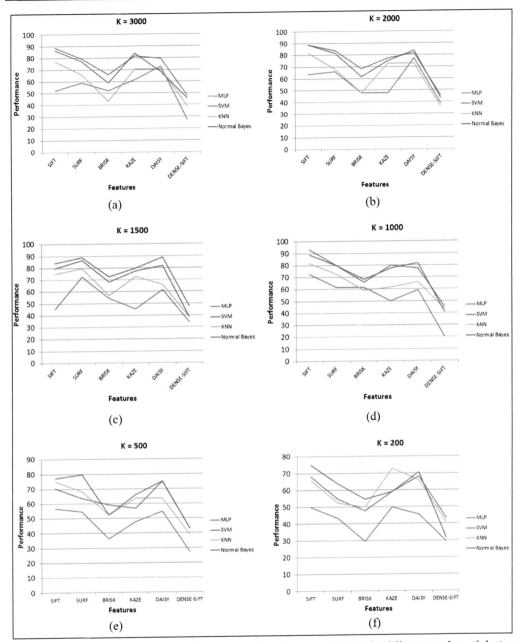

Relationship between the performance of features and machine algorithms under different numbers of clusters

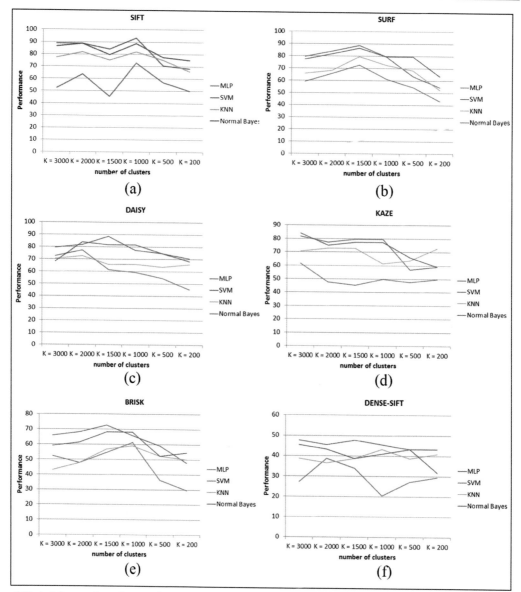

Effect of the number of centroids on the performance of features according to different machine algorithms

Evaluation with different features

In the figure, *Relationship between the performance of features and machine algorithms under different numbers of clusters*, we have evaluated six features. SIFT gives the best results in most cases. DAISY is comparable to SIFT. In some cases, KAZE also gives good results. DENSE-SIFT is not a good choice for our facial expression problem since the results are poor. Moreover, the computation cost for DENSE features is really high. In conclusion, SIFT is still the most stable choice. However, SIFT is under patent. You may want to look at DAISY or KAZE. We recommend you do the evaluation on your data and choose the most suitable feature.

Evaluation with a different number of clusters

In the figure, *Effect of the number of centroids on the performance of features according to different machine algorithms*, we made a graph to visualize the effects of the number of clusters on performance. As you can see, the number of clusters differs between features. In SIFT, KAZE, and BRISK, the best number of clusters is 1,000. However, in SURF, DAISY, and DENSE-SIFT, 1,500 is a better choice. Basically, we don't want the number of clusters to be too large. The computation cost in kmeans increases with a larger number of clusters, especially in DENSE-SIFT.

System overview

In this section, we will explain the process to apply the trained model in your application. Given a face image, we detect and process each face separately. Then, we find landmarks and extract the face region. The image features are extracted and passed to kmeans to obtain a 1,000-dimensional feature vector. PCA is applied to reduce the dimension of this feature vector. The learned machine learning model is used to predict the expression of the input face.

The following figure shows the complete process to predict the facial expression of a face in an image:

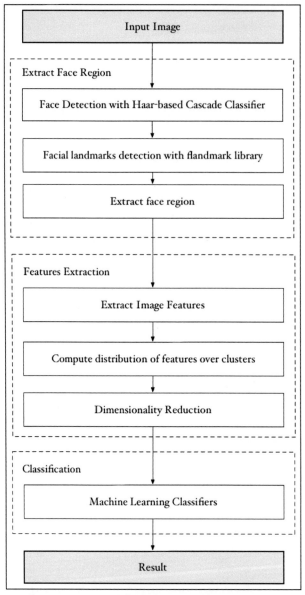

The process to predict a facial expression in a new image

Further reading

We have introduced a basic system for facial expression. If you are really interested in this topic, you may want to read this section for more guidance on how to improve the performance of the system. In this section, we will introduce you to compiling the `opencv_contrib` module, the Kaggle facial expression dataset, and the k-cross validation approach. We will also give you some suggestions on how to get better feature extraction.

Compiling the opencv_contrib module

In this section, we will introduce the process for compiling `opencv_contrib` in Linux-based systems. If you use Windows, you can use the Cmake GUI with the same options.

First, clone the `opencv` repository to your local machine:

```
git clone https://github.com/Itseez/opencv.git --depth=1
```

Second, clone the `opencv_contrib` repository to your local machine:

```
git clone https://github.com/Itseez/opencv_contrib --depth=1
```

Change directory to the `opencv` folder and make a build directory:

```
cd opencv
mkdir build
cd build
```

Build OpenCV from source with opencv_contrib support. You should change `OPENCV_EXTRA_MODULES_PATH` to the location of `opencv_contrib` on your machine:

```
cmake -D CMAKE_BUILD_TYPE=RELEASE -D CMAKE_INSTALL_PREFIX=/usr/local -D
OPENCV_EXTRA_MODULES_PATH=~/opencv_contrib/ ..
make -j4
make install
```

Kaggle facial expression dataset

Kaggle is a great community of data scientists. There are many competitions hosted by Kaggle. In 2013, there was a facial expression recognition challenge.

At the moment, you can go to the following link to access the full dataset:
`https://www.kaggle.com/c/challenges-in-representation-learning-facial-expression-recognition-challenge/`

The dataset consists of 48x48 pixel grayscale images of faces. There are 28,709 training samples, 3,589 public test images and 3,589 images for final test. The dataset contains seven expressions (Anger, Disgust, Fear, Happiness, Sadness, Surprise and Neutral). The winner achieved a score of 69.769 %. This dataset is huge so we think that our basic system may not work out of the box. We believe that you should try to improve the performance of the system if you want to use this dataset.

Facial landmarks

In our facial expression system, we use face detection as a pre-processing step to extract the face region. However, face detection is prone to misalignment, hence, feature extraction may not be reliable. In recent years, one of the most common approaches has been the usage of facial landmarks. In this kind of method, the facial landmarks are detected and used to align the face region. Many researchers use facial landmarks to extract the facial components such as the eyes, mouth, and so on, and do feature extractions separately.

What are facial landmarks?

Facial landmarks are predefined locations of facial components. The figure below shows an example of a 68 points system from the iBUG group (http://ibug.doc.ic.ac.uk/resources/facial-point-annotations)

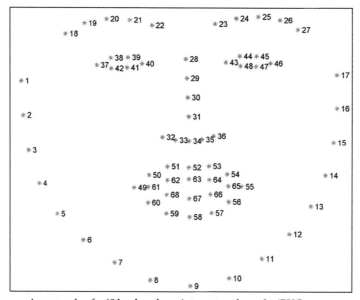

An example of a 68 landmarks points system from the iBUG group

How do you detect facial landmarks?

There are several ways to detect facial landmarks in a face region. We will give you a few solutions so that you can start your project easily

- **Active Shape Model**: This is one of the most common approaches to this problem. You may find the following library useful:

  Stasm: `https://github.com/cxcxcxcx/asmlib-opencv`

- **Face Alignment by Explicit Regression by Cao et al**: This is one of the latest works on facial landmarks. This system is very efficient and highly accurate. You can find an open source implementation at the following hyperlink: `https://github.com/soundsilence/FaceAlignment`

How do you use facial landmarks?

You can use facial landmarks in many ways. We will give you some guides:

- You can use facial landmarks to align the face region to a common standard and extract the features vectors as in our basic facial expression system.

- You can extract features vectors in different facial components such as eyes and mouths separately and combine everything in one feature vector for classification.

- You can use the location of facial landmarks as a feature vector and ignore the texture in the image.

- You can build classification models for each facial component and combine the prediction in a weighted manner.

Improving feature extraction

Feature extraction is one of the most important parts of facial expression. It is better to choose the right feature for your problem. In our implementation, we have only used a few features in OpenCV. We recommend that you try every possible feature in OpenCV. Here is the list of supported features in Open CV: BRIEF, BRISK, FREAK, ORB, SIFT, SURF, KAZE, AKAZE, FAST, MSER, and STAR.

There are other great features in the community that might be suitable for your problem, such as LBP, Gabor, HOG, and so on.

K-fold cross validation

K-fold cross validation is a common technique for estimating the performance of a classifier. Given a training set, we will divide it into k partitions. For each fold i of k experiments, we will train the classifier using all the samples that do not belong to fold i and use the samples in fold i to test the classifier.

The advantage of k-fold cross validation is that all the examples in the dataset are eventually used for training and validation.

It is important to divide the original dataset into the training set and the testing set. Then, the training set will be used for k-fold cross validation and the testing set will be used for the final test.

Cross validation combines the prediction error of each experiment and derives a more accurate estimate of the model. It is very useful, especially in cases where we don't have much data for training. Despite a high computation time, using a complex feature is a great idea if you want to improve the overall performance of the system.

Summary

This chapter showed the complete process of a facial expression system in OpenCV 3. We went through each step of the system and gave you a lot of alternative solutions for each step. This chapter also made an evaluation of the results based on features and learning algorithms.

Finally, this chapter gave you a few hints for further improvement including a great facial expression challenge, a facial landmarks approach, some features suggestions, and k-fold cross validation.

4
Panoramic Image Stitching Application Using Android Studio and NDK

Panorama is an interesting subject in application development. In OpenCV, the stitching module can easily create a panorama image from a sequence of images. One benefit of the stitching module is that the sequence of images don't have to be in order and can be in any direction. However, in the OpenCV Android SDK, the stitching module does not exist. Therefore, we must use the stitching module in the C++ interface. Luckily, Android provides the **Native Development Kit (NDK)** to support native development in C/C++. In this chapter, we will guide you through the steps to capture camera frames from Java and process the data in OpenCV C++ with the NDK.

In this chapter, you will learn:

- How to make a complete panorama stitching application
- How to use Java Native Interface (JNI) to use OpenCV C++ in Android Studio
- How to use the stitching module to create a panorama image

Introducing the concept of panorama

A panorama image gives the viewer a much broader field of view than a normal image and allows them to fully experience a scene. By extending the range of panorama to 360 degrees, viewers can simulate turning their head around. A panorama image can be created by stitching a sequence of overlapping images.

The following figure shows a demonstration of a panorama image captured with our application.

A panorama image captured in an horizontal direction

In order to capture a panorama image, you must capture many images of the scene at different angles, as in the following figure. For example, you take your first picture at the left side of the room. Then, you move the phone straight to a new angle to start capturing. All the images will be stitched together to create a panorama image.

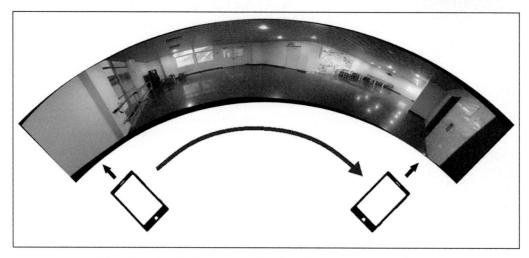

Illustration showing how you pan the phone to create a panorama image

Normally, a panorama application only supports capturing images in horizontal. With the stitching module in OpenCV, we can extend the height of an image by capturing more images in both directions. The following figure shows an image that can be captured by changing the camera view in a horizontal and vertical direction.

A panorama image captured in both directions

In this chapter, we will implement a panorama application in Android using OpenCV 3.0.0. The chapter contains two main sections:

- **Android section**: We will implement the user interface in Android Studio. In this chapter, we only implement the panorama capture activity with two buttons, **Capture** and **Save**. When the panorama is captured, we will save it to the phone's internal storage.

- **OpenCV section**: We will show the process to integrate OpenCV to Android Studio with NDK/JNI and implement the code to create a panorama image from a sequence of images captured in the Android section.

In the following sections, we will show the process to create a user interface in Android Studio. If you want to review the OpenCV code, you can go to the *Integrating OpenCV into the Android Studio* section and come back to this later.

The Android section – an application user interface

In this section, we will show you a basic user interface to capture and save the panorama to the internal storage. Basically, the user will see a fullscreen of the camera preview image. When the user presses the **Capture** button, the application will capture the current scene and put the captured image on an overlay layer above the current view. Therefore, the user knows what they have just captured and can change the phone position to capture the next image.

The following is a screenshot of the application when the user opens it and after the user captures an image:

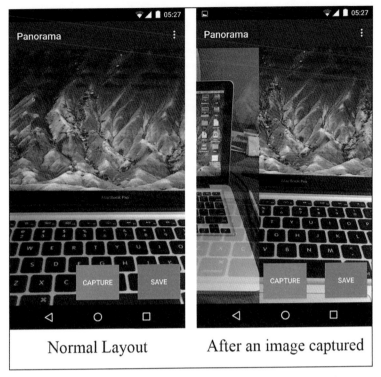

An example of the user interface before and after a user captures an image

The setup activity layout

First, we will create a new Android project with a blank activity in Android Studio. Then, we will edit the layout xml for MainActivity in `app/src/main/res/layout/activity_main.xml` as follows:

```xml
<RelativeLayout    xmlns:android="http://schemas.android.com/apk/res/
android"
    xmlns:tools="http://schemas.android.com/tools"
    android:layout_width="match_parent"
    android:layout_height="match_parent"
    tools:context=".MainActivity">
    <SurfaceView
        android:id="@+id/surfaceView"
        android:layout_width="match_parent"
        android:layout_height="match_parent"
        />
    <SurfaceView
        android:id="@+id/surfaceViewOnTop"
        android:layout_width="match_parent"
        android:layout_height="match_parent"
        />
    <Button
        android:id="@+id/capture"
        android:text="Capture"
        android:layout_width="wrap_content"
        android:layout_height="70dp"
        android:layout_alignParentBottom="true"
        android:layout_centerHorizontal="true"
        android:layout_marginBottom="10dp"
        android:padding="10dp"
        android:textColor="#FFF"
        android:background="@android:color/holo_blue_dark"
        />
    <Button
        android:id="@+id/save"
        android:text="Save"
        android:layout_width="wrap_content"
        android:layout_height="70dp"
        android:padding="10dp"
        android:textColor="#FFF"
        android:background="@android:color/holo_purple"
        android:layout_marginRight="10dp"
```

```
            android:layout_alignTop="@+id/capture"
            android:layout_alignParentRight="true"
            android:layout_alignParentEnd="true" />
    </RelativeLayout>
```

In this layout xml file, we have two SurfaceViews—one for the camera preview and one for the overlay layer. We also have two buttons—one for capturing the image and one for saving the panorama image to the internal storage.

Capturing the camera frame

In this section, we will implement the process to capture camera frames and view it on a SurfaceView with the ID `surfaceView`.

At the begin of the `MainActivity` class, we will create some objects to work with the layout:

```
public class MainActivity extends ActionBarActivity {
    private Button captureBtn, saveBtn; // used to interact with
capture and save Button in UI
    private SurfaceView mSurfaceView, mSurfaceViewOnTop; // used to
display the camera frame in UI
    private Camera mCam;
    private boolean isPreview; // Is the camera frame displaying?
    private boolean safeToTakePicture = true; // Is it safe to capture
a picture?
```

In the preceding code, we created two buttons and two `SurfaceViews` to interact with the user interface. We also create a Camera object, `mCam`, to open the camera. In our implementation, we will open the camera and get the video frame in the Android approach. OpenCV also provides some other approaches to open the camera. However, we found that they may not work well on all Android devices, so we prefer using the camera with Android approach. In this chapter, we only need the Camera object from the Android API. The advantage of this approach is that you can expect it to work on almost any Android device. The disadvantage is that you have to do some conversion from camera byte array to Android Bitmap to display on the UI and to OpenCV Mat to do the image processing.

 If you want to experience OpenCV classes to interact with the camera, you may want to check *Chapter 7, Gyroscopic Video Stabilization*, of this book.

In the `onCreate` function, we set up these objects as follows:

```
@Override
protected void onCreate(Bundle savedInstanceState){
    super.onCreate(savedInstanceState);
    setContentView(R.layout.activity_main);

    isPreview = false;
    mSurfaceView = (SurfaceView)findViewById(R.id.surfaceView);
    mSurfaceView.getHolder().addCallback(mSurfaceCallback);

    mSurfaceViewOnTop = (SurfaceView)findViewById(R.
id.surfaceViewOnTop);
    mSurfaceViewOnTop.setZOrderOnTop(true);     // necessary
    mSurfaceViewOnTop.getHolder().setFormat(PixelFormat.TRANSPARENT);

    captureBtn = (Button) findViewById(R.id.capture);
    captureBtn.setOnClickListener(captureOnClickListener);

    saveBtn = (Button) findViewById(R.id.save);
    saveBtn.setOnClickListener(saveOnClickListener);
}
```

First, we initialize `isPreview` to false and assign `mSurfaceView` to `SurfaceView` in the layout. Then, we get the holder of `mSurfaceView` and add a callback to it. The variable `mSurfaceCallback` is an instance of `SurfaceHolder.Callback` that we will create later. We also assign `mSurfaceViewOnTop` to the other SurfaceView in the layout, since we want this SurfaceView to be an overlay layer on the camera view. We need to set the Z order to be true and set the holder format to `TRANSPARENT`. Finally, we set up the capture and save buttons, and set the corresponding `OnClickListener`. In the next part, we will work on displaying the camera frame on the `SurfaceView`. So we will just create a basic `OnClickListener` as follows:

```
View.OnClickListener captureOnClickListener = new View.
OnClickListener() {
    @Override
    public void onClick(View v) {
    }
};
View.OnClickListener saveOnClickListener = new View.OnClickListener()
{
    @Override
    public void onClick(View v) {
    }
};
```

Using the Camera API to get the camera frame

As we said before, we will use the Android API to get the camera frame in Android. Currently, there are two versions of Camera API, android.hardware.Camera and android.hardware.camera2. We will use android.hardware.Camera because it supports most of the Android devices up to Android 4.4. In Android 5.0 and later, this API is deprecated and replaced by camera2. We can still use android. hardware.Camera on Android 5.0. If you want to target Android 5.0, we recommend you to try camera2 in your application.

In order to use the camera, we need to add the following lines to AndroidManifest. xml to gain the permissions to the camera. Besides, we also request the permission to write to storage as we will save the panorama image to internal storage.

```
<uses-feature android:name="android.hardware.camera" />
<uses-permission android:name="android.permission.CAMERA" />
<uses-permission android:name="android.permission.WRITE_EXTERNAL_
STORAGE" />
```

We want to set the mSurfaceView to display the camera frame, so we will set up the camera parameters in the callback of mSurfaceView. We need to create the variable mSurfaceCallback as follows:

```
SurfaceHolder.Callback mSurfaceCallback = new SurfaceHolder.Callback()
{
    @Override
    public void surfaceCreated(SurfaceHolder holder) {
        try {
            // Tell the camera to display the frame on this
surfaceview
            mCam.setPreviewDisplay(holder);
        } catch (IOException e) {
            e.printStackTrace();
        }
    }
    @Override
    public void surfaceChanged(SurfaceHolder holder, int format, int
width, int height) {
        // Get the default parameters for camera
        Camera.Parameters myParameters = mCam.getParameters();
        // Select the best preview size
        Camera.Size myBestSize = getBestPreviewSize( myParameters );
        if(myBestSize != null){
            // Set the preview Size
```

```
                    myParameters.setPreviewSize(myBestSize.width, myBestSize.
height);
                    // Set the parameters to the camera
                    mCam.setParameters(myParameters);
                    // Rotate the display frame 90 degree to view in portrait
mode
                    mCam.setDisplayOrientation(90);
                    // Start the preview
                    mCam.startPreview();
                    isPreview = true;
                }
            }
            @Override
            public void surfaceDestroyed(SurfaceHolder holder) {
            }
        };
```

In this code, we call the `setPreviewDisplay` method in the `surfaceCreated` function to tell the camera to display the camera frame on `mSurfaceView`. After this, in the `surfaceChanged` function, we set the camera parameters, change the display orientation to 90 degrees and start the preview process. The function `getBestPreviewSize` is a function to get the preview size that has the biggest number of pixels. The `getBestPreviewSize` is simple, as follows:

```
    private Camera.Size getBestPreviewSize(Camera.Parameters parameters){
        Camera.Size bestSize = null;
        List<Camera.Size> sizeList = parameters.
getSupportedPreviewSizes();
        bestSize = sizeList.get(0);
        for(int i = 1; i < sizeList.size(); i++){
            if((sizeList.get(i).width * sizeList.get(i).height) >
                    (bestSize.width * bestSize.height)){
                bestSize = sizeList.get(i);
            }
        }
        return bestSize;
    }
```

Finally, we need to add some code to open the camera in `onResume` and release the camera in `onPause`:

```
    @Override
    protected void onResume() {
        super.onResume();
```

```
    mCam = Camera.open(0); // 0 for back camera
}
@Override
protected void onPause() {
    super.onPause();
    if(isPreview){
        mCam.stopPreview();
    }
    mCam.release();
    mCam = null;
    isPreview = false;
}
```

At this moment, we can install and run the application on a real device. The following figure shows a screenshot of our application on a Nexus 5 running Android 5.1.1:

A screenshot of the application in Camera Preview mode on Nexus 5 running Android 5.1.1

In our application, we don't want the layout to rotate so we set the activity orientation to portrait mode. It's optional. If you want to do this, you can simply change your activity in `AndroidManifest.xml` as follows:

```
<activity
    android:screenOrientation="portrait"
    android:name=".MainActivity"
    android:label="@string/app_name" >
```

Implementing the Capture button

In this section, we will show you how to implement the `OnClickListener` of the **Capture** button. When the user clicks on the **Capture** button, we want the application to take a picture of the current scene. With the Camera API, we can use the `takePicture` function to capture a picture. The benefit of this function is that the resolution of the output image is very high. For example, when our application runs on Nexus 5, even though the previewing size is 1920x1080, the resolution of the captured image is 3264x2448. We change `captureOnClickListener` as follows:

```
View.OnClickListener captureOnClickListener = new View.
OnClickListener() {
    @Override
    public void onClick(View v) {
        if(mCam != null && safeToTakePicture){
            // set the flag to false so we don't take two picture at a
same time
            safeToTakePicture = false;
            mCam.takePicture(null, null, jpegCallback);
        }
    }
};
```

In the `onClick` function, we check whether the camera is initialized and the flag `safeToTakePicture` is `true`. Then, we set the flag to `false` so that we don't take two pictures at the same time. The `takePicture` function of the Camera instance requires three parameters. The first and second parameters are shutter call back and raw data call back respectively. These functions may be called differently on different devices so we don't want to use them and set them to null. The last parameter is the callback that is called when the camera saves the picture in the JPEG format.

```
Camera.PictureCallback jpegCallback = new Camera.PictureCallback() {
    public void onPictureTaken(byte[] data, Camera camera) {
        // decode the byte array to a bitmap
```

```
        Bitmap bitmap = BitmapFactory.decodeByteArray(data, 0, data.
length);
        // Rotate the picture to fit portrait mode
        Matrix matrix = new Matrix();
        matrix.postRotate(90);
        bitmap = Bitmap.createBitmap(bitmap, 0, 0, bitmap.getWidth(),
bitmap.getHeight(), matrix, false);

        // TODO: Save the image to a List to pass them to OpenCV
method

        Canvas canvas = null;
        try {
            canvas = mSurfaceViewOnTop.getHolder().lockCanvas(null);
            synchronized (mSurfaceViewOnTop.getHolder()) {
                // Clear canvas
                canvas.drawColor(Color.TRANSPARENT, PorterDuff.Mode.
CLEAR);

                // Scale the image to fit the SurfaceView
                float scale = 1.0f * mSurfaceView.getHeight() /
bitmap.getHeight();
                Bitmap scaleImage = Bitmap.createScaledBitmap(bitmap,
(int)(scale * bitmap.getWidth()), mSurfaceView.getHeight() , false);
                Paint paint = new Paint();
                // Set the opacity of the image
                paint.setAlpha(200);
                // Draw the image with an offset so we only see one
third of image.
                canvas.drawBitmap(scaleImage, -scaleImage.getWidth() *
2 / 3, 0, paint);
            }
        } catch (Exception e) {
            e.printStackTrace();
        } finally {
            if (canvas != null) {
                mSurfaceViewOnTop.getHolder().
unlockCanvasAndPost(canvas);
            }
        }
        // Start preview the camera again and set the take picture
flag to true
```

```
            mCam.startPreview();
            safeToTakePicture = true;
        }
    };
```

First, `onPictureTaken` provides a byte array of the captured image, so we would want to decode it to an instance of Bitmap. Because the camera sensor captured the image in landscape mode, we would want to apply a rotation matrix to obtain the image in the portrait mode. Then, we would want to save this image to pass a sequence of images to the OpenCV stitching module. Since this code needs the OpenCV library, we will implement this part later. After this, we will obtain the canvas of the overlay `SurfaceView` and try to draw the image on the screen. The following is a demonstration of the overlay layer on top of the previewing layer. Finally, we will start the preview process again and also set the `safeToTakePicture` flag to `true`.

A screenshot of the application after the user captured an image on a Nexus 5 running Android 5.1.1

Implementing the Save button

Currently, the **Save** button is fairly simple. We will assume that when the user clicks on the **Save** button, we will start a new thread to perform the image processing task:

```
View.OnClickListener saveOnClickListener = new View.OnClickListener()
{
    @Override
    public void onClick(View v) {
        Thread thread = new Thread(imageProcessingRunnable);
        thread.start();
    }
};
```

In `imageProcessingRunnable`, we would want to show a processing dialog at the start of the process and close the dialog when everything is completed. In order to accomplish this, we will first create an instance of `ProgressDialog`:

```
ProgressDialog ringProgressDialog;
```

Then, `imageProcessingRunnable` is implemented as:

```
private Runnable imageProcessingRunnable = new Runnable() {
    @Override
    public void run() {
        showProcessingDialog();
        // TODO: implement OpenCV parts
        closeProcessingDialog();
    }
};
```

We will simply call `showProcessingDialog` to show the progressing dialog and call `closeProcessingDialog` to close the dialog. The steps in between are quite complex and requires lots of OpenCV functions, so we keep this part for a later section. The functions to show and close the progress dialog are as follows:

```
private void showProcessingDialog(){
    runOnUiThread(new Runnable() {
        @Override
        public void run() {
            mCam.stopPreview();
            ringProgressDialog = ProgressDialog.show(MainActivity.
this, "", "Panorama", true);
```

```
                    ringProgressDialog.setCancelable(false);
            }
        });
    }

    private void closeProcessingDialog(){
        runOnUiThread(new Runnable() {
            @Override
            public void run() {
                mCam.startPreview();
                ringProgressDialog.dismiss();
            }
        });
    }
```

In `showProcessingDialog`, we will stop the camera preview to reduce unnecessary computation cost on the device, whereas in `closeProcessingDialog`, we start the camera preview again to allow the user to capture more panorama images. We must put these codes in `runOnUiThread` since these codes interact with the UI elements.

In the following section, we will show you how to implement the remaining parts of our application with OpenCV.

Integrating OpenCV into the Android Studio

In this section, we will show you the steps to integrate OpenCV in the Android Studio with the Native Development Kit and use the OpenCV stitching module in C++ to create the final panorama image. We will also do some computations with OpenCV Android SDK Java to show how the interaction goes about between Java and C++ interfaces.

Compiling OpenCV Android SDK to the Android Studio project

Officially, the OpenCV Android SDK is an Eclipse project, which means we can't simply use it in our Android Studio project. We need to convert the OpenCV Android SDK to an Android Studio project and import it as a module to our application.

We assume that you have downloaded the latest OpenCV for Android from `http://opencv.org/downloads.html`. At the time of writing, we now have OpenCV for Android 3.0.0.

Let's extract the downloaded file to your favorite path, for example, `/Volumes/Data/OpenCV/OpenCV-android-sdk`.

Then, we need to open a new Android Studio window and select **Import project** (Eclipse ADT, Gradle, and so on). In the popup window, you should select the `java` folder at `OpenCV-android-sdk/sdk/java` and click on **OK**.

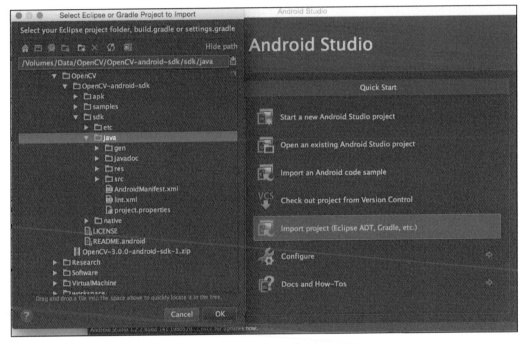

Import project visualization

In the next window, we will choose a path to store the new OpenCV SDK project. In our case, we choose /Volumes/Data/OpenCV/opencv-java and click on **Next**.

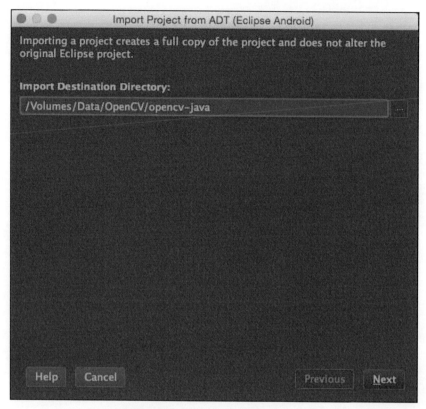

Select import destination visualization

In the last window, we will simply click on **Finish** and wait until Android Studio completes the Gradle build process. Basically, Gradle is the default build system of Android Studio. At this step, we want to make sure that the OpenCV SDK can be compiled successfully. One of the common errors is that you haven't downloaded the required Android SDK. The error message is very straightforward. You can follow the message to solve the problem. In our case, there is no problem as in the following screenshot.

Build competition visualization

At this time, we can close this project and open our Panorama project.

Setting up the Android Studio to work with OpenCV

In order to use OpenCV in our project, we need to import the OpenCV Android SDK to our project. With this SDK, we can use the OpenCV Java API and perform image processing tasks easily. Moreover, we must make a further step to tell Android Studio to compile OpenCV C++ code to use OpenCV in the Native Development Kit (NDK). We will split this section into three subsections: Importing the Android SDK, Creating a Java-C++ interaction, and Compiling OpenCV C++.

Importing the OpenCV Android SDK

We assume that you have opened the Panorama project. We need to import the converted OpenCV Android SDK in the previous section as follows:

File | New | Import Module

In the **New Module** window, we will select the source directory to the converted project. In our case, we will choose `/Volumes/Data/OpenCV/opencv-java`. Then, we'll check the import checkbox, change the module name to `:opencv-java`, as shown in the following screenshot and click **Finish**:

A new module window

Next, we need to modify `build.gradle` in the `app` folder to add one line to the `dependencies` section:

```
dependencies {
    compile fileTree(dir: 'libs', include: ['*.jar'])
    compile 'com.android.support:appcompat-v7:22.1.1'

    compile project(":opencv-java")
}
```

Finally, we must sync the project with the button **Sync Project with Gradle Files**.

> If you only need the OpenCV Java Interface and don't want to use
> OpenCV C++, you must copy the `libs` folder at `OpenCV-android-`
> `sdk/sdk/native/libs` to your `app/src/main` folder. Then, you
> must add the following `loadLibrary` code to your class file:
>
> ```
> static {
>         //If you use OpenCV 2.*, use "opencv_java"
>         System.loadLibrary("opencv_java3");
> }
> ```

Creating a Java and C++ interaction with Java Native Interface (JNI)

Before we start the compile process, we will create a class file named
`NativePanorama.java` and add a method to the `NativePanorama` class:

```
public class NativePanorama {
    public native static void processPanorama(long[]
imageAddressArray, long outputAddress);
}
```

The `processPanorama` method will receive an array of long addresses of each image
and a long address of an output image.

You must rebuild the project in order to follow the ensuing steps. The detailed
explanation is in the next paragraph:

- Use the `javah` command line to create a C++ header
- Create a `.cpp` file for the newly created header in the `jni` folder to
  implement the function in C++

You may notice the keyword `native` before the `processPanorama` method. This
means that we will use this method to interact between Java and C++ in our
application. Therefore, we need to create some headers and source files to implement
our C++ code. We must follow **Java Native Interface (JNI)** to use C++ code, so the
process may be a bit complex and out of the scope of this book.

In the following parts, we will show you the steps to use OpenCV C++.

> If you want to understand JNI, you may want to take a look at the JNI documentation found at:
>
> http://docs.oracle.com/javase/7/docs/technotes/
> guides/jni/
>
> Also, have a look at the JNI tips from API guides found at:
>
> http://developer.android.com/training/articles/perf-
> jni.html

First, we will use the `javah` command in the terminal to create the corresponding C++ header for the `processPanorama` method. In order to do this, you need to open the terminal on your machine, then change the directory to the folder `app/src/main` in your Android application and run the following command:

```
javah -d jni -classpath ../../build/intermediates/classes/debug/ com.
example.panorama.NativePanorama
```

You only need to verify the package name and the name of the class file, `NativePanorama`. The command will not display anything on the terminal, as shown in the following figure. You may want to rebuild the project if you encounter the following error: **Error: Could not find class file for 'com.example. panorama.NativePanorama'**.

```
Quans-MacBook-Pro:main quanhua92$ javah -d jni -classpath ../../build/intermediates/classes/debug/
com.example.panorama.NativePanorama
Quans-MacBook-Pro:main quanhua92$
```

The terminal after using the javah command

As the result of the `javah` command, we now have a folder named `jni` in our `app/src/main` folder with a file `com_example_panorama_NativePanorama.h`. This header contains a function to work with Java Interface. When `processPanorama` is called, this function will run in C++.

Next, we will create a source file named `com_example_panorama_NativePanorama.cpp` in the `jni` folder. We recommend that you should copy the function declaration from the header file to the source file and add the parameter names as follows:

```
#include "com_example_panorama_NativePanorama.h"
JNIEXPORT void JNICALL Java_com_example_panorama_NativePanorama_
processPanorama
  (JNIEnv * env, jclass clazz, jlongArray imageAddressArray, jlong
outputAddress) {
}
```

The only thing left is that we need to compile OpenCV C++ SDK to use it in the preceding source file.

Compiling OpenCV C++ with NDK/JNI

In order to use OpenCV in C++ code, we need to compile OpenCV C++ and use an `Android.mk` file as the make file to build and link our C++ file with OpenCV library. However, Android Studio doesn't support `Android.mk` out of the box. We need to do lots of things to make this happen.

First, we will open the `local.properties` file and set `ndk.dir` to be your path to the Android NDK folder. In our case, the `local.properties` will look like this:

```
sdk.dir=/Users/quanhua92/Library/Android/sdk
ndk.dir=/Users/quanhua92/Software/android-ndk-r10e
```

 You can get the Android NDK at: `https://developer.android.com/ndk/index.html`

Secondly, we open the `build.gradle` file in our app folder and add this line at the top:

```
import org.apache.tools.ant.taskdefs.condition.Os
```

Then, we need to add the following code between the `defaultConfig` tag and `buildType` tag to create a new Gradle task to build C++ code.

```
// begin NDK OPENCV
sourceSets.main {
    jni.srcDirs = [] //disable automatic ndk-build call
}
task ndkBuild(type: Exec, description: 'Compile JNI source via NDK') {
    def rootDir = project.rootDir
    def localProperties = new File(rootDir, "local.properties")
    Properties properties = new Properties()
    localProperties.withInputStream { instr ->
        properties.load(instr)
    }
    def ndkDir = properties.getProperty('ndk.dir')
    if (Os.isFamily(Os.FAMILY_WINDOWS)) {
        commandLine "$ndkDir\\ndk-build.cmd",
                'NDK_PROJECT_PATH=build/intermediates/ndk',
                'NDK_LIBS_OUT=src/main/jniLibs',
                'APP_BUILD_SCRIPT=src/main/jni/Android.mk',
```

```
                    'NDK_APPLICATION_MK=src/main/jni/Application.mk'
        } else {
            commandLine "$ndkDir/ndk-build",
                    'NDK_PROJECT_PATH=build/intermediates/ndk',
                    'NDK_LIBS_OUT=src/main/jniLibs',
                    'APP_BUILD_SCRIPT=src/main/jni/Android.mk',
                    'NDK_APPLICATION_MK=src/main/jni/Application.mk'
        }
    }
    tasks.withType(JavaCompile) {
        compileTask -> compileTask.dependsOn ndkBuild
    }
    //end
```

You may want to look at the following figure for a screenshot of our build.gradle.

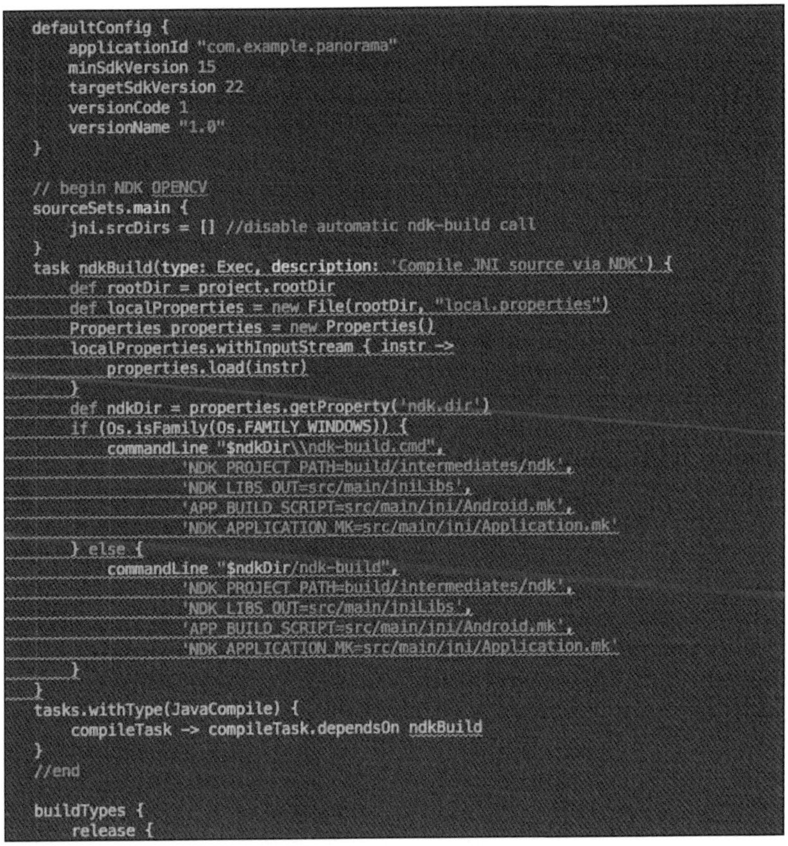

A screenshot of our build.gradle

Next, we create a file named `Application.mk` in the `jni` folder and put the following lines in it:

```
APP_STL := gnustl_static
APP_CPPFLAGS := -frtti -fexceptions
APP_ABI := all
APP_PLATFORM := android-16
```

Finally, we create a file named `Android.mk` in the `jni` folder and set up this file as below to use OpenCV in our C++ code. You may need to change the OPENCVROOT variable to the location of OpenCV-android-sdk in your machine:

```
LOCAL_PATH := $(call my-dir)

include $(CLEAR_VARS)
#opencv
OPENCVROOT:= /Volumes/Data/OpenCV/OpenCV-android-sdk
OPENCV_CAMERA_MODULES:=on
OPENCV_INSTALL_MODULES:=on
OPENCV_LIB_TYPE:=SHARED
include ${OPENCVROOT}/sdk/native/jni/OpenCV.mk

LOCAL_SRC_FILES := com_example_panorama_NativePanorama.cpp
LOCAL_LDLIBS += -llog
LOCAL_MODULE := MyLib

include $(BUILD_SHARED_LIBRARY)
```

With the preceding `Android.mk`, Android Studio will build OpenCV into `libopencv_java3.so` and build our C++ code into `libMyLib.so` in the folder app/src/main/jniLibs. We have to open our `MainActivity.java` and load this library to use in our application as follows:

```
public class MainActivity extends ActionBarActivity {
    static{
        System.loadLibrary("opencv_java3");
        System.loadLibrary("MyLib");
    }
```

 If you use OpenCV Android SDK Version 2.*, you should load `opencv_java` instead of `opencv_java3`.

Implementing the OpenCV Java code

In this section, we will show you OpenCV in Java side to prepare the data for the stitching module in the OpenCV C++ side.

First, we will create a list to store all of the captured images when the user presses the **Capture** button:

```
private List<Mat> listImage = new ArrayList<>();
```

Then, in the onPictureTaken method of the jpegCallback variable, we want to convert the captured Bitmap into an OpenCV Mat and store in this listImage list. You need to add these lines before the drawing parts with Canvas:

```
Mat mat = new Mat();
Utils.bitmapToMat(bitmap, mat);
listImage.add(mat);
```

Finally, when the user clicks the **Save** button, we would want to send the address of the images in listImage to the OpenCV C++ code to perform the stitching process.

In imageProcessingRunnable, we will add these codes after the showProcessingDialog function call:

```
try {
    // Create a long array to store all image address
    int elems=  listImage.size();
    long[] tempobjadr = new long[elems];
    for (int i=0;i<elems;i++){
        tempobjadr[i]=  listImage.get(i).getNativeObjAddr();
    }
    // Create a Mat to store the final panorama image
    Mat result = new Mat();
    // Call the OpenCV C++ Code to perform stitching process
    NativePanorama.processPanorama(tempobjadr, result.
getNativeObjAddr());

    // Save the image to external storage
    File sdcard = Environment.getExternalStorageDirectory();
    final String fileName = sdcard.getAbsolutePath() + "/opencv_" +
System.currentTimeMillis() + ".png";
    Imgcodecs.imwrite(fileName, result);
```

```
        runOnUiThread(new Runnable() {
            @Override
            public void run() {
                Toast.makeText(getApplicationContext(), "File saved at: "
+ fileName, Toast.LENGTH_LONG).show();
            }
        });

        listImage.clear();
    } catch (Exception e) {
        e.printStackTrace();
    }
}
```

In the preceding code, we will create a long array to store all the native addresses of each Mat image. Then, we will pass this long array and the native address of a Mat result, to store the panorama image. The OpenCV C++ code will run to perform stitching with the stitching module. After this, we save the result into the external storage and make a simple toast to indicate to the user that the panorama is saved. Finally, we clear the listImage list to start a new section.

Implementing the OpenCV C++ code

At this moment, we want to implement the processPanorama in OpenCV C++. The implementation is really simple; we will only edit the com_example_panorama_ NativePanorama.cpp file as follows:

```
#include "com_example_panorama_NativePanorama.h"
#include "opencv2/opencv.hpp"
#include "opencv2/stitching.hpp"

using namespace std;
using namespace cv;

JNIEXPORT void JNICALL Java_com_example_panorama_NativePanorama_
processPanorama
    (JNIEnv * env, jclass clazz, jlongArray imageAddressArray, jlong
outputAddress){
    // Get the length of the long array
    jsize a_len = env->GetArrayLength(imageAddressArray);
```

```
    // Convert the jlongArray to an array of jlong
    jlong *imgAddressArr = env->GetLongArrayElements(imageAddressArr
ay,0);
    // Create a vector to store all the image
    vector< Mat > imgVec;
    for(int k=0;k<a_len;k++)
    {
      // Get the image
      Mat & curimage=*(Mat*)imgAddressArr[k];
      Mat newimage;
      // Convert to a 3 channel Mat to use with Stitcher module
      cvtColor(curimage, newimage, CV_BGRA2RGB);
      // Reduce the resolution for fast computation
      float scale = 1000.0f / curimage.rows;
      resize(newimage, newimage, Size(scale * curimage.rows, scale *
curimage.cols));
      imgVec.push_back(newimage);
    }
    Mat & result  = *(Mat*) outputAddress;
    Stitcher stitcher = Stitcher::createDefault();
    stitcher.stitch(imgVec, result);
    // Release the jlong array
    env->ReleaseLongArrayElements(imageAddressArray, imgAddressArr ,0);
  }
```

In the preceding code, we converted the long array of image addresses into images and pushed into a vector called imgVec. We also resized the image for fast computation. The stitching module is really easy to use.

First, we will create an instance of Stitcher.

```
    Stitcher stitcher = Stitcher::createDefault();
```

Then, we use this stitcher to stitch our vector image of Mat. The panorama image will be saved into a resultant Mat.

The following screenshot shows an example of a panorama image processed with the default configuration:

A sample image captured in the corridor

Application showcase

In this section, we show some panorama images captured with our application. You can see that the application is capable of processing panorama images in both horizontal and vertical directions.

First, this is an image captured from the fifth floor of a building. We took this picture through a window glass so the light was dim. However, the panorama is good because there are many details so the feature matcher can do a great job.

A sample image captured by the application

The following screenshot is an image captured in the evening on a balcony. The region on the top-left corner of the panorama is bad since this only contains a blank wall and the sky. Therefore, there were too little features to compare between images. Hence, the final panorama is not perfect in this region.

A sample image captured by the application in the evening

The following screenshot was captured through a window. The lower half of the image is good. However, the sky still has some problems due to the lack of features, as in the previous image.

Another sample image captured by the application in the evening

The following image was shot in a courtyard in front of the building in the afternoon. The lighting was good and there were many details, so the final panorama is perfect.

A sample image captured by the application in the afternoon

This image was taken at the same period with the previous image. However, this image was captured with a wide range of angles and the light was different at each shot. Therefore, the lighting in the final panorama is not consistent.

Another sample image captured by the application in the afternoon

Further improvement

In this section, we will show some improvements that you can consider while creating a fully featured panorama application.

First, you can make a better user interface for the user to capture a panorama image. The current user interface doesn't show that the application can capture images in both directions. A suggestion is to use the motion sensors (accelerometer and gyroscope) in the Android API to obtain the rotation of the device and adjust the position of the overlay image.

 Motion Sensors API documentation is available at http://developer. android.com/guide/topics/sensors/sensors_motion.html.

Secondly, the current application resizes the captured image to decrease computation time. You may want to change some parameters of the Stitcher to have better performance. We suggest that you look at the documentation of the stitching module for more details. In our implementation, we will use the Stitcher class for simplification. However, there is a detailed sample in the OpenCV repository at `samples/cpp/stitching_detailed.cpp`, where they show many options to improve the stability and quality of the final panorama.

 The detailed sample of using the stitching module is available at `https://github.com/Itseez/opencv/blob/master/samples/cpp/stitching_detailed.cpp`.

Thirdly, you can change the logic of our application to perform real-time stitching. That means we make a stitching image whenever there are two captured images. Then, we show the result with the help of a 360-degree user interface so that the user can know which is the missing region, if any.

Summary

This chapter showed a complete panorama application in Android Studio where OpenCV 3 is used in both the Java interface and the C++ interface with the support of the Native Development Kit (NDK). The chapter also introduced us to how to use the Android Camera API with the OpenCV library. Also, the chapter illustrated some basic implementation with the OpenCV 3 stitching module to perform image stitching.

5
Generic Object Detection for Industrial Applications

This chapter will introduce you to the world of generic object detection, with a closer look at the advantages that industrial applications yield compared to the standard academic research cases. As many of you will know, OpenCV 3 contains the well-known **Viola and Jones algorithm** (embedded as the CascadeClassifier class), which was specifically designed for robust face detection. However, the same interface can efficiently be used to detect any desired object class that suits your needs.

More information on the Viola and Jones algorithm can be found in the following publication:

Rapid object detection using a boosted cascade of simple features, Viola P. and Jones M., (2001). In Computer Vision and Pattern Recognition, 2001 (CVPR 2001). Proceedings of the 2001 IEEE Computer Society Conference on (Vol. 1, pp. I-511). IEEE.

This chapter assumes that you have a basic knowledge of the cascade classification interface of OpenCV 3. If not, here are some great starting points for understanding this interface and the basic usage of the supplied parameters and software:

- http://docs.opencv.org/master/modules/objdetect/doc/cascade_classification.html
- http://docs.opencv.org/master/doc/tutorials/objdetect/cascade_classifier/cascade_classifier.html
- http://docs.opencv.org/master/doc/user_guide/ug_traincascade.html

Or you can simply read one of the PacktPub books that discuss this topic in more detail such as *Chapter 3, Training a Smart Alarm to Recognize the Villain and His Cat*, of the *OpenCV for Secret Agents* book by Joseph Howse.

In this chapter, I will take you on a tour through specific elements that are important when using the Viola and Jones face detection framework for generic object detection. You will learn how to adapt your training data to the specific situation of your setup, how to make your object detection model rotation invariant, and you will find guidelines on how to improve the accuracy of your detector by smartly using environment parameters and situational knowledge. We will dive deeper into the actual object class model and explain what happens, combined with some smart tools for visualizing the actual process of object detection. Finally, we will look at GPU possibilities, which will lead to faster processing times. All of this will be combined with code samples and example use cases of general object detection.

Difference between recognition, detection, and categorization

For completely understanding this chapter, it is important that you understand that the Viola and Jones detection framework based on cascade classification is actually an object categorization technique and that it differs a lot from the concept of object recognition. This leads to a common mistake in computer vision projects, where people do not analyze the problem well enough beforehand and thus wrongfully decide to use this technique for their problems. Take into consideration the setup described in the following figure, which consists of a computer with a camera attached to it. The computer has an internal description of four objects (plane, cup, car, and snake). Now, we consider the case where three new images are supplied to the camera of the system.

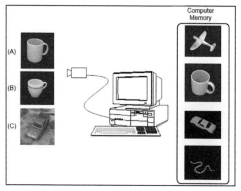

A simple computer vision setup

In the case that image A is presented to the system, the system creates a description of the given input image and tries to match it with the descriptions of the images in the computer memory database. Since that specific cup is in a slightly rotated position, the descriptor of the cup's memory image will have a closer match than the other object images in memory and thus this system is able to successfully recognize the known cup. This process is called **object recognition**, and is applied in cases where we know exactly which object we want to find in our input image.

> *"The goal of object recognition is to match (recognize) a specific object or scene. Examples include recognizing a specific building, such as the Pisa Tower, or a specific painting, such as the Mona Lisa. The object is recognized despite changes in scale, camera viewpoint, illumination conditions and partial occlusion."*
>
> *– Andrea Vedaldi and Andrew Zisserman*

However, this technique has some downsides. If an object is presented to the system that doesn't have a description in the image database, the system will still return the closest match and thus the result could be very misleading. To avoid this we tend to put a threshold on the matching quality. If the threshold is not reached, we simply do not provide a match.

When image B is presented to the same system, we experience a new problem. The difference between the the given input image and the cup image in memory is so large (different size, different shape, different print, and so on) that the descriptor of image B will not be matched to the description of the cup in memory, again a large downside of object recognition. The problems even rise further, when image C is presented to the system. There, the known car from computer memory is presented to the camera system, but it is presented in a completely different setup and background than the one in memory. This could lead to the background influencing the object descriptor so much that the object is not recognized anymore.

Object detection goes a bit further; it tries to find a given object in varying setups by learning a more object specific description instead of just a description of the image itself. In a situation where the detectable object class becomes more complex, and the variation of an object is large over several input images — we are no longer talking about single object detection, but rather about detecting a class of objects — this is where **object categorization** comes into play.

With object categorization, we try to learn a generic model for the object class that can handle a lot of variation inside the object class, as shown in the following figure:

An example of object classes with lots of variation: cars and chairs/sofas

Inside such a single object class, we try to cope with different forms of variation, as seen in the following figure:

Variation within a single object class: illumination changes, object pose, clutter, occlusions, intra-class appearance, and viewpoint

It is very important to make sure that your application actually is of the third and latter case if you plan to use the Viola and Jones object detection framework. In that case, the object instances you want to detect are not known beforehand and they have a large intra-class variance. Each object instance can have differences in shape, color, size, orientation, and so on. The Viola and Jones algorithm will model all that variance into a single object model that will be able to detect any given instance of the class, even if the object instance has never been seen before. And this is the large power of object categorization techniques, where they generalize well over a set of given object samples to learn specifics for the complete object class.

These techniques allow us to train object detectors for more complex classes and thus make object categorization techniques ideal to use in industrial applications such as object inspection, object picking, and so on, where typically used threshold-based segmentation techniques seem to fail due this large variation in the setup.

If your application does not handle objects in these difficult situations, then consider using other techniques such as object recognition if it suits your needs!

Before we start with the real work, let me take the time to introduce to you the basic steps that are common in object detection applications. It is important to pay equal attention to all the steps and definitely not to try and skip some of them for gaining time. These would all influence the end result of the object detector interface:

1. **Data collection**: This step includes collecting the necessary data for building and testing your object detector. The data can be acquired from a range of sources going from video sequences to images captured by a webcam. This step will also make sure that the data is formatted correctly to be ready to be passed to the training stage.

2. **The actual model training**: In this step, you will use the data gathered in the first step to train an object model that will be able to detect that model class. Here, we will investigate the different training parameters and focus on defining the correct settings for your application.

3. **Object detection**: Once you have a trained object model, you can use it to try and detect object instances in the given test images.

4. **Validation**: Finally, it is important to validate the detection result of the third step, by comparing each detection with a manually defined ground truth of the test data. Various options for efficiency and accuracy validation will be discussed.

Let's continue by explaining the first step, the data collection in more detail, which is also the first subtopic of this chapter.

Smartly selecting and preparing application specific training data

In this section, we will discuss how much training samples are needed according to the situational context and highlight some important aspects when preparing your annotations on the positive training samples.

Let's start by defining the principle of object categorization and its relation to training data, which can be seen in the following figure:

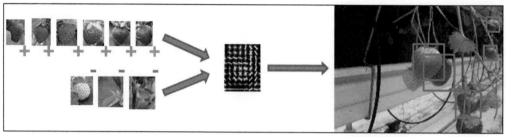

An example of positive and negative training data for an object model

The idea is that the algorithm takes a set of positive object instances, which contain the different presentations of the object you want to detect (this means object instances under different lighting conditions, different scales, different orientations, small shape changes, and so on) and a set of negative object instances, which contains everything that you do not want to detect with your model. Those are then smartly combined into an object model and used to detect new object instances in any given input image as seen in the figure above.

The amount of training data

Many object detection algorithms depend heavily on large quantities of training data, or at least that is what is expected. This paradigm came to existence due to the academic research cases, mainly focusing on very challenging cases such as pedestrian and car detection. These are both object classes where a huge amount of intra-class variance exists, resulting in:

- A very large positive and negative training sample set, leading up to thousands and even millions of samples for each set.

- The removal of all information that pollutes the training set, rather than helping it, such as color information, and simply using feature information that is more robust to all this intra-class variation such as edge information and pixel intensity differences.

As a result, models were trained that successfully detect pedestrians and cars in about every possible situation, with the downside that training them required several weeks of processing.. However, when you look at more industrial specific cases, such as the picking of fruit from bins or the grabbing of objects from a conveyor belt, you can see that the amount of variance in objects and background is rather limited compared to these very challenging academic research cases. And this is a fact that we can use to our own advantage.

We know that the accuracy of the resulting object model is highly dependent on the training data used. In cases where your detector needs to work in all possible situations, supplying huge amounts of data seems reasonable. The complex learning algorithms will then decide which information is useful and which is not. However, in more confined cases, we could build object models by considering what our object model actually needs to do.

For example, the Facebook DeepFace application, used for detecting faces in every possible situation using the neural networks approach uses 4.4 million labeled faces.

More information on the DeepFace algorithm can be found in:

Deepface: Closing the gap to human-level performance in face verification, Taigman Y., Yang M., Ranzato M. A., and Wolf L. (2014, June). In Computer Vision and Pattern Recognition (CVPR), 2014, IEEE Conference on (pp. 1701-1708).

We therefore suggest using only meaningful positive and negative training samples for your object model by following a set of simple rules:

- For the positive samples, only use **natural occurring samples**. There are many tools out there that create artificially rotated, translated, and skewed images to turn a small training set into a large training set. However, research has proven that the resulting detector is less performant than simply collecting positive object samples that cover the actual situation of your application. Better use a small set of decent **high quality object samples**, rather than using a large set of low quality non-representative samples for your case.

- For the negative samples, there are two possible approaches, but both start from the principle that you collect negative samples in the situation where your detector will be used, which is very different from the normal way of training object detects, where just a large set of random samples not containing the object are being used as negatives.
    - Either point a camera at your scene and start grabbing random frames to sample negative windows from.

- ° Or use your positive images to your advantage. Cut out the actual object regions and make the pixels black. Use those masked images as negative training data. Keep in mind that in this case the ratio between background information and actual object occurring in the window needs to be large enough. If your images are filled with object instances, cutting them will result in a complete loss of relevant background information and thus reduce the discriminative power of your negative training set.

- Try to use a very small set of negative windows. If in your case only 4 or 5 background situations can occur, then there is no need to use 100 negative images. Just take those five specific cases and sample negative windows from them.

Efficiently collecting data in this way ensures that you will end up with a very robust model for your specific application! However, keep in mind that this also has some consequences. The resulting model will not be robust towards different situations than the ones trained for. However, the benefit in training time and the reduced need of training samples completely outweighs this downside.

 Software for negative sample generation based on OpenCV 3 can be found at `https://github.com/OpenCVBlueprints/OpenCVBlueprints/tree/master/chapter_5/source_code/generate_negatives/`.

You can use the negative sample generation software to generate samples like you can see in the following figure, where object annotations of strawberries are removed and replaced by black pixels.

An example of the output of the negative image generation tool, where annotations are cut out and replaced by black pixels

As you can see, the ratio between the object pixels and the background pixels is still large enough in order to ensure that the model will not train his background purely based on those black pixel regions. Keep in mind that avoiding the approach of using these black pixelated images, by simply collecting negative images, is always better. However, many companies forget this important part of data collection and just end up without a negative data set meaningful for the application. Several tests I performed proved that using a negative dataset from random frames from your application have a more discriminative negative power than black pixels cutout based images.

Creating object annotation files for the positive samples

When preparing your positive data samples, it is important to put some time in your annotations, which are the actual locations of your object instances inside the larger images. Without decent annotations, you will never be able to create decent object detectors. There are many tools out there for annotation, but I have made one for you based on OpenCV 3, which allows you to quickly loop over images and put annotations on top of them.

 Software for object annotation based on OpenCV 3 can be found at
`https://github.com/OpenCVBlueprints/OpenCVBlueprints/tree/master/chapter_5/source_code/object_annotation/`.

The OpenCV team was kind enough to also integrate this tool into the main repository under the apps section. This means that if you build and install the OpenCV apps during installation, that the tool is also accessible by using the following command:

```
/opencv_annotation -images <folder location> -annotations <output file>
```

Using the software is quite straightforward:

1. Start by running the CMAKE script inside the GitHub folder of the specific project. After running CMAKE, the software will be accessible through an executable. The same approach applies for every piece of software in this chapter. Running the CMAKE interface is quite straightforward:

   ```
   cmakemake
   ```

   ```
   ./object_annotation -images <folder location> -annotations <output
   file>
   ```

2. This will result in an executable that needs some input parameters, being the location of the positive image files and the output detection file.

 Keep in mind to always assign the absolute path of all files!

3. First, parse the content of your positive image folder to a file (by using the supplied `folder_listing` software inside the object annotation folder), and then follow this by executing the annotation command:

```
./folder_listing –folder <folder> -images <images.txt>
```

4. The folder listing tool should generate a file, which looks exactly like this:

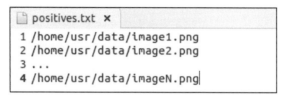

A sample positive samples file generated by the folder listing tool

5. Now, fire up the annotation tool with the following command:

```
./object_annotation –images <images.txt> -annotations
<annotations.txt>
```

6. This will fire up the software and give you the first image in a window, ready to apply annotations, as shown in the following figure:

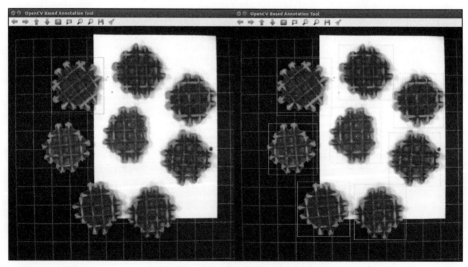

A sample of the object annotation tool

7. You can start by selecting the top-left corner of the object, then moving the mouse until you reach the bottom right corner of the object, which can be seen in the left part of the preceding figure. However, the software allows you to start your annotation from each possible corner. If you are unhappy with the selection, then reapply this step, until the annotation suits your needs.

8. Once you agree on the selected bounding box, press the button that confirms a selection, which is key C by default. This will confirm the annotation, change its color from red to green, and add it to the annotations file. Be sure only to accept an annotation if you are 100% sure of the selection.

9. Repeat the preceding two steps for the same image until you have annotated every single object instance in the image, as seen in the right part of the preceding example image. Then press the button that saves the result and loads in the following image, which is the *N* key by default.

10. Finally, you will end up with a file called annotations.txt, which combines the location of the image files together with the ground truth locations of all object instances that occur inside the training images.

> If you want to adapt the buttons that need to be pressed for all the separate actions, then open up the object_annotation.cpp file and browse to line 100 and line 103. There you can adapt the ASCII values assigned to the button you want to use for the operation.
>
> An overview of all ASCII codes assigned to your keyboard keys can be found at http://www.asciitable.com/.

The output from the software is a list of object detections in a *.txt file for each folder of positive image samples, which has a specific structure as seen in the following figure:

```
positive_annotations.txt  ×
1 /home/usr/data/image1.png 6 43 90 111 96 43 189 110 96 57 289 111 99 231 321
2                           102 108 230 209 100 91 223 101 101 93
3 /home/usr/data/image2.png 8 98 129 89 93 95 274 102 96 197 196 92 95 220 87
4                           90 88 311 158 102 109 394 82 102 102 423 239 94 109
5                           281 293 107 91
6 ...
7 /home/usr/data/imageN.png 6 138 20 148 129 162 165 146 137 337 164 138 137 309
8                           9 136 128 186 333 146 141 356 326 135 133
```

An example of an object annotation tool

It starts with the absolute file location of each image in the folder. There was a choice of not using relative paths since the file will then be fully dependent on the location where it is stored. However, if you know what you are doing, then using relative file locations in relation to the executable should work just fine. Using the absolute path makes it more universal and more failsafe. The file location is followed by the number of detections for that specific image, which allows us to know beforehand how many ground truth objects we can expect. For each of the objects, the (x, y) coordinates are stored to the top-left corner combined with the width and the height of the bounding box. This is continued for each image, which is each time a new line appears in the detection output file.

 It is important for further model training that each set of ground truth values captured from other annotation systems is first converted to this format in order to ensure the decent working of the cascade classifier software embedded in OpenCV 3.

A second point of attention when processing positive training images containing object instances, is that you need to pay attention to the way you perform the actual placement of the bounding box of an object instance. A good and accurately annotated ground truth set will always give you a more reliable object model and will yield better test and accuracy results. Therefore, I suggest using the following points of attention when performing object annotation for your application:

- Make sure that the bounding box contains the complete object, but at the same time avoid as much background information as possible. The ratio of object information compared to background information should always be larger than 80%. Otherwise, the background could yield enough features to train your model on and the end result will be your detector model focusing on the wrong image information.

- Viola and Jones suggests using squared annotations, based on a 24x24 pixel model, because it fits the shape of a face. However, this is not mandatory! If your object class is more rectangular like, then do annotate rectangular bounding boxes instead of squares. It is observed that people tend to push rectangular shaped objects in a square model size, and then wonder why it is not working correctly. Take, for example, the case of a pencil detector, where the model dimensions will be more like 10x70 pixels, which is in relation to the actual pencil dimensions.

- Try doing concise batches of images. It is better to restart the application 10 times, than to have a system crash when you are about to finish a set of 1,000 images with corresponding annotations. If somehow, the software or your computer fails it ensures that you only need to redo a small set.

Parsing your positive dataset into the OpenCV data vector

Before the OpenCV 3 software allows you to train a cascade classifier object model, you will need to push your data into an OpenCV specific data vector format. This can be done by using the provided sample creation tool of OpenCV.

> The sample creation tool can be found at `https://github.com/Itseez/opencv/tree/master/apps/createsamples/` and should be built automatically if OpenCV was installed correctly, which makes it usable through the `opencv_createsamples` command.

Creating the sample vector is quite easy and straightforward by applying the following instruction from the command line interface:

```
./opencv_createsamples -info annotations.txt -vec images.vec -bg
negatives.txt -num amountSamples -w model_width -h model_height
```

This seems quite straightforward, but it is very important to make no errors in this step of the setup and that you carefully select all parameters if you want a model that will actually be able to detect something. Let's discuss the parameters and instruct where to focus on:

- `-info`: Add here the annotation file that was created using the object annotation software. Make sure that the format is correct, that there is no empty line at the bottom of the file and that the coordinates fall inside the complete image region. This annotation file should only contain positive image samples and **no negative image samples** as some online tutorials suggest. This would train your model to recognize negative samples as positives, which is not what we desire.

- `-vec`: This is the data format OpenCV will use to store all the image information and is the file that you created using the create samples software provided by OpenCV itself.

- `-num`: This is the actual number of annotations that you have inside the vector file over all the images presented to the algorithm. If you have no idea anymore how many objects you have actually annotated, then run the annotation counter software supplied.

> The sample counting tool can be found at `https://github.com/OpenCVBlueprints/OpenCVBlueprints/tree/master/chapter_5/source_code/count_samples/` and can be executed by the following command:
>
> `./count_samples -file <annotations.txt>`

- -w and -h: These are the two parameters that specify the final model dimensions. Keep in mind that these dimensions will immediately define the smallest object that you will be able to detect. Keep the size of the actual model therefore smaller than the smallest object you want to detect in your test images. Take, for example, the Viola and Jones face detector, which was trained on samples of 24x24 pixels, and will never be able to detect faces of 20x20 pixels.

When looking to the OpenCV 3 documentation on the "create samples" tool, you will see a wide range of extra options. These are used to apply artificial rotation, translation, and skew to the object samples in order to create a large training dataset from a limited set of training samples. This only works well when applying it to objects on a clean single color background, which can be marked and passed as the transparency color. Therefore, we suggest not to use these parameters in real-world applications and provide enough training data yourself using all the rules defined in the previous section.

If you have created a working classifier with, for example, 24x24 pixel dimensions and you still want to detect smaller objects, then a solution could be to upscale your images before applying the detector. However, keep in mind that if your actual object is, for example, 10x10 pixels, then upscaling that much will introduce tons of artifacts, which will render your model detection capabilities useless.

A last point of attention is how you can decide which is an effective model size for your purpose. On the one hand, you do not want it to be too large so that you can detect small object instances, on the other hand, you want enough pixel information so that separable features can be found.

You can find a small code snippet that can help you out with defining these ideal model dimensions based on the average annotation dimensions at the following location:
`https://github.com/OpenCVBlueprints/OpenCVBlueprints/tree/master/chapter_5/source_code/average_dimensions/.`

Basically, what this software does is it takes an annotation file and processes the dimensions of all your object annotations. It then returns an average width and height of your object instances. You then need to apply a scaling factor to assign the dimensions of the smallest detectable object.

For example:

- Take a set of annotated apples in an orchard. You got a set of annotated apple tree images of which the annotations are stored in the apple annotation file.

- Pass the apple annotation file to the software snippet which returns you the average apple width and apple height. For now, we suppose that the dimensions for $[w_{average} \ h_{average}]$ are [60 60].

- If we would use those [60 60] dimensions, then we would have a model that can only detect apples equal and larger to that size. However, moving away from the tree will result in not a single apple being detected anymore, since the apples will become smaller in size.

- Therefore, I suggest reducing the dimensions of the model to, for example, [30 30]. This will result in a model that still has enough pixel information to be robust enough and it will be able to detect up to half the apples of the training apples size.

- Generally speaking, the rule of thumb can be to take half the size of the average dimensions of the annotated data and ensure that your largest dimension is not bigger than 100 pixels. This last guideline is to ensure that training your model will not increase exponentially in time due to the large model size. If your largest dimension is still over 100 pixels, then just keep halving the dimensions until you go below this threshold.

You have now prepared your positive training set. The last thing you should do is create a folder with the negative images, from which you will sample the negative windows randomly, and apply the folder listing functionality to it. This will result in a negative data referral file that will be used by the training interface.

Parameter selection when training an object model

Once you have built a decent training samples dataset, which is ready to process, the time has arrived to fire up the cascade classifier training software of OpenCV 3, which uses the Viola and Jones cascade classifier framework to train your object detection model. The training itself is based on applying the boosting algorithm on either Haar wavelet features or Local Binary Pattern features. Several types of boosting are supported by the OpenCV interface, but for convenience, we use the frequently used AdaBoost interface.

If you are interested in knowing all the technical details of the feature calculation, then have a look at the following papers which describe them in detail:

- **HAAR**: Papageorgiou, Oren and Poggio, "A general framework for object detection", International Conference on Computer Vision, 1998.
- **LBP**: T. Ojala, M. Pietikäinen, and D. Harwood (1994), "Performance evaluation of texture measures with classification based on Kullback discrimination of distributions", Proceedings of the 12th IAPR International Conference on Pattern Recognition (ICPR 1994), vol. 1, pp. 582 - 585.

This section will discuss several parts of the training process in more detail. It will first elaborate on how OpenCV runs its cascade classification process. Then, we will take a deeper look at all the training parameters provided and how they can influence the training process and accuracy of the resulting model. Finally, we will open up the model file and look in more detail at what we can find there.

Training parameters involved in training an object model

It is important to pay attention when carefully selecting your training parameters. In this subsection, we will discuss the relevance of some of the training parameters used when training and suggest some settings for general testing purposes. The following subsection will then discuss the output and the quality of the resulting classifier.

First, start by downloading and compiling the cascade classifier training application which is needed for generating an object detection model using the Viola and Jones framework.

The cascade classification training tool can be found at `https://github.com/Itseez/opencv/tree/master/apps/traincascade/`. If you build the OpenCV apps and installed them, then it will be directly accessible by executing the `./train_cascade` command.

If you run the application without the parameters given, then you will get a print of all the arguments that the application can take. We will not discuss every single one of them, but focus on the most delicate ones that yield the most problems when training object models using the cascade classifier approach. We will give some guidelines as how to select correct values and where to watch your steps. You can see the output parameters from the cascade classifier training interface in the following figure:

```
Usage: opencv_traincascade
  -data <cascade_dir_name>
  -vec <vec_file_name>
  -bg <background_file_name>
  [-numPos <number_of_positive_samples = 2000>]
  [-numNeg <number_of_negative_samples = 1000>]
  [-numStages <number_of_stages = 20>]
  [-precalcValBufSize <precalculated_vals_buffer_size_in_Mb = 256>]
  [-precalcIdxBufSize <precalculated_idxs_buffer_size_in_Mb = 256>]
  [-baseFormatSave]
--cascadeParams--
  [-stageType <BOOST(default)>]
  [-featureType <{HAAR(default), LBP, HOG}>]
  [-w <sampleWidth = 24>]
  [-h <sampleHeight = 24>]
--boostParams--
  [-bt <{DAB, RAB, LB, GAB(default)}>]
  [-minHitRate <min_hit_rate> = 0.995>]
  [-maxFalseAlarmRate <max_false_alarm_rate = 0.5>]
  [-weightTrimRate <weight_trim_rate = 0.95>]
  [-maxDepth <max_depth_of_weak_tree = 1>]
  [-maxWeakCount <max_weak_tree_count = 100>]
--haarFeatureParams--
  [-mode <BASIC(default) | CORE | ALL
--lbpFeatureParams--
--HOGFeatureParams--
```

The opencv_traincascade input parameters in OpenCV 3

- -data: This parameter contains the folder where you will output your training results. Since the creation of folders is OS specific, OpenCV decided that they will let users handle the creation of the folder. If you do not make it in advance, training results will not be stored correctly. The folder will contain a set of XML files, one for the training parameters, one for each trained stage and finally a combined XML file containing the object model.

- `-numPos`: This is the amount of positive samples that will be used in training each stage of weak classifiers. Keep in mind that this number is not equal to the total amount of positive samples. The classifier training process (discussed in the next subtopic) is able to reject positive samples that are wrongfully classified by a certain stage limiting further stages to use that positive sample. A good guideline in selecting this parameter is to multiply the actual amount of positive samples, retrieved by the sample counter snippet, with a factor of 0.85.

- `-numNeg`: This is the amount of negative samples used at each stage. However, this is not the same as the amount of negative images that were supplied by the negative data. The training samples negative windows from these images in a sequential order at the model size dimensions. Choosing the right amount of negatives is highly dependent on your application.

  ○ If your application has close to no variation, then supplying a small number of windows could simply do the trick because they will contain most of the background variance.

  ○ On the other hand, if the background variation is large, a huge number of samples would be needed to ensure that you train as much random background noise as possible into your model.

  ○ A good start is taking a ratio between the number of positive and the number of negative samples equaling 0.5, so double the amount of negative versus positive windows.

  ○ Keep in mind that each negative window that is classified correctly at an early stage will be discarded for training in the next stage since it cannot add any extra value to the training process. Therefore, you must be sure that enough unique windows can be grabbed from the negative images. For example, if a model uses 500 negatives at each stage and 100% of those negatives get correctly classified at each stage, then training a model of 20 stages will need 10,000 unique negative samples! Considering that the sequential grabbing of samples does not ensure uniqueness, due to the limited pixel wise movement, this amount can grow drastically.

- `-numStages`: This is the amount of weak classifier stages, which is highly dependent on the complexity of the application.

  ○ The more stages, the longer the training process will take since it becomes harder at each stage to find enough training windows and to find features that correctly separate the data. Moreover, the training time increases in an exponential manner when adding stages.

- ○ Therefore, I suggest looking at the reported acceptance ratio that is outputted at each training stage. Once this reaches values of 10^(-5), you can conclude that your model will have reached the best descriptive and generalizing power it could get, according to the training data provided.

- ○ Avoid training it to levels of 10^(-5) or lower to avoid overtraining your cascade on your training data. Of course, depending on the amount of training data supplied, the amount of stages to reach this level can differ a lot.

- `-bg`: This refers to the location of the text file that contains the locations of the negative training images, also called the negative samples description file.

- `-vec`: This refers to the location of the training data vector that was generated in the previous step using the create_samples application, which is built-in to the OpenCV 3 software.

- `-precalcValBufSize` and `-precalcIdxBufSize`: These parameters assign the amount of memory used to calculate all features and the corresponding weak classifiers from the training data. If you have enough RAM memory available, increase these values to 2048 MB or 4096 MB, which will speed up the precalculation time for the features drastically.

- `-featureType`: Here, you can choose which kind of features are used for creating the weak classifiers.

  - ○ HAAR wavelets are reported to give higher accuracy models.

  - ○ However, consider training test classifiers with the LBP parameter. It decreases training time of an equal sized model drastically due to the integer calculations instead of the floating point calculations.

- `-minHitRate`: This is the threshold that defines how much of your positive samples can be misclassified as negatives at each stage. The default value is 0.995, which is already quite high. The training algorithm will select its stage threshold so that this value can be reached.

  - ○ Making it 0.999, as many people do, is simply impossible and will make your training stop probably after the first stage. It means that only 1 out of 1,000 samples can be wrongly classified over a complete stage.

  - ○ If you have very challenging data, then lowering this, for example, to 0.990 could be a good start to ensure that the training actually ends up with a useful model.

- `-maxFalseAlarmRate`: This is the threshold that defines how much of your negative samples need to be classified as negatives before the boosting process should stop adding weak classifiers to the current stage. The default value is 0.5 and ensures that a stage of weak classifier will only do slightly better than random guessing on the negative samples. Increasing this value too much could lead to a single stage that already filters out most of your given windows, resulting in a very slow model at detection time due to the vast amount of features that need to be validated for each window. This will simply remove the large advantage of the concept of early window rejection.

The parameters discussed earlier are the most important ones to dig into when trying to train a successful classifier. Once this works, you can increase the performance of your classifier even more, by looking at the way boosting forms its weak classifiers. This can be adapted by the `-maxDepth` and `-maxWeakCount` parameters. However, for most cases, using **stump weak classifiers** (single layer decision trees) on single features is the best way to start, ensuring that single stage evaluation is not too complex and thus fast at detection time.

The cascade classification process in detail

Once you select the correct training parameters, you can start the cascade classifier training process, which will build your cascade classifier object detection model. In order to fully understand the cascade classification process that builds up your object model, it is important to know how OpenCV does its training of the object model, based on the boosting process.

Before we do this, we will have a quick look at the outline of the boosting principle in general.

More information on the boosting principle can be found in

Freund Y., Schapire R., and Abe N (1999). A short introduction to boosting. Journal-Japanese Society For Artificial Intelligence, 14(771-780), 1612

The idea behind boosting is that you have a very large pool of features that can be shaped into classifiers. Using all those features for a single classifier would mean that every single window in your test image will need to be processed for all these features, which will take a very long time and make your detection slow, especially if you consider how many negative windows are available in a test image. To avoid this, and to reject as many negative windows as fast as possible, boosting selects the features that are best at separating the positive and negative data and combines them into classifiers, until the classifier does a bit better than random guessing on the negative samples. This first step is called a weak classifier. Boosting repeats this process until the combination of all these weak classifiers reach the desired accuracy of the algorithm. The combination is called the strong classifier. The main advantage of this process is that tons of negative samples will already be discarded by the few early stages, with only evaluating a small set of features, thus decreasing detection time a lot.

We will now try to explain the complete process using the output generated by the cascade training software embedded in OpenCV 3. The following figure illustrates how a strong cascade classifier is built from a set of stages of weak classifiers.

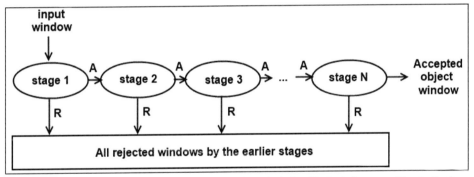

A combination of weak classifier stages and early rejection of misclassified windows resulting in the famous cascade structure

The cascade classifier training process follows an iterative process to train subsequent stages of weak classifiers (1…N). Each stage consists of a set of weak classifiers, until the criteria for that specific stage have been reached. The following steps are an overview of what is happening at training each stage in OpenCV 3, according to the input parameters given and the training data provided. If you are interested in more specific details of each subsequent step, then do read the research paper of Viola and Jones (you can have a look at the citation on the first page of this chapter) on cascade classifiers. All steps described here are subsequently repeated for each stage until the desired accuracy for the strong classifier is reached. The following figure shows how such a stage output looks like:

```
===== TRAINING 0-stage =====
<BEGIN
POS count : consumed    100 : 100
NEG count : acceptanceRatio     1000 : 1
Precalculation time: 1
+----+----------+----------+
|  N |    HR    |    FA    |
+----+----------+----------+
|   1|        1|         1|
+----+----------+----------+
|   2|        1|         1|
+----+----------+----------+
|   3|        1|    0.221|
+----+----------+----------+
END>
Training until now has taken 0 days 0 hours 14 minutes 46 seconds.

===== TRAINING 1-stage =====
<BEGIN
POS count : consumed    100 : 100
NEG count : acceptanceRatio     1000 : 0.28393
Precalculation time: 2
+----+----------+----------+
|  N |    HR    |    FA    |
+----+----------+----------+
|   1|        1|         1|
+----+----------+----------+
|   2|        1|         1|
+----+----------+----------+
|   3|        1|         1|
+----+----------+----------+
|   4|        1|    0.388|
+----+----------+----------+
END>
Training until now has taken 0 days 0 hours 34 minutes 19 seconds.
```

An example output of a classifier stage training

Step 1 – grabbing positive and negative samples

You will notice that the first thing the training does is grabbing training samples for the current stage—first the positive samples from the data vector you supplied, and then the random negative window samples from the negative images that you supplied. This will be outputted for both steps as:

```
POS:number_pos_samples_grabbed:total_number_pos_samples_needed
NEG:number_neg_samples_grabbed:acceptanceRatioAchieved
```

If no positive samples can be found anymore, an error will be generated and training will be stopped. The total number of samples needed will increase once you start discarding positives that are no longer useful. The grabbing of the negatives for the current stage can take much longer than the positive sample grabbing since all windows that are correctly classified by the previous stages are discarded and new ones are searched. The deeper you go into the amount of stages, the harder this gets. As long as the number of samples grabbed keeps increasing (and yes, this can be very slow, so be patient), your application is still running. If no more negatives are found, the application will end training and you will need to lower the amount of negatives for each stage or add extra negative images.

The acceptance ratio that is achieved by the previous stage is reported after the grabbing of the negative windows. This value indicates whether the model trained until now is strong enough for your detection purposes or not!

Step 2 – precalculation of integral image and all possible features from the training data

Once we have both positive and negative window-sized samples, the precalculation will calculate every single feature that is possible within the window size and apply it for each training sample. This can take some time according to the size of your model and according to the amount of training samples, especially when knowing that a model of 24x24 pixels can yield more than 16,000 features. As suggested earlier, assigning more memory can help out here or you could decide on selecting LBP features, of which the calculation is rather fast compared to HAAR features.

All features are calculated on the integral image representation of the original input window. This is done in order to speed up the calculation of the features. The paper by Viola and Jones explains in detail why this integral image representation is used.

The features calculated are dumped into a large feature pool from which the boosting process can select the features needed to train the weak classifiers that will be used within each stage.

Step 3 – firing up the boosting process

Now, the cascade classifier training is ready for the actual boosting process. This happens in several small steps:

- Every possible weak classifier inside the feature pool is being calculated. Since we use stumps, which are basically weak classifiers based on single feature to create a decision tree, there are as many weak classifiers as features. If you prefer, you can decide to train actual decision trees with a predefined maximum depth, but this goes outside of the scope of this chapter.

- Each weak classifier is trained in order to minimize the misclassification rate on the training samples. For example, when using Real AdaBoost as a boosting technique, the Gini index is minimized.

> More information on the Gini index, used for the misclassification rate on the training samples can be found in:
>
> Gastwirth, J. L. (1972). The estimation of the Lorenz curve and Gini index. The Review of Economics and Statistics, 306-316.

- The weak classifier with the lowest misclassification rate is added as the next weak classifier to the current stage.

- Based on the weak classifiers that are already added to the stage, the algorithm calculates the overall stage threshold, which is set so that the desired hit rate is guaranteed.

- Now, the weights of the samples are adapted based on their classification in the last iteration, which will yield a new set of weak classifiers in the next iteration, and thus the whole process can start again.

- During the combination of the weak classifiers inside a single stage, which is visualized in the training output, the boosting process makes sure that:
    ◦ The overall stage threshold does not drop below the minimum hit rate that was selected by the training parameters.
    ◦ The false alarm rate on the negative samples decreases compared to the previous stage.

- This process continues until:
    ◦ The false acceptance ratio on the negative samples is lower than the maximum false alarm rate set. The process then simply starts training a new stage of weak classifiers for the detection model.

- ○ The required stage false alarm rate is reached, which is `maxFalseAlarmRate^#stages`. This will yield an end to the model training since the model satisfies our requirements and better results cannot be achieved anymore. This will not happen often, since this value drops rather quickly, and after several stages, this would mean that you correctly classify more than 99% of your positive and negative samples all together.

- ○ The hit rate drops below the stage specific minimal hit rate, which is the `minHitRate^#stages`. At this stage, too many positives get wrongly classified and the maximum performance for your model is reached.

Step 4 – saving the temporary result to a stage file

After training each stage, the stage specific details about the weak classifiers and the thresholds are stored in the data folder, in a separate XML file. If the desired number of stages has been reached, then these subfiles are combined into a single cascade XML file.

However, the fact that every stage is stored separately means that you can stop the training at any time and create an in-between object detection model, by simply restarting the training command, but changing the `-numStages` parameter to the stage value on which you want to check the model's performance. This is ideal when you want to perform an evaluation on a validation set to ensure that your model does not start overfitting on the training data!

The resulting object model explained in detail

It has been observed that many users of the cascade classifier algorithm embedded in OpenCV 3 do not know the meaning of the inner construction of the object model which is stored in the XML files, which sometimes leads to wrong perceptions of the algorithm. This subsection will explain each internal part of the trained object models. We will discuss a model based on stump-typed weak classifiers, but the idea is practically the same for any other type of weak classifiers inside a stage, such as decision trees. The biggest difference is that the weight calculation inside the model gets more complex as compared to when using stump features. As to the weak classifiers structure inside each stage, this will be discussed for both HAAR- and LBP-based features since these are the two most used features inside OpenCV for training cascade classifiers.

The two models that will be used for explaining everything can be found at

- `OpenCVsource/data/haarcascades/haarcascade_frontalface_default.xml`
- `OpenCVsource/data/lbpcascades/lbpcascade_frontalface.xml`

The first part of each XML stored model describes the parameters that specify the characteristics of the model itself and some of the important training parameters. Subsequently, we can find the type of training that is used, which is limited to boosting for now, and the type of features used for building the weak classifiers. We also have the width and height of the object model that will be trained, the parameters of the boosting process, which include the type of boosting used, the selected minimum hit ratio, and the selected maximum false acceptance rate. It also contains information about how the weak classifier stages are built, in our case as a combination of one feature deep trees, called stumps, with a maximum of 100 weak classifiers on a single stage. For the HAAR wavelet based model, we can then see which features are used, being only the basic upright features or the combined rotated 45-degree set.

After the training-specific parameters, it starts to get interesting. Here, we find more information about the actual structure of the cascade classifier object model. The amount of stages is described, and then iteratively the model sums up the training results and thresholds for each separate stage which were generated by the boosting process. The basic structure of an object model can be seen here:

```
<stages>
    <_>
        <maxWeakCount></maxWeakCount>
        <stageThreshold</stageThreshold>
        <weakClassifiers>
            <!-- tree 0 -->
            <_>
                <internalNodes></internalNodes>
                <leafValues></leafValues></_>
            <!-- tree 1 -->
            <_>
                <internalNodes></internalNodes>
                <leafValues></leafValues></_>
            <!-- tree 2 -->
```

```
        ... ... ...
      <!-- stage 1 -->
        ... ... ...
  </stages>
  <features>
        ... ... ...
  </features>
```

We start with an empty iteration tag for each stage. At each stage the number of weak classifiers that were used are defined, which in our case shows how many single layer decision trees (stumps) were used inside the stage. The stage threshold defines the threshold on the final stage score for a window. This is generated by scoring the window with each weak classifier and then summing and weighing the results for the complete stage. For each single weak classifier, we collect the internal structure, based on the decision nodes and layers used. The values present are the boosting values used for creating the decision tree and the leaf values, which are used to score a window that is evaluated by the weak classifier.

The specifics for the internal node structure are different for HAAR wavelets and -based features. The storage of the leaf scores is equal. The values of the internal nodes, however, specify the relation to the bottom part of the code, which contains the actual features area, and which are also different for both the HAAR and the LBP approach. The difference between both techniques can be seen in the following sections, grabbing for both models the first tree of the first stage and a part of the feature set.

HAAR-like wavelet feature models

The following are two code snippets from the HAAR wavelet feature-based model, containing the internal node structure and the features structure:

```
<internalNodes>
0 -1 445 -1.4772760681807995e-02
</internalNodes>
... ... ...
<_>
    <rects>
        <_>23 10 1 3 -1.</_>
        <_>23 11 1 1 3.</_>
    </rects>
    <tilted>0</tilted>
</_>
```

For the internal nodes, there are four values present at each node:

- **Node left and node right**: These values indicate that we have a stump with two leafs.

- **The node feature index**: This points the index of the feature used at this node according to its position inside the features list of that model.

- **The node threshold**: This is the threshold that is set on the feature value for this weak classifier, which is learned from all the positive and negative samples in this stage of training. Since we are looking at models with stump based weak classifiers, this is also the stage threshold, which is set in the boosting process.

The features inside the HAAR-based model are described by a set of rectangles, which can be up to three rectangles, so as to calculate every possible feature from a window. Then, there is a value indicating if the feature itself is tilted over 45 degrees or not. For each rectangle, which is a partial feature value, we have:

- The location of the rectangle, which is defined by upper-left corner x and y coordinates and the width and height of the rectangle.

- The weight for that specific partial feature. These weights are used to combine both partial feature rectangles into a predefined feature. These weights allow us to represent each feature with less rectangles than is actually necessary. An example of this can be seen in the following figure:

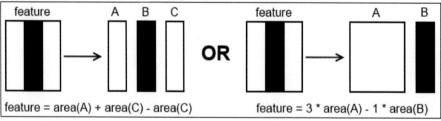

A three rectangle feature can be represented by a two rectangle weighted combination reducing the need of an extra area calculation

The feature sum is finally calculated by first summing all values of the pixels inside the rectangle and then multiplying it with the weight factor. Finally, those weighted sums are combined together to yield as a final feature value. Keep in mind that all the coordinates retrieved for a single feature are in relation to the window/model size and not the complete image which is processed.

Local binary pattern models

The following are two code snippets from the LBP feature-based model, containing the internal node structure and the features structure:

```
<internalNodes>
0 -1 46 -67130709 -21569 -1426120013 -1275125205 -21585
-16385 587145899 -24005
</internalNodes>
... ... ...
<_>
    <rect>0 0 3 5</rect>
</_>
```

For the internal nodes, there are 11 values present at each node:

- **Node left and node right**: These values indicate that we have a stump with two leafs, which is identical to the HAAR-based model. If a more complex tree structure is used, these values will expand.

- **The node feature index**: This points to the index of the feature used at this node according to its position inside the features list of that model.

- **Eight 32-bit values**: These values together in the combined form of a 256-bit LUT are calculated by comparing all subrectangle regions to the center subrectangle, as illustrated in the following figure, and which is used as a threshold to yield 1 or 0 as an outcome for the descriptor of the feature.

For the features inside the LBP based model, we have the dimensions (x, y, w, h) of a single subrectangle region (the top-left subrectangle) out of the nine that are needed for the LBP feature to be evaluated, as seen here:

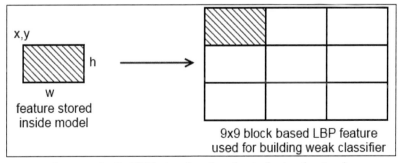

An example of a LBP feature-based on the single stored rectangle

Visualization tool for object models

However, there is nothing better than seeing your trained object model visualized on the object you have been training for. Therefore, I programmed a code snippet that takes a model and a base image and visualizes the complete model detection process on top of it.

 The software for visualizing Haar wavelet or LBP models can be found at `https://github.com/OpenCVBlueprints/OpenCVBlueprints/tree/master/chapter_5/source_code/visualize_models/`.

The software takes in several input arguments, such as the model location, the image where the visualization needs to happen, and the output folder where the results need to be stored. However, in order to use the software correctly, there are some points of attention:

- The model needs to be HAAR wavelet or LBP feature based. Deleted because this functionality is no longer supported in OpenCV 3.

- You need to supply an image that is an actual model detection for visualization purposes and resize it to the model scale or a positive training sample from the training data. This is to ensure that a feature of your model is placed at the correct location.

- Inside the code, you can adapt the visualization scales, one being for the video output of your model and one for the images that represent the stages.

The following two figures illustrate the visualization result of the Haar wavelet and LBP feature based frontal face model respectively, both incorporated into the OpenCV 3 repository under the data folder. The reason for the low image resolution of the visualization is quite obvious. The training process happens on a model scale; therefore, I wanted to start from an image of that size to illustrate that specific details of an object get removed, while general specifics of the object class still occur to be able to differentiate classes.

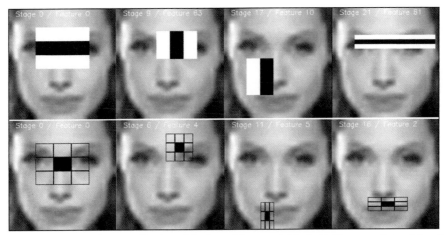

A set of frames from the video visualization of the frontal face model for both Haar wavelet and Local Binary Pattern features

The visualizations for example also clearly show that an LBP model needs less features and thus less weak classifiers to separate the training data successfully, which yields a faster model at detection time.

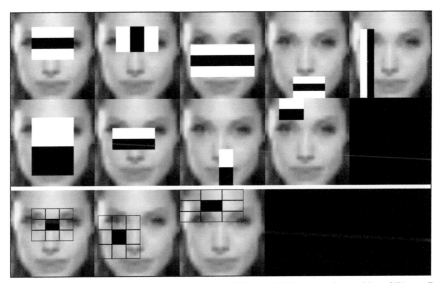

A visualization of the first stage of the frontal face model for both Haar wavelet and Local Binary Pattern features

Using cross-validation to achieve the best model possible

Making sure that you get the absolute best model given your training, testing the data can be done by applying a cross validation approach, such as the leave-one-out approach. The idea behind this is that you combine both training and test set and vary the test set that you use from the larger set. With each random test set and training set, you build a separate model and you perform the evaluation using precision-recall, which is discussed further in this chapter. Finally, the model that provides the best result could be adopted as a final solution. Thus, it could mitigate the impact of an error due to a new instance that is not represented in the training set.

 More information on the topic of cross validation can be found in Kohavi R. (1995, August), a study of cross-validation and bootstrap for accuracy estimation and model selection in Ijcai (Vol. 14, No. 2, pp. 1137-1145).

Using scene specific knowledge and constraints to optimize the detection result

Once your cascade classifier object model is trained, you can use it to detect instances of the same object class in new input images, which are supplied to the system. However, once you apply your object model, you will notice that there are still false positive detections and objects that are not found. This section will cover techniques to improve your detection results, by removing, for example, most of the false positive detections with scene-specific knowledge.

Using the parameters of the detection command to influence your detection result

If you apply an object model to a given input image, you must consider several things. Let's first take a look at the detection function and some of the parameters that can be used to filter out your detection output. OpenCV 3 supplies three possible interfaces. We will discuss the benefits of using each one of them.

Interface 1:

```
void CascadeClassifier::detectMultiScale(InputArray image,
vector<Rect>& objects, double scaleFactor=1.1, int minNeighbors=3, int
flags=0, Size minSize=Size(), Size maxSize=Size())
```

The first interface is the most basic one. It allows you to fast evaluate your trained model on a given test image. There are several elements on this basic interface that will allow you to manipulate the detection output. We will discuss these parameters in some more detail and highlight some points of attention when selecting the correct value.

scaleFactor is the scale step used to downscale the original image in order to create the image pyramid, which allows us to perform multiscale detections using only a single scale model. One downside is that this doesn't allow you to detect objects that are smaller than the object size. Using a value of 1.1 means that in each step the dimensions are reduced by 10% compared to the previous step.

- Increasing this value will make your detector run faster since it has less scale levels to evaluate, but it will yield the risk of losing detections that are in between scale steps.

- Decreasing the value will make your detector run slower, since more scale levels need to be evaluated, but it will increase the chance of detecting objects that were missed before. Also, it will yield more detections on an actual object, resulting in a higher certainty.

- Keep in mind that adding scale levels also gives rise to more false positive detections, since those are bound to each layer of the image pyramid.

A second interesting parameter to adapt for your needs is the `minNeighbors` parameter. It describes how many overlapping detections occur due to the sliding window approach. Each detection overlapping by more than 50% with another will be merged together as a sort of nonmaxima suppression.

- Putting this value on 0 means that you will get all detections generated by the windows that get through the complete cascade. However, due to the sliding window approach (with steps of 8 pixels) many detections will happen for a single window, due to the nature of cascade classifiers, which train in some variance on object parameters in order to better generalize over an object class.

- Adding a value means that you want to count how many windows there should be, at least those combined by the nonmaxima suppression in order to keep the detection. This is interesting since an actual object should yield far more detections than a false positive. So, increasing this value will reduce the number of false positive detections (which have a low amount of overlapping detections) and keep the true detections (which have a large amount of overlapping detections).

- A downside is that on a certain point, actual objects with a lower certainty of detections and thus less overlapping windows will disappear while some false positive detections might still stand.

Use the `minSize` and `maxSize` parameters to effectively reduce the scale space pyramid. In an industrial setup with, for example, a fixed camera position, such as a conveyor belt setup, you can in most cases guarantee that objects will have certain dimensions. Adding scale values in this case and thus defining a scale range will decrease processing time for a single image a lot, by removing undesired scale levels. As an extra advantage, all false positive detections on those undesired scales will also disappear. If you leave these values blank, the algorithm will start building the image pyramid at input image dimensions, in a bottom-up manner, downscale in steps equaling the scale percentage, until one of the dimensions is smaller than the largest object dimension. This will be the top of the image pyramid, which is also the place where later, at the detection time, the detection algorithm will start running its object detector.

Interface 2:

```
void CascadeClassifier::detectMultiScale(InputArray image,
vector<Rect>& objects, vector<int>& numDetections, double
scaleFactor=1.1, int minNeighbors=3, int flags=0, Size minSize=Size(),
Size maxSize=Size())
```

The second interface brings a small addition, by adding the `numDetections` parameter. This allows you to put the `minNeighbors` value on 1, applying the merging of overlapping windows as nonmaxima suppression, but at the same time returning you a value of the overlapping windows, which were merged. This value can be seen as a certainty score of your detection. The higher the value, the better or the more certain the detection.

Interface 3:

```
void CascadeClassifier::detectMultiScale(InputArray image,
std::vector<Rect>& objects, std::vector<int>& rejectLevels,
std::vector<double>& levelWeights, double scaleFactor=1.1, int
minNeighbors=3, int flags=0, Size minSize=Size(), Size maxSize=Size(),
bool outputRejectLevels=false )
```

A downside of this interface is that 100 windows with a very small certainty of detection on an individual basis can simply out rule a single detection with a very high individual certainty of detection. This is where the third interface can bring us the solution. It allows us to look at the individual scores of each detection window (described by the threshold value of the last stage of the classifier). You can then grab all those values and threshold the certainty score of those individual windows. When applying nonmaxima suppression in this case, the threshold values of all overlapping windows are combined.

Keep in mind that if you want to try out the third interface in OpenCV 3.0, you have to put the parameter `outputRejectLevels` on `true`. If you do not do this, then the level weights matrix, which has the threshold scores, will not be filled.

Software illustrating the two most used interfaces for object detection can be found at `https://github.com/OpenCVBlueprints/OpenCVBlueprints/tree/master/chapter_5/source_code/detect_simple` and `https://github.com/OpenCVBlueprints/OpenCVBlueprints/tree/master/chapter_5/source_code/detect_score` OpenCV detection interfaces change frequently and that it is possible that new interfaces are already available which are not discussed here..

Increasing object instance detection and reducing false positive detections

Once you have chosen the most appropriate way of retrieving the object detections for your application, you can evaluate the proper output of your algorithm. Two of the most common problems found after training an object detector are:

- Object instances that are not being detected.
- Too much false positive detections.

The reason for the first problem can be explained by looking at the generic object model that we trained for the object class based on positive training samples of that object class. This lets us conclude that the training either:

- Did not contain enough positive training samples, making it impossible to generalize well over new object samples. In this case, it is important to add those false negative detections as positive samples to the training set and retrain your model with the extra data. This principle is called "reinforced learning".

- We overtrained our model to the training set, again reducing the generalization of the model. To avoid this, reduce the model in stages and thus in complexity.

The second problem is quite normal and happens more than often. It is impossible to supply enough negative samples and at the same time ensure that there will not be a single negative window that could still yield a positive detection at a first run. This is mainly due to the fact that it is very hard for us humans to understand how the computer sees an object based on features. On the other hand, it is impossible to grasp every possible scenario (lighting conditions, interactions during the production process, filth on the camera, and so on) at the very start when training an object detector. You should see the creation of a good and stable model as an iterative process.

 An approach to avoid the influence of lighting conditions can be to triplicate the training set by generating artificial dark and artificial bright images for each sample. However, keep in mind the disadvantages of artificial data as discussed in the beginning of this chapter.

In order to reduce the amount of false positive detections, we generally need to add more negative samples. However, it is important not to add randomly generated negative windows, since the extra knowledge that they would bring to the model would, in most cases, simply be minimal. It is better to add meaningful negative windows that can increase the quality of the detector. This is known as **hard negative mining** using a **bootstrapping** process. The principle is rather simple:

1. Start by training a first object model based on your initial training set of positive and negative window samples.

2. Now, collect a set of negative images, which are either specific to your application (if you want to train an object detector specific to your setup) or which are more general (if you want your object detector to work in versatile conditions).

3. Run your detector on that set of negative images, with a low certainty threshold and save all found detections. Cut them out of the supplied negative images and rescale them towards the object model size dimensions.

4. Now, retrain your object model, but add all the found windows to your negative training set in order to ensure that your model will now be trained with this extra knowledge.

This will ensure that the accuracy of your model goes up by a fair and decent amount depending on the quality of your negative images.

When adding the found extra and useful negative samples, add them to the top of your `background.txt` file! This forces the OpenCV training interface to first grab these more important negative samples before sampling all the standard negative training images provided! Be sure that they have exactly the required model size so that they can only be used once as a negative training sample.

Obtaining rotation invariance object detection

A large downside to the current OpenCV cascade classifier implementation is that it only supports multiscale single rotation object detection. Many industrial applications that could actually use object detection do not know the orientation of the object beforehand and thus rotation invariant multiscale object detection would be much more interesting. Therefore, I will guide you through some techniques for applying multiscale rotation invariant object detection, by simply using the provided functionality in OpenCV.

OpenCV 3 also provides other techniques that are able to perform multiscale rotation invariant object categorization like the Bag of Visual Words approach. A good tutorial on this technique can be found at https://gilscvblog.wordpress.com/2013/08/23/bag-of-words-models-for-visual-categorization/.

There are three main ideas when trying to achieve rotation invariant object detection:

- Train a single object model with all possible orientations of the object as training data.
- Train multiple detectors for multiple orientations and then combine the outputs of all detectors together into a single output for a frame.
- Use a single rotation detector on a rotated object space and then warp back each found detection to the original frame.

The first approach is rather risky, especially if you do not know exactly what your algorithm will do with the provided training data. If you have an object that is of nature rotation invariant on its contours, such as a circle or ball-shaped object, then this could be a good approach. It will simply reject or ignore orientation specific information on its inner structure since not all samples will have the same feature value ranges inside the object, and will in turn focus only on object edge information. The figure *Example of the object annotation tool* illustrates a case of detecting cookies, of which the outer contour is 360 degrees rotation invariant, and thus, in this case, a single model can be used for all possible orientations.

However, this approach has several downsides:

- If the contour doesn't have enough object specific details, then it could trigger a lot of false positive detections on background structures with the same contour properties.

- If you want to differ between two similar object classes, then this will not work if the outer contours are rather similar since many of the other object specific features will simply be lost.

- If your object is not rotation invariant on its contour, then your features will have to be too generic to trigger a high hit rate on all your positive samples, and thus your model will generalize too much. This will result in a huge amount of false positive detections and a model that detects a lot of items that are actually no object instances.

The second approach is a bit more interesting. Research has proven that a single cascade classifier can handle rotations from about -10 to +10 degrees towards the original orientation of the model; however, it does vary a lot over different object classes. This enables us to basically cover the whole 360 degrees that an object can be in, with the use of about 18 models. This approach would request you to warp all training samples before training each specific orientation assigned model. Again, this technique has several downsides:

- You have to find optimal training parameters for each model. It is not guaranteed that the training parameters applied for the standard orientation will yield the same results if applied for a rotation of 45 degrees.

- You need to train 18 models! Depending on the complexity of your objects and the amount of training data this can take a very long time, especially with HAAR wavelet features. This is the time that you cannot spend on optimizing a single orientation model.

- If you rotate an image, then you will have to fill up blank space around the image in order not to lose image information. However, this creates artificial borders, which will not occur in your application. If your model trains on those regions, the result will be very poor. This is one of the major reasons why I suggest most people should also discard this second approach.

In the third approach, we will simply create a 3D rotational representation of our input image over the different orientations. I will supply you with a code snippet that can do this for you and discuss it step by step.

Software for performing rotation invariant object detection based on the described third approach can be found at `https://github.com/OpenCVBlueprints/OpenCVBlueprints/tree/master/chapter_5/source_code/rotation_invariant_detection/`.

The biggest advantage of this approach is that you only need to train a single orientation model and can put your time in updating and tweaking that single model in order to make it as efficient as possible. Another advantage is that you can combine all the detections in different rotations, by providing some overlap, and then increase the certainty of a detection, by smartly removing false positives that do not get detections over multiple orientations. So basically, it is kind of a trade-off between benefits and downsides of the approach.

However, there are still some downsides to this approach:

- You will need to apply a multiscale detector to each layer of your 3D representation matrix. This will definitely increase the search time for object instances compared to single orientation object detection.
- You will create false positive detections on each orientation, which will also be warped back, thus increasing the total number of false positive detections.

Let's take a deeper look at parts of the source code used for performing this rotation invariance and explain what is actually happening. The first interesting part can be found in the creation of the 3D matrix of rotated images:

```
// Create the 3D model matrix of the input image
Mat image = imread(input_image);
int steps = max_angle / step_angle;
vector<Mat> rotated_images;
cvtColor(rotated, rotated, COLOR_BGR2GRAY);
```

```
equalizeHist( rotated, rotated );
for (int i = 0; i < steps; i ++){
    // Rotate the image
    Mat rotated = image.clone();
    rotate(image, (i+1)*step_angle, rotated);
    // Preprocess the images

    // Add to the collection of rotated and processed images
    rotated_images.push_back(rotated);
}
```

Basically, what we do is read the original image, create a vector of Mat objects that can contain each rotated input image, and apply the rotation function on top of it. As you will notice, we immediately apply all preprocessing which is needed for efficient object detection using the cascade classifier interface such as rendering the image to grayscale values and applying a histogram equalization in order to cope a bit with illumination changes.

The rotate function can be seen here:

```
void rotate(Mat& src, double angle, Mat& dst)
{
    Point2f pt(src.cols/2., src.rows/2.);
    Mat r = getRotationMatrix2D(pt, angle, 1.0);
    warpAffine(src, dst, r, cv::Size(src.cols, src.rows));
}
```

This code first calculates a rotation matrix based on the angle, which is expressed in degrees, that we want to be rotated and then applies an affine transformation based on this rotation matrix. Keep in mind that rotating an image like this can lead to an information loss of objects at the borders. This code example assumes your objects will occur at the center of the image and thus this does not influence the result. You can avoid this by enlarging the original image by adding black borders to that. The width and height of the image are equal so that the image information loss is minimal. This can be done by adding the following code right behind the reading of the original input image:

```
Size dimensions = image.size();
if(dimensions.rows > dimensions.cols){
    Mat temp = Mat::ones(dimensions.rows, dimensions.rows, image.
        type()) * 255;
    int extra_rows = dimensions.rows - dimensions.cols;
    image.copyTo(temp(0, extra_rows/2, image.rows, image.cols));
    image = temp.clone();
}
```

```
if(dimensions.cols > dimensions.rows){
    Mat temp = Mat::ones(dimensions.cols, dimensions.cols, image.
        type()) * 255;
    int extra_cols = dimensions.cols - dimensions.rows;
    image.copyTo(temp(extra_cols/2, 0, image.rows, image.cols));
    image = temp.clone();
}
```

This code will simply expand the original image to match a square region depending on the largest dimension.

Finally, on each level of the 3D image representation, a detection is performed and the found detections are warped back to the original image using a similar approach as warping the original image:

1. Take the four corner points of the found detection in the rotated image and add them into a matrix for rotation warping (code line 95-103).

2. Apply the inverse transformation matrix based on the angle of the current rotated image (code line 106-108).

3. Finally, draw a rotated rectangle on the information of the rotated four matrix points (code line 111-128).

The following figure shows the exact result of applying a rotation invariant face detection to an image with faces in multiple orientations.

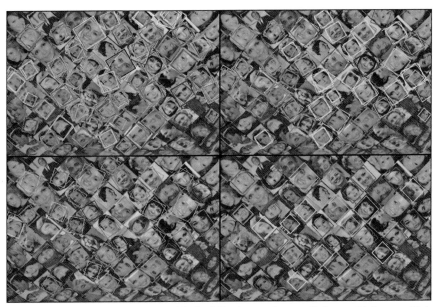

Rotation invariant face detection starting with the following angle steps [1 degree, 10 degrees, 25 degrees, 45 degrees]

We see that four times the suggested technique is applied to the same input image. We played around with the parameters in order to see the influence on detection time and the detections returned. In all cases, we applied a search from 0 to 360 degrees, but changed the angle step in between each stage of the 3D rotation matrix from 0 to 45 degrees.

Applied angle step	Total time for executing all detections
1 degree	220 seconds
10 degrees	22.5 seconds
25 degrees	8.6 seconds
45 degrees	5.1 seconds

As we can see, the detection time is reduced drastically when increasing the step of the angle. Knowing that an object model on itself could cover at least 20 degrees in total, we can easily reduce the step in order to significantly decrease the processing time.

2D scale space relation

Another large advantage that we can exploit in industrial cases is the fact that many of these setups have a fixed camera position. This is interesting when the objects that need to be detected follow a fixed ground plane, like in the case of pedestrians or objects passing by on a conveyor belt. If these conditions exist, then there is actually a possibility to model the scale of an object at each position in the image. This yields two possible advantages:

- First of all, you can use this knowledge to effectively reduce the number of false positive detections while still keeping your certainty threshold low enough so that low certainty and good detection still stick around. This can be done in some sort of post-processing step after the object detection phase.

- Secondly, this knowledge can be used to effectively reduce the detection time and search space for object candidates inside the image pyramid.

Let's start by focusing on the following case, illustrated in the following figure. Consider the fact that we want to create a pedestrian detection and that we have an existing model for doing so. We have a 360-degree camera mounted on top of a car and are grabbing those cycloramic images at continuous intervals. The cycloramas are now passed on towards the computer vision component that needs to define if a pedestrian is actually occurring in the image. Due to the very large resolution of such a 360-degree cyclorama, the image pyramid will be huge, leading to a lot of false positive detections and a very long processing time.

An example of the Viola and Jones cascade classifier pedestrian detection model in OpenCV 3 based on HAAR features

The example clearly shows that when applying the detector it is very hard to find a decent score threshold to only find pedestrians and no longer have a bunch of false positive detections. Therefore, we took a base set of 40 cycloramic images and manually annotated each pedestrian inside, using our object annotation tool. If we then visualized the annotation heights of the bounding box in function of the x position location of appearance in the image, we could derive the following relation, as shown in the following graph:

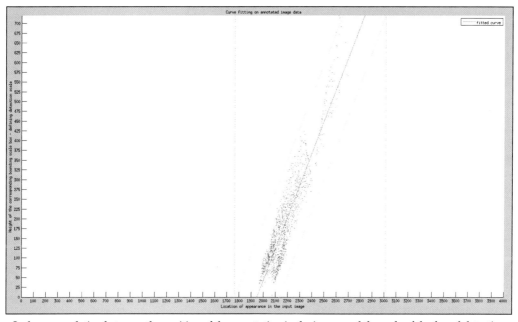

Scale space relation between the position of the annotation in the image and the scale of the found detection

The red dots in this figure are all possible ground truth annotations that we retrieved from the test bench of 40 cycloramas. The red line is the linear relation that we fitted to the data and which describes more or less which scale should be detected on which location in the image. However, we do know that there could be a small variation on that specific scale as defined by the green borders, in order to contain as much of the annotations as possible. We used the rule of assigning a Gaussian distribution and thus agree that in the range [-3sigma,+3sigma] 98% of all detections should fall. We then apply the minimal and maximal value according to our ranges and define a region where objects can occur naturally, assigned with the blue borders and visualized in the following picture:

Possible locations of pedestrians walking in the same ground plane and fully visible by the camera system

This means that if we run a detector on this input image, we already can eliminate more than 50% of the image because training data clearly shows that a pedestrian cannot occur in that location. This reduces the search space quite a lot! The only downside to this approach of limiting the search space with an image mask is that people on, for example, balconies will simply be ignored. But again, in this application, it was not necessary to find these people since they are not in the same ground plane.

We then finally combined everything we know from this chapter together. We applied a scale space relation for all possible scales that can occur, already only inside the mask area because objects cannot exist outside of it in our application. We then lowered the score threshold to have more detections and to ensure that we have detected as many pedestrians as possible before applying our filtering based on the scale-space relation. The result can be shown here. It clearly shows that there are applications where the contextual information can increase your detection rates a lot!

The complete pipeline: 1) detection with low threshold, 2) applying the mask and removing a lot of false positives, 3) enforcing the scale space location to remove extra false positive detections

Performance evaluation and GPU optimizations

We are heading towards the end of this chapter, but before we end, I would like to address two small but still important topics. Let's start by discussing the evaluation of the performance of cascade classifier object detection models by using not only a visual check but by actually looking at how good our model performs over a larger dataset.

Object detection performance testing

We will do this by using the concept of precision recall curves. They differ a bit from the more common ROC curves from the statistics field, which have the downside that they depend on true negative values, and with sliding windows applications, this value becomes so high that the true positive, false positive, and false negative values will disappear in relation to the true negatives. Precision-recall curves avoid this measurement and thus are better for creating an evaluation of our cascade classifier model.

Precision = TP / (TP + FP) and *Recall = TP / (TP + FN)* with a true positive (TP) being an annotation that is also found as detection, a false positive (FP) being a detection for which no annotation exist, and a false negative (FN) being an annotation for which no detection exists.

These values describe how good your model works for a certain threshold value. We use the certainty score as a threshold value. The **precision** defines how much of the found detections are actual objects, while the **recall** defines how many of the objects that are in the image are actually found.

Software for creating PR curves over a varying threshold can be found at `https://github.com/OpenCVBlueprints/OpenCVBlueprints/tree/master/chapter_5/source_code/precision_recall/`.

The software requires several input elements:

- First of all, you need to collect a validation/test set that is independent of the training set because otherwise you will never be able to decide if your model was overfitted for a set of training data and thus worse for generalizing over a set of class instances.

- Secondly, you need an annotation file of the validation set, which can be seen as a ground truth of the validation set. This can be made with the object annotation software that is supplied with this chapter.

- Third, you need a detection file created with the detection software that also outputs the score, in order to be able to vary over those retrieved scores. Also, ensure that the nonmaxima suppression is only set at 1 so that detections on the same location get merged but none of the detections get rejected.

When running the software on such a validation set, you will receive a precision recall result file as shown here. Combined with a precision recall coordinate for each threshold step, you will also receive the threshold itself, so that you could select the most ideal working point for your application in the precision recall curve and then find the threshold needed for that!

coordinates.txt			
1	0.617763	0.997093	-5
2	0.617763	0.997093	-4.9
3	0.617763	0.997093	-4.8
4	0.617763	0.997093	-4.7
5	0.617763	0.997093	-4.6
6	0.617763	0.997093	-4.5
7	0.617763	0.997093	-4.4
8	0.617763	0.997093	-4.3
9	0.617763	0.997093	-4.2
10	0.617763	0.997093	-4.1
11	0.617763	0.997093	-4
12	0.618008	0.997081	-3.9
13	0.618008	0.997081	-3.8
14	0.619882	0.996987	-3.7

Precision recall results for a self trained cascade classifier object model

This output can then be visualized by software packages such as MATLAB (http://nl.mathworks.com/products/matlab/) or Octave (http://www.gnu.org/software/octave/), which have better support for graph generation than OpenCV. The result from the preceding file can be seen in the following figure. A MATLAB sample script for generating those visualizations is supplied together with the precision recall software.

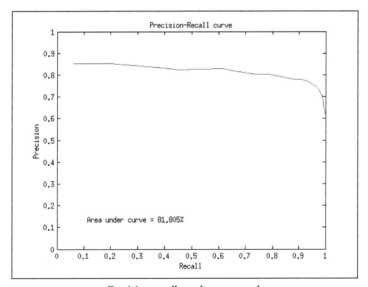

Precision recall results on a graph

Looking at the graph, we see that both precision and recall have a scale of [0 1]. The most ideal point in the graph would be the upper-right corner (precision=1/recall=1), which would mean that all objects in the image are found and that no false positive detections are found. So basically, the closer the slope of your graph goes towards the upper right corner, the better your detector will be.

In order to add a value of accuracy to a certain curve of the precision recall graph (when comparing models with different parameters), the computer vision research community uses the principle of the area under the curve (AUC), expressed in a percentage, which can also be seen in the generated graph. Again, getting an AUC of 100% would mean that you have developed the ideal object detector.

Optimizations using GPU code

To be able to reconstruct the experiments done in the discussion about GPU usage, you will need to have an NVIDIA GPU, which is compatible with the OpenCV CUDA module. Furthermore, you will need to rebuild OpenCV with different configurations (which I will highlight later) to get the exact same output.

The tests from my end were done with a Dell Precision T7610 computer containing an Intel Xeon(R) CPU that has two processors, each supporting 12 cores and 32 GB of RAM memory. As GPU interface, I am using an NVIDIA Quadro K2000 with 1 GB of dedicated on-board memory.

Similar results can be achieved with a non-NVIDIA GPU through OpenCL and the newly introduced T-API in OpenCV 3. However, since this technique is fairly new and still not bug free, we will stick to the CUDA interface.

OpenCV 3 contains a GPU implementation of the cascade classifier detection system, which can be found under the CUDA module in. This interface could help to increase the performance when processing larger images. An example of that can be seen in the following figure:

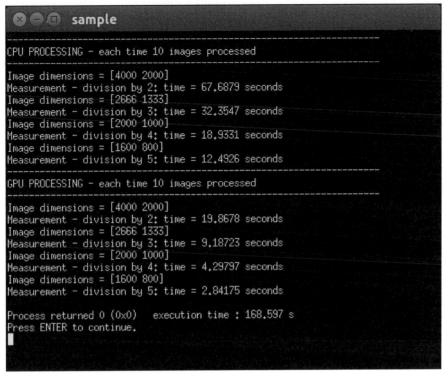

CPU-GPU comparison without using any CPU optimizations

 These results were obtained by using the software that can be retrieved from https://github.com/OpenCVBlueprints/OpenCVBlueprints/tree/master/chapter_5/source_code/CPU_GPU_comparison/.

For achieving this result, I built OpenCV without any CPU optimization and CUDA support. For this, you will need to disable several CMAKE flags, thus disabling the following packages: IPP, TBB, SSE, SSE2, SSE3, SSE4, OPENCL, and PTHREAD. In order to avoid any bias from a single image being loaded at a moment that the CPU is doing something in the background, I processed the image 10 times in a row.

The original input image has a size of 8000x4000 pixels, but after some testing, it seemed that the `detectMultiScale` function on GPU would require memory larger than the dedicated 1 GB. Therefore, we only run tests starting from having the image size as 4000*2000 pixels. It is clear that, when processing images on a single core CPU, the GPU interface is way more efficient, even if you take into account that at each run, it needs to push data from memory to the GPU and get it back. We still get a speedup of about 4-6 times.

However, the GPU implementation is not always the best way to go, as we will prove by a second test. Let's start by summing up some reasons why the GPU could be a bad idea:

- If your image resolution is small, then it is possible that the time needed to initialize the GPU, parse the data towards the GPU, process the data, and grab it back to memory will be the bottleneck in your application and will actually take longer than simply processing it on the CPU. In this case, it is better to use a CPU-based implementation of the detection software.

- The GPU implementation does not provide the ability to return the stage weights and thus creating a precision recall curve based on the GPU optimized function will be difficult.

- The preceding case was tested with a single core CPU without any optimizations, which is actually a bad reference nowadays. OpenCV has been putting huge efforts into making their algorithms run efficiently on CPU with tons of optimizations. In this case, it is not for granted that a GPU with the data transfer bottleneck will still run faster.

To prove the fact that a GPU implementation can be worse than a CPU implementation, we built OpenCV with the following freely available optimization parameters: IPP (free compact set provided by OpenCV), TBB, SSE2, SSE3, SSE4 (SSE instructions selected automatically by the CMAKE script for my system), pthread (for using parallel for loop structures), and of course, with the CUDA interface.

We will then run the same software test again, as shown here.

```
⊗ ⊖ ⊡  sample
-------------------------------------------------------------------
CPU PROCESSING - each time 10 images processed
-------------------------------------------------------------------
Image dimensions = [4000 2000]
Measurement - division by 2: time = 12.517 seconds
Image dimensions = [2666 1333]
Measurement - division by 3: time = 5.79939 seconds
Image dimensions = [2000 1000]
Measurement - division by 4: time = 3.47494 seconds
Image dimensions = [1600 800]
Measurement - division by 5: time = 2.26352 seconds
-------------------------------------------------------------------
GPU PROCESSING - each time 10 images processed
-------------------------------------------------------------------
Image dimensions = [4000 2000]
Measurement - division by 2: time = 19.9184 seconds
Image dimensions = [2666 1333]
Measurement - division by 3: time = 9.18187 seconds
Image dimensions = [2000 1000]
Measurement - division by 4: time = 4.31584 seconds
Image dimensions = [1600 800]
Measurement - division by 5: time = 2.87771 seconds

Process returned 0 (0x0)   execution time : 61.211 s
Press ENTER to continue.
```

CPU-GPU comparison with basic CPU optimizations provided by OpenCV 3.0

We will clearly see now that using the optimizations on my system yield a better result on CPU than on GPU. In this case, one would make a bad decision by only looking at the fact that he/she has a GPU available. Basically, this proves that you should always pay attention to how you will optimize your algorithm. Of course, this result is a bit biased, since a normal computer does not have 24 cores and 32 GB of RAM memory, but seeing that the performance of personal computers increase every day, it will not take long before everyone has access to these kind of setups.

I even took it one step further, by taking the original image of 8000*4000 pixels, which has no memory limits on my system for the CPU due to the 32 GB or RAM, and performed the software again on that single size. For the GPU, this meant that I had to break down the image into two parts and process those. Again, we processed 10 images in a row. The result can be seen in the following image:

```
-----------------------------------------------------------------
CPU-GPU PROCESSING on the original, 10 times
-----------------------------------------------------------------
CPU Measurement - [8000x4000] pixels: time = 21.446 seconds
GPU Measurement - [8000x4000] pixels: time = 70.4371 seconds
```

Comparison of an 8000x4000 pixel processed on GPU versus multicore CPU

As you can see, there is still a difference of the GPU interface taking about four times as long as the CPU interface, and thus in this case, it would be a very bad decision to select a GPU solution for the project, rather than a multicore CPU solution.

Practical applications

If you are still wondering what the actual industrial applications for this object detection software could be, then take a look at the following:

Examples of industrial object detection

This is a quick overview of the applications that I used this software for to get accurate locations of detected objects:

- Dummy test cases containing rotation invariant detection of both cookies and candies on a set of different backgrounds.

- Automated detection and counting of microorganisms under a microscope instead of counting them yourself.

- Localization of strawberries for ripeness classification.

- Localization of road markings in an aerial imagery for automated creation of a GIS (Geographic Information System) based on the retrieved data.

- Rotation invariant detection of peppers (green, yellow, and red combined) on a conveyor belt combined with the detection of the stoke for effective robot gripping.

- Traffic sign detection for ADAS (Automated Driver Assist System) systems.

- Orchid detection for automated classification orchid species.

- Pedestrian detection and tracking in NIR images for security applications.

So, as you can see, the possibilities are endless! Now, try to come up with your own application and conquer the world with it.

Let's wrap up the chapter with a critical note on object detection using the Viola and Jones object categorization framework. As long as your application is focusing on detecting one or two object classes, then this approach works fairly well. However, once you want to tackle multiclass detection problems, it might be good to look for all the other object categorization techniques out there and find a more suitable one for your application, since running a ton of cascade classifiers on top of a single image will take forever.

Some very promising object categorization frameworks that are in research focus at the moment, or that are a solid base for newer techniques, can be found below. They might be an interesting starting point for people wanting to go further than the OpenCV possibilities.

- Dollár P., Tu Z., Perona P., and Belongie S (2009, September), Integral Channel Features. In BMVC (Vol. 2, No. 3, p. 5)
- Dollár P., Appel R., Belongie S., and Perona P (2014), Fast feature pyramids for object detection. Pattern Analysis and Machine Intelligence, IEEE transactions on, 36(8), 1532-1545.
- Krizhevsky A., Sutskever I., and Hinton G. E (2012), Imagenet classification with deep convolutional neural networks. In Advances in neural information processing systems (pp. 1097-1105).
- Felzenszwalb P. F., Girshick R. B., McAllester D., and Ramanan D (2010), Object detection with discriminatively trained part-based models. Pattern Analysis and Machine Intelligence, IEEE Transactions on, 32(9), 1627-1645.

Summary

This chapter brought together a wide variety of tips and tricks concerning the cascade classifier object detection interface in OpenCV 3 based on the Viola and Jones framework for face detection. We went through each step of the object detection pipeline and raised attention to points where it can go wrong. This chapter supplied you with tools to optimize the result of your cascade classifier for any desired object model, while at the same time suggesting optimal parameters to choose from.

Finally, some scene specific examples were used to illustrate that a weaker trained object model can also perform well if you use the knowledge of the scene to remove false positive detections.

6
Efficient Person Identification Using Biometric Properties

The rise of digital media is greater than ever. People are placing more and more of their personal information on digital carriers like laptops, smartphones, and tablets. However, many of these systems do not provide efficient identification and authentication systems to ensure that strangers cannot access your personal data. This is where biometrics-based identification systems come into play and try to make your data more secure and less vulnerable to malicious people.

These identification systems can be used to lock down your computer, avoid people getting into a secure room, and so on, but, with technology improving each day, we are only one step away from further digitalizing our personal lives. How about using your facial expressions to unlock your door? How about opening your car with your fingerprint? The possibilities are endless.

Many techniques and algorithms are already available in open source computer vision and machine learning packages like OpenCV to efficiently use these personal identification properties. Of course, this opens up the possibility for enthusiastic computer vision programmers to create many different applications based on these techniques.

In this chapter, we will focus on techniques that use individual biometrics in order to create personal authentication systems that outperform standard available login systems based on passwords. We will take a deeper look at iris and fingerprint recognition, face detection, and face recognition.

We will first discuss the main principles behind each biometric technique, and then we'll show an implementation based on the OpenCV 3 library. For some of the biometrics, we will make use of the available open source frameworks out there. All datasets used to demonstrate the techniques are available for free online for research purposes. However, if you want to apply them to a commercial application, be sure to check their licenses!

Finally, we will illustrate how you can combine several biometric classifications to increase the chance of successfully identifying a specific person based on the probability of the individual biometrics.

At the end of this chapter, you will be able to create a fully functional identification system that will help you to avoid your personal details being stolen by any malicious party out there.

Biometrics, a general approach

The general idea behind identifying a person using a biometric property is the same for all biometrics out there. There are several steps that we should follow in the correct order if we want to achieve decent results. Moreover, we will point out some major points inside these general steps that will help you improve your recognition rate with extreme measures.

Step 1 – getting a good training dataset and applying application-specific normalization

The key to most biometric identification systems is to collect a system training dataset that is representative of the problem for which you will actually use the system. Research has proven that there is something called **dataset bias**, which means that if you train a system on a training set with a specific setup, environmental factors, and recording devices, and then apply that system to a test set which has been taken from a completely different setup with different environmental factors (like lighting sources) and different recording devices, then this will produce a decrease in performance of up to 25%. This is a very large setback in performance, since you want to make sure that your identification system runs with top performance.

Therefore, there are several things to consider when creating your training set for your identification system:

- You should only collect training data with the **known setup** that will be used when applying the biometric recognition. This means that you need to decide on hardware before you start training models and classifiers.

- For biometric login systems, it is important to **constrain your data** as much as possible. If you can eliminate lighting changes, different background setups, movement, non-equal positioning, and so on, then you can drastically improve the performance of your application.

- Try to **normalize your data** orientation-wise. If you align all your training data to the same position, you avoid introducing undesired variance in a single person's description of the biometric. Research in this field has proven that this can increase recognition rates by more than 15%!

- Use **multiple training instances** of a single biometric and use the average biometric description for authenticating a person. Single-shot training systems have the downside that slight differences between two biometric recordings have a large influence on the classification rate. Single-shot learning is still a very active research topic, and there is yet to be found a very stable solution to this problem.

How to apply this normalization for specific techniques will be discussed in the corresponding subtopics; for example, in the case of face recognition, since it can actually depend a lot on the techniques used. Once you get a good training set, with sufficient samples, you are ready to move to the second step.

Keep in mind that there will be cases where applying constraints is not always a good way to go. Consider a laptop login system based on biometric features that only works with the lights on like face detection and recognition. That system would not work when somebody was working in a dark room. In that case, you would reconsider your application and ensure that there were enough biometric checks irrelevant to the changing light. You could even check the light intensity yourself through the webcam and disable the face check if you could predict that it would fail.

The simplification of the application and circumstances involves simplifying the algorithm discussed in this chapter, leading to better performance in these constrained scenarios.

Step 2 – creating a descriptor of the recorded biometric

Once you get the required training data to build your biometric identification system, it is important to find a way to uniquely describe each biometric parameter for each individual. This description is called a "unique feature vector" and it has several benefits compared to the original recorded image:

- A full scale RGB image with high resolution (which is used a lot in biometrics recording) contains a lot of data. If we applied the classification to the complete image it would be:
    - Computationally very expensive.
    - Not as unique as desired, since regions over different persons can be identical or very similar.

- It reduces the important and unique information in an input image to a sparse representation based on keypoints which are unique features of each image.

Again, how you construct the feature descriptor depends on which biometric you want to use to authenticate. Some approaches are based on Gabor filter banks, local binary pattern descriptions, and keypoint descriptors such as SIFT, SURF, and ORB. The possibilities are, again, endless. It all depends on getting the best description for your application. We will make suggestions for each biometric, but a more exhaustive search will need to be done to find the best solution for your application.

Step 3 – using machine learning to match the retrieved feature vector

Each feature vector created from step 2 needs to be unique to ensure that a machine learning technique based on these feature vectors can differentiate between the biometrics of different test subjects. Therefore, it is important to have a descriptor with enough dimensions. Machine learning techniques are way better at separating data in high dimensional spaces than humans are, while they fail at separating data at low dimension feature spaces, for which a human brain outperforms the system.

Selecting the best machine learning approach is very cumbersome. In principle, different techniques offer similar results, but getting the best one is a game of trial and error. You can apply parameter optimization inside each machine learning approach to get even better results. This optimization would be too detailed for this chapter. People interested in this should take a deeper look at **hyper parameter optimization** techniques.

Some interesting publications about this hyper parameter optimization problem can be found below:

- Bergstra J. S., Bardenet R., Bengio Y., and Kégl B. (2011), *Algorithms for hyper-parameter optimization*, in Advances in Neural Information Processing Systems (pp. 2546-2554).
- Bergstra J. and Bengio Y. (2012), *Random search for hyper-parameter optimization*, The Journal of Machine Learning Research, 13(1), 281-305.
- Snoek J., Larochelle H., and Adams R. P. (2012), *Practical Bayesian optimization of machine learning algorithms*, in Advances in Neural Information Processing Systems (pp. 2951-2959).

There are many machine learning techniques in OpenCV 3. Some of the most frequently used techniques can be found below in order of complexity:

- **Similarity matching** using distance metrics.

- **K-Nearest neighbors search**: A multi (K) class classification based on distance (Euclidean, Hamming, and so on) calculations between feature vectors in a high dimensional space.

- **Naïve Bayes classifier**: A binary classifier that uses Bayesian learning to differentiate between different classes.

- **Support vector machines**: Mostly used as a binary classifier learning approach, but can be adapted to a multi-class classifier system. This approach depends on the separation of data in high dimensional spaces by looking for optimal separation plains between training data clouds and separating margins.

- **Boosting and random forests**: Techniques that combine several weak classifiers or learners into a complex model able to separate binary and multi-class problems.

- **Artificial neural networks**: A group of techniques that use the power of combining huge amounts of neurons (like the small cells in the brain) that learn connections and decisions based on examples. Due to their steeper learning curve and complex optimization steps, we will discard their use in this chapter.

 If you are interested in using neural networks for your classification problems, then take a look at this OpenCV documentation page:
`http://docs.opencv.org/master/d0/dce/`
`classcv_1_1ml_1_1ANN__MLP.html`

Step 4 – think about your authentication process

Once you have a machine learning technique that outputs a classification for your input feature vector, you need to retrieve a certainty. This certainty is needed to be sure how certain a classification result is. For example, if a certain output has a match for both entry 2 and entry 5 in a database, then you will need to use the certainty to be sure of which of the two matches you should continue with.

Here, it is also important to think about how your authentication system will operate. It can either be a one-versus-one approach, where you match each database entry with your test sample until you get a high enough matching score, or a one-versus-all approach, where you match the complete database, then look at the retrieved score for each match and take the best match possible.

One-versus-one can be seen as an iterative version of one-versus-all. They usually use the same logic; the difference is in the data structure used during the comparison. The one-versus-all approach requires a more complex way of storing and indexing the data, while one-versus-one uses a more brute-force approach.

 Keep in mind that both techniques can yield different results due to the fact that a false positive match is always possible in machine learning.

Imagine an input test query for your system. Using one-versus-one matching, you would stop analyzing the database when you had a high enough match. However, if further down the road there was a match yielding an even higher score, then this one would be discarded. With the one-versus-all approach, this could be avoided, so in many cases it is better to apply this one-versus-all approach.

To give an example of which approach to use in a given case, imagine a door to a secret lab. If you want to check if a person is allowed to enter the lab, then a one-versus-all approach is required to make sure that you match all database entries and that the highest matching score has a certainty above a certain threshold. However, if this final secret lab door is only used to select who is already allowed to enter the room, then a one-versus-one approach is sufficient.

In order to avoid problems with two individuals who have very similar descriptors for a single biometric, multiple biometrics are combined to reduce the occurrence of false positive detections. This will be discussed further at the end of this chapter, when we combine multiple biometrics in an effective authentication system.

Face detection and recognition

Most existing authentication systems start by detecting a face and trying to recognize it by matching it to a database of known people who use the system. This subsection will take a closer look at that. We will not dive into every single parameter of the software.

If you want more information about complete face detection and the recognition pipeline for both people and cats, then take a look at one of the PacktPub books called *OpenCV for Secret Agents*. It looks at the complete process in more detail.

If you want a very detailed explanation of the parameters used for the face detection interface in OpenCV based on the cascade classification pipeline from Viola and Jones, then I suggest going to *Chapter 5, Generic Object Detection for Industrial Applications*, which discusses the interface generalized for generic object detection.

Whenever you are focusing on an authentication system, you want to make sure that you are familiar with the different sub-tasks that need to be applied, as seen in the figure *An example of face detection software and the cut-out face region* in the section *Face detection using the Viola and Jones boosted cascade classifier algorithm*.

1. You should start by using a **general face detector**. This is used to find faces in any given input; for example, from your webcam. We will use the Viola and Jones face detector inside OpenCV, trained with a cascade classifier based on AdaBoost.

2. Secondly, you should perform some normalization on the image. In our case, we will apply some grayscaling, histogram equalization, and some alignment based on eye and mouth detection.

3. Finally, the data needs to be passed to a face recognizer interface. We will discuss the different options briefly (LBPH, Eigenfaces, and Fisherfaces) and walk you through it. This will return the selected user from the database we use to match to.

We will discuss the possible advantages, disadvantages, and risks of possible approaches at all stages. We will also suggest several open source packages that give you the chance to further optimize the approach if you want to.

Software for this subsection can be found at the following location: `https://github.com/OpenCVBlueprints/OpenCVBlueprints/tree/master/chapter_6/source_code/face/`

Face detection using the Viola and Jones boosted cascade classifier algorithm

Most webcam setups nowadays provide a high resolution RGB image as input. However, keep in mind that, for all OpenCV based operations, OpenCV formats the input as a BGR image. Therefore, we should apply some pre-processing steps to the output image before applying a face detector.

- Start by converting the image to a grayscale image. The Viola and Jones approach uses a HAAR wavelet or local binary pattern-based features, which are both independent of color. Both feature types look for regions of changing pixel intensities. Therefore, we can omit this extra color information and reduce the amount of data that needs to be processed.

- Reduce the resolution of the image. This depends on the webcam output format but, keeping in mind that processing time increases exponentially with increasing resolution, a ratio of 640x360 is more than enough for face detection.

- Apply **histogram equalization** to the image to cover invariance under different illuminations. Basically, this operation tries to flatten the intensity histogram of the complete image. The same was done when training the detection models in OpenCV 3 and doing the same works here.

It is always good to use different input and output containers for algorithms, since inline operations tend to do very nasty things to the output. Avoid problems by declaring an extra variable if you are not sure that inline replacement is supported.

The following code snippet illustrates this behavior:

```
Mat image, image_gray, image_hist;
VideoCapture webcam(0);
Webcam >> image;
resize(image, image, Size(640,360));
cvtColor(image, image_gray, COLOR_BGR2GRAY);
equalizeHist(image_gray, image_hist);
```

Once you have done all the preprocessing, you can apply the following code to have an operational face detector on your input image:

```
CascadeClassifier cascade('path/to/face/model/');
vector<Rect> faces;
cascade.detectMultiScale(image_hist, faces, 1.1, 3);
```

You can now draw the retrieved rectangles on top of the image to visualize the detections.

 If you want to know more about used parameters or retrieved detections, have a look at *Chapter 5, Generic Object Detection for Industrial Applications*, which discusses this interface in much more detail.

The face detections will look like the figure below:

An example of face detection software and the cut-out face region

Finally, you should cut out the detected face regions so that they can be passed to the interfaces that will process the image. The best approach is to grab these face regions from the original resized image, as seen in the preceding figure, and not from the visualization matrix, to avoid the red border being cut out and polluting the face image.

```
for(int i=0; i<faces.size(); i++){
    Rect current_face = faces[i];
    Mat face_region = image( current_face ).clone();
    // do something with this image here
}
```

The software for executing this face detection can be found at:
`https://github.com/OpenCVBlueprints/OpenCVBlueprints/`
`tree/master/chapter_6/source_code/face/face_detection/`.

Data normalization on the detected face regions

If you are only interested in a basic test setup, then face normalization steps are not really necessary. They are mainly used for improving the quality of your face recognition software.

A good way to start is to reduce the amount of variation in the image. You can already apply conversion to grayscale and histogram equalization to remove information from the image, as described in the previous subtopic. This would be enough if you wanted a simple test setup, but it would require the person to keep their head positioned in the same way as the training data was grabbed for that person. If not, then the slight variation in the data due to a different head position would be enough to trigger a false positive match with another person in the database.

To avoid this, and to increase the quality of the following face recognition system, we propose applying face alignment. This can be done in several ways.

- As a basic approach, one could run an eye and mouth detector based on the existing OpenCV detectors, and use the centers of the detections as a way to align faces.

For a very detailed explanation, refer to chapter 8 of *Mastering OpenCV* by Shervan Emami (`https://github.com/MasteringOpenCV/code/tree/master/Chapter8_FaceRecognition`). He discusses several ways to align faces using eye detection.

Also, have a look at the section *Finding the face region in the image* in *Chapter 3, Recognizing Facial Expressions with Machine Learning*.

- A more advanced approach would be to apply a facial landmark detector and use all those points to normalize and align the faces.

 If you are interested in more advanced techniques, take a look at the flandmark library (`http://cmp.felk.cvut.cz/~uricamic/flandmark/`). More information about using the facial landmark techniques can be found in *Chapter 3, Recognizing Facial Expressions with Machine Learning*, which discusses how to install this library, configure the software, and then run it on any given face image.

A good discussion about face alignment can be found at the following OpenCV Q&A forum: `http://answers.opencv.org/question/24670/how-can-i-align-face-images/`. Multiple active forum users have gathered their OpenCV knowledge to come up with a very promising alignment technique, based on basic facial landmark techniques.

The most basic alignment can be carried out by using the following approach:

1. Start by detecting the two eyes using the provided eye cascades.
2. Find the center points of both eye detections.
3. Calculate the angle between both eyes.
4. Rotate the image around its own center.

The following code does this:

```
CascadeClassifier eye('../haarcascades/haarcascade_eye.xml');
vector<Rect> eyes_found;
eye.detectMultiScale(face_region, eyesfound, 1.1, 3);
// Now let us assume only two eyes (both eyes and no FP) are found
double angle = atan( double(eyes_found[0].y - eyes_found[1].y) /
double(eyes_found[0].x - eyes_found[1].x) ) * 180 / CV_PI;
```

```
Point2f pt(image.cols/2, image.rows/2);
Mat rotation = getRotationMatrix2D(pt, angle, 1.0);
Mat rotated_face;
warpAffine(face_region, rotated_face, rotation, Size(face_region.cols,
face_region.rows));
```

The software for executing this face normalization can be found at:

```
https://github.com/OpenCVBlueprints/
OpenCVBlueprints/tree/master/chapter_6/source_code/
face/face_normalisation/
```

This will result in what is illustrated below. You can clearly see that the eye positions are aligned, even if it is for a short time. You will need this software for the AT&T database, which has these small variations, if you want to achieve better performance.

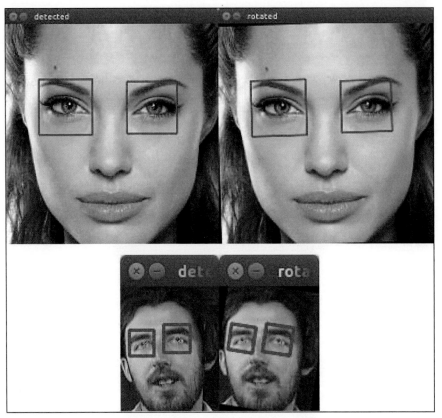

An example of the face alignment output

However, this basic approach causes problems.

- It will fail if you do not identify two eyes, so you should make a built-in check to avoid that and leave the image as it is if you cannot locate the eyes.

- The eye detector generates false positive detections, which could result in very bad alignment of images.

 For people who want to go a step further and include more complex algorithms, take a look at the research of Erik Learned-Miller, who provides an open access tool to perform face alignment without using eye detectors, based on the entropy of face images (`http://vis-www.cs.umass.edu/faceAlignment/`).

Various face recognition approaches and their corresponding feature space

Here, we will discuss how a face recognition system is built and how you can do it with OpenCV 3.

 We should thank Philipp Wagner of Bytefish for providing the guidelines to facial recognition using OpenCV using the samples included in the OpenCV repository. They have been released under the BSD license, which allows you to use them in a closed source application.

As mentioned in the introduction, we need to go to an intermediate state of face representation before we can apply face recognition. Based on pure pixel values, research has proven that faces are not unique enough unless you gather a tremendous amount of facial features, which makes it even more complex. Therefore, we will make a derivate face representation, based on a single feature descriptor, for each person represented in a specific feature space, so that it is easier to separate different faces from each other. There are three possibilities, namely:

- **Eigenfaces**: Eigenvalue decomposition through PCA.
- **Fisherfaces**: Linear discriminant analysis using the Fisher criterion.
- **LBPH**: Local binary pattern histogram comparison.

The basic idea behind each approach is that we reduce the high dimensionality of the facial data to a lower-dimensional data representation, which aids us in better retrieving a correct match to our pre-created database.

If you want the face module in OpenCV 3 to work properly, you should:

- Build OpenCV with the opencv_contrib repository activated, especially the face module.

- Make sure that your source file includes the header to the face module, like this: `#include "opencv2/face.hpp"`.

- Make sure that you include the correct namespace by adding this line of code: `using namespace cv::face;`. If you don't, you will have to add this prefix to each face module function that is used below.

Before explaining each method using the OpenCV 3 interface, I would like to stress that it is important that, at this stage, you should have your face images ready in a database. This means that you should have:

- A training database containing faces, with labels for each of the people you want to have access to the system

- A set of testing images containing unlabeled faces, which you will use to evaluate the performance of the system itself

We will use the AT&T database for face recognition. This was created by the Cambridge University Computer Laboratory and can be downloaded from `http://www.cl.cam.ac.uk/research/dtg/attarchive/facedatabase.html`.

Remember that, if you want to use this database as an example for your application, you should acknowledge the lab for providing it. The database contains 40 subjects, each having a set of images taken under different lighting conditions, with different facial expressions, and even with different facial details like wearing glasses, and is therefore a very interesting database to work with.

The software repository for this chapter contains the AT&T database, together with the necessary data files for further processing it with the software. Paths might change, and you should adapt the files accordingly.

If you prefer to make your own data, then it is better to align it with the structure of the current database so that you have other subjects to test your system with. In the following subtopics, I will add some of the code needed to get the representation and recognition results for this face recognition project.

To be able to do anything useful with the OpenCV face recognizer interface, you need to make sure that your training data has the following structure, obtained from your software. This can be grabbed from a CSV file or in any way you want it incorporated inside your program.

- You need a vector of matrices to store all the training images. This can be in the format `vector<Mat> faces`.

- You need a vector of integers containing the labels that you want to assign to each training sample. This can be in the format `vector<int> labels`.

- Make sure that you know which label corresponds to which person. This should be handled by your software design, as the interface will, at the end, just return this label for the best match.

- Make sure that each sample has the same dimensions, or the training will not work properly.

- Make sure that the test sample has the same dimensions as the training data. A detection test sample should always be rescaled to the training model dimensions.

Make sure that, if you want to test the accuracy of your system, you make separate training and testing data. This can be done by splitting your original faces and label vectors into two separate parts, or just by creating different vectors as you please. Now, let's discuss the three interfaces available with the OpenCV-based software.

Eigenface decomposition through PCA

PCA, or principal component analysis, handles the given image as a high-dimensional representation, and represents the given image in a lower-dimensional representation by looking at the principle axes of maximum variance, also called the principal components or eigenvalues. It basically re-projects every single image point onto all of the axes used in the dimensionality reduction.

> The software for executing this face detection can be found at:
> `https://github.com/OpenCVBlueprints/OpenCVBlueprints/`
> `tree/master/chapter_6/source_code/face/face_`
> `recognition_eigen/`

To build an Eigenface recognizer interface, you should use the following code snippet:

```
Ptr<BasicFaceRecognizer> face_model = createEigenFaceRecognizer();
```

This will generate an Eigenface-based model ready for training, which will use all eigenvectors (which could be slow) and without a certainty threshold. To be able to use them, you need to use an overloaded interface of the face recognizer.

- ```
  Ptr< BasicFaceRecognizer > face_model =
  createEigenFaceRecognizer(20);
  ```

- ```
  Ptr< BasicFaceRecognizer > face_model =
  createEigenFaceRecognizer(20, 100.0);
  ```

Here, you need to make a decision on what you actually want to achieve. The training will be fast with a low number of eigenvectors, but the accuracy will be lower. To increase the accuracy, increase the number of eigenvectors used. Getting the correct number of eigenvectors is quite cumbersome since it depends a lot on the training data used. As a heuristic, you could train a recognizer with a low number of eigenvectors, test the recognition rate on a test set, and then increase the number of eigenvectors as long as you do not reach the recognition rate goal.

Then, the model can be learned with the following code:

```
// train a face recognition model
vector<Mat> faces;
vector<int> labels;
Mat test_image = imread("/path/to/test/image.png");
// do not forget to fill the data before training
face_model.train(faces, labels);
// when you want to predict on a new image given, using the model
int predict = modelàpredict(test_image);
```

If you want to have a bit more information on the prediction, like the prediction confidence, then you can replace the last line with:

```
int predict = -1; // a label that is unexisting for starters
double confidence = 0.0;
modelàpredict(test_image, predict, confidence);
```

This is a basic setup. The things that you need to remember to improve the quality of your model are:

- Generally the more training faces of a person you have, the better a new sample of that person will be recognized. However, keep in mind that your training samples should contain as many different situations as possible, regarding lighting conditions, facial hair, attributes, and so on.

- Increasing the number of eigenvectors used for projecting increases accuracy, but it also makes the algorithm slower. Finding a good trade-off is very important for your application.

- To avoid fraud getting in by the best match from the database principle, you can use the confidence scores to threshold out matches that are not secure enough

If you want to do further research on the algorithm specifics, I suggest reading a paper that describes the technique in more detail:

Turk, Matthew, and Alex P. Pentland. "Face recognition using eigenfaces" Computer Vision and Pattern Recognition, 1991. Proceedings CVPR'91., IEEE Computer Society Conference on. IEEE, 1991.

If you want to play along with the internal data of the Eigenface-based model, you can retrieve interesting information using the following code:

```
// Getting the actual eigenvalues (reprojection values on the
eigenvectors for each sample)
Mat eigenvalues = face_model->getEigenValues();
// Get the actual eigenvectors used for projection and dimensionality
reduction
Mat eigenvectors = face_model->getEigenVectors();
// Get the mean eigenface
Mat mean = face_model->getMean();
```

Some output results on the samples that we used for testing can be seen in the figure below. Remember that, if you want to show these images, you will need to transform them to the [0 255] range. The OpenCV 3 FaceRecognizer guide shows clearly how you should do this. The jet color space is often used to visualize Eigenfaces data.

The complete and detailed OpenCV 3 FaceRecognizer interface guide can be found at the following web page, and discusses further use of these parameters in more depth than this chapter:

`http://docs.opencv.org/master/da/d60/tutorial_face_main.html`

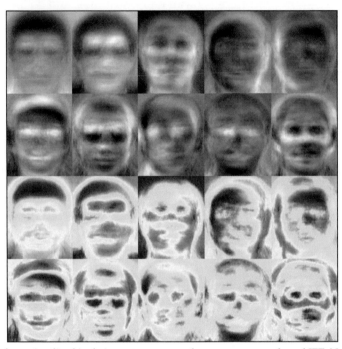

The first ten Eigenfaces visualized in their most common color spaces, grayscale and JET. Note the influence of the background.

Linear discriminant analysis using the Fisher criterion

The downside of using the Eigenface decomposition is that the transformation is optimal if you think about the pure reconstruction of the given data, however, the technique does not take into account class labels. This could lead to a case where the axes of maximal variance are actually created by external sources rather than the faces themselves. In order to cope with this problem, the technique of using LDA, or linear discriminant analysis, was introduced, based on the Fisher criterion. This minimizes variance within a single class, while maximizing variance between classes at the same time, which makes the technique more robust in the long run.

The software for executing this face detection can be found at:

```
https://github.com/OpenCVBlueprints/
OpenCVBlueprints/tree/master/chapter_6/
source_code/face/face_recognition_fisher/
```

To build a LDA face recognizer interface using the Fisher criteria, you should use the following code snippet in OpenCV 3:

```
// Again make sure that the data is available
vector<Mat> faces;
vector<int> labels;
Mat test_image = imread("/path/to/test/image.png");
// Now train the model, again overload functions are available
Ptr<BasicFaceRecognizer> face_model = createFisherFaceRecognizer();
face_modelàtrain(faces, labels);
// Now predict the outcome of a sample test image
int predict = face_modelàpredict(test_image);
```

If you want to get more specific properties of the model, this can be achieved with property-specific functions, as depicted below. Remember that, if you want to show these images, you will need to transform them to the [0 255] range. The bone color space is often used to visualize Fisherfaces data.

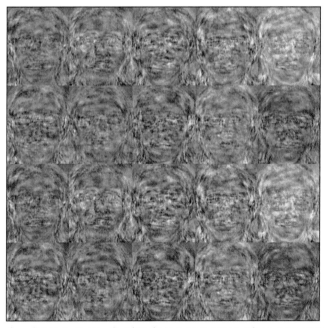

The first 10 Fisherface dimensions, visualized in their most common color spaces, grayscale and BONE.

> Note that the background influence is minimal for these Fisherfaces compared to the previous Eigenfaces technique. This is the main advantage of Fisherfaces over Eigenfaces.

It is nice to know that both Eigenfaces and Fisherfaces support the reconstruction of any given input inside the Eigenspace or Fisherspace at a certain point in mapping onto the dimensions selected. This is done by applying the following code:

```
// Get the eigenvectors or fishervectors and the mean face
Mat mean = face_modelàgetMean();
Mat vectors = face_modelàgetEigenValues();
// Then apply the partial reconstruction
// Do specify at which stage you want to look
int component_index = 5;
Mat current_slice = vectors.col(component_index);
// Images[0] is the first image and used for reshape properties
Mat projection = cv::LDA::subspaceProject(current_slice, mean,
images[0].reshape(1,1));
Mat reconstruction = cv::LDA::subspaceReconstruct(current_slice, mean,
projection);
// Then normalize and reshape the result if you want to visualize, as
explained on the web page which I referred to.
```

> The software for executing this face detection can be found at:
> https://github.com/OpenCVBlueprints/
> OpenCVBlueprints/tree/master/chapter_6/source_
> code/face/face_recognition_projection/

This will result in the output shown in the figure below. We re-project one of the test subjects at different stages in the Eigenspace, subsequently adding 25 eigenvectors to the representation. Here, you can clearly see that we have succeeded in reconstructing the individual in 12 steps. We can apply a similar procedure to the Fisherfaces. However, due to the fact that Fisherfaces have lower dimensionality, and the fact that we only look for features to distinguish between labels, we cannot expect a reconstruction that is as pure as it is with Eigenfaces.

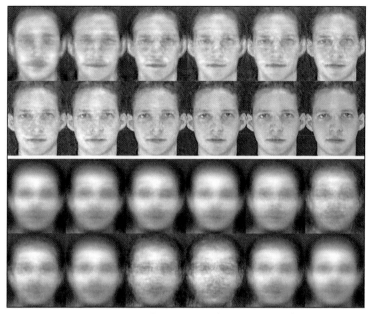

Reprojection result for both Eigenfaces and Fisherfaces

If you want to do further research on the algorithm specifics, I suggest reading a paper that describes the technique in more detail:

Belhumeur Peter N., João P. Hespanha, and David J. Kriegman, *Eigenfaces vs. fisherfaces: Recognition using class specific linear projection*, Pattern Analysis and Machine Intelligence, IEEE Transactions on 19.7 (1997): 711-720.

Local binary pattern histograms

Instead of simply reducing the dimensionality to universal axes, another approach is the use of local feature extraction. By looking at local features rather than a complete global description of the feature, researchers have tried to cope with problems like partial occlusion, illumination, and small sample size. The use of local binary pattern intensity histograms is a technique that looks at local face information rather than looking at global face information for a single individual. Local binary patterns have their origin in texture analysis and have proven to be efficient at face recognition by focusing on very specific local textured areas. This measure is more prone to changing lighting conditions than the previous techniques.

The software for executing this face detection can be found at:
```
https://github.com/OpenCVBlueprints/
OpenCVBlueprints/tree/master/chapter_6/source_
code/face/face_recognition_LBPH/
```

The LBPH features are illustrated below. They clearly show a more local feature description than Eigenfaces or Fisherfaces.

Example face image and its ELBP projection

 The software for executing this LBPH face projection can be found at:
```
https://github.com/OpenCVBlueprints/OpenCVBlueprints/
tree/master/chapter_6/source_code/face/face_to_ELBP/
```

To build a LBP face recognizer interface using histograms of local binary patterns, you should use the following code snippet in OpenCV 3:

```cpp
// Again make sure that the data is available
vector<Mat> faces;
vector<int> labels;
Mat test_image = imread("/path/to/test/image.png");
```

```
// Now train the model, again overload functions are available
Ptr<LBPHFaceRecognizer> face_model = createLBPHFaceRecognizer();
face_modelàtrain(faces, labels);
// Now predict the outcome of a sample test image
int predict = face_modelàpredict(test_image);
```

The LBPH interface also has an overload function, but this time related to the structure of the LBPH pattern and not the projection axes. This can be seen below:

```
// functionality createLBPHFaceRecognizer(radius, neighbors, grid_X,
grid_Y, treshold)
cv::createLBPHFaceRecognizer(1,8,8,8,123.0);
// Getting the properties can be done using the getInt function.
int radius = model->getRadius();
int neighbors = model->getNeighbors();
int grid_x = model->getGridX();
int grid_y = model->getGridY();
double threshold = model->getThreshold();
```

Again, the function can operate with or without a threshold being set in advance. Getting or setting the parameters of the model can also be done using the specific getter and setter functions.

If you want to do further research on the algorithm specifics, I suggest reading a paper that describes the technique in more detail:

Ahonen Timo, Abdenour Hadid, and Matti Pietikäinen, *Face recognition with local binary patterns*, Computer vision-eccv 2004, Springer Berlin Heidelberg, 2004. 469-481.

We provided functionality for each of the above three interfaces, also calculating the number of test samples classified correctly and the ones classified incorrectly, as shown below. In the case of LBPH, this means that we have a correct classification rate on the test samples of 96.25%, which is quite amazing with the very limited training data of only eight samples per person.

Total correct: 77 / Total wrong: 3

The number of correctly classified samples is outputted after each run.

The problems with facial recognition in its current OpenCV 3 based implementation

The techniques discussed enable us to recognize a face and link it to a person in the dataset. However, there are still some problems with this system that should be addressed:

- When using the Eigenfaces system, it is a general rule that the more Eigenvectors you use, the better the system will become, and the higher the accuracy will be. Defining how many dimensions you need to get a decent recognition result is frustrating, since it depends on how the data is presented to the system. The more variation there is in the original data, the more challenging the task will be, and thus the more dimensions you will need. The experiments of Philipp Wagner have shown that, in the AT&T database, about 300 Eigenvectors should be enough.

- You can apply thresholding to both Eigenfaces and Fisherfaces. This is a must if you want to be certain of classification accuracy. If you do not apply this, then the system will basically return the best match. If a given person is not part of the dataset, then you want to avoid this, and that can be done by calling the interface with a threshold value!

- Keep in mind that, with all face recognition systems, if you train them with data in one setup and test them with data containing completely different situations and setups, then the drop in accuracy will be huge.

- If you build a recognition system based on 2D image information, then frauds will be able to hack it by simply printing a 2D image of the person and presenting it to the system. In order to avoid this, either include 3D knowledge or add extra biometrics.

More information on adding 3D information to avoid fraud attempts can be found in the following publications:

Akarun Lale, B. Gokberk, and Albert Ali Salah, *3D face recognition for biometric applications*, Signal Processing Conference, 2005 13th European. IEEE, 2005.

Abate Andrea F., et al, *2D and 3D face recognition: A survey*, Pattern Recognition Letters 28.14 (2007): 1885-1906.

However, this topic is too specific and complex for the scope of this chapter, and will thus not be discussed further.

Fingerprint identification, how is it done?

In the previous section, we discussed the use of the first biometric, which is the face of the person trying to log in to the system. However, since we mentioned that using a single biometric is risky, it is better to add secondary biometric checks to the system, like a fingerprint. There are several off-the-shelf fingerprint scanners that are quite cheap and return you a scanned image. However, you will still have to write your own registration software for these scanners, and this can be done with OpenCV. Examples of such fingerprint images can be found below:

Examples of single individual thumbprints from different scanners

This dataset can be downloaded from the FVC2002 competition website released by the University of Bologna. The website (`http://bias.csr.unibo.it/fvc2002/databases.asp`) contains four databases of fingerprints available for public download in the following format:

- Four fingerprint capturing devices, DB1 - DB4
- For each device, the prints of 10 individuals are available
- For each person, eight different positions of prints were recorded

We will use this publicly available dataset to build our system. We will focus on the first capturing device, using up to four fingerprints from each individual for training the system and making an average descriptor of the fingerprint. Then, we will use the other four fingerprints to evaluate our system and make sure that the person is still recognized by our system.

You can apply the same approach to the data grabbed from the other devices if you want to investigate the difference between a system that captures binary images and one that captures grayscale images. However, we will provide techniques for doing the binarization yourself.

Implementing the approach in OpenCV 3

 The complete fingerprint software for processing fingerprints obtained from a fingerprint scanner can be found at:
`https://github.com/OpenCVBlueprints/OpenCVBlueprints/`
`tree/master/chapter_6/source_code/fingerprint/`
`fingerprint_process/`

In this subsection, we will describe how you can implement this approach in the OpenCV interface. We start by grabbing the image from the fingerprint system and applying binarization. This enables us to remove any noise from the image, as well as helping us to make the contrast better between the skin and the wrinkled surface of the finger:

```
// Start by reading in an image
Mat input = imread("/data/fingerprints/image1.png", IMREAD_GRAYSCALE);
// Binarize the image, through local thresholding
Mat input_binary;
threshold(input, input_binary, 0, 255, THRESH_BINARY | THRESH_OTSU);
```

The Otsu thresholding will automatically choose the best generic threshold for the image to obtain a good contrast between foreground and background information. This is because the image contains a bimodal distribution (which means that we have an image with two peak histograms) of pixel values. For that image, we can take an approximate value in the middle of those peaks as the threshold value (for images that are not bimodal, binarization won't be accurate). Otsu allows us to avoid using a fixed threshold value, making the system more compatible with capturing devices. However, we do acknowledge that, if you only have one capturing device, then playing around with a fixed threshold value may result in a better image for that specific setup. The result of the thresholding can be seen below.

In order to make the thinning from the next skeletization step as effective as possible, we need to invert the binary image.

Comparison of grayscale and binarized fingerprint images

Once we have a binary image, we are ready to calculate our feature points and feature point descriptors. However, in order to improve the process a bit more, it is better to skeletize the image. This will create more unique and stronger interest points. The following piece of code can apply the skeletization on top of the binary image. The skeletization is based on the Zhang-Suen line-thinning approach.

> Special thanks to @bsdNoobz of the OpenCV Q&A forum, who supplied this iteration approach.

```cpp
#include <opencv2/imgproc.hpp>
#include <opencv2/highgui.hpp>

using namespace std;
using namespace cv;

// Perform a single thinning iteration, which is repeated until the
skeletization is finalized
void thinningIteration(Mat& im, int iter)
{
    Mat marker = Mat::zeros(im.size(), CV_8UC1);
    for (int i = 1; i < im.rows-1; i++)
    {
```

```
        for (int j = 1; j < im.cols-1; j++)
        {
            uchar p2 = im.at<uchar>(i-1, j);
            uchar p3 = im.at<uchar>(i-1, j+1);
            uchar p4 = im.at<uchar>(i, j+1);
            uchar p5 = im.at<uchar>(i+1, j+1);
            uchar p6 = im.at<uchar>(i+1, j);
            uchar p7 = im.at<uchar>(i+1, j-1);
            uchar p8 = im.at<uchar>(i, j-1);
            uchar p9 = im.at<uchar>(i-1, j-1);

            int A  = (p2 == 0 && p3 == 1) + (p3 == 0 && p4 == 1) +
                     (p4 == 0 && p5 == 1) + (p5 == 0 && p6 == 1) +
                     (p6 == 0 && p7 == 1) + (p7 == 0 && p8 == 1) +
                     (p8 == 0 && p9 == 1) + (p9 == 0 && p2 == 1);
            int B  = p2 + p3 + p4 + p5 + p6 + p7 + p8 + p9;
            int m1 = iter == 0 ? (p2 * p4 * p6) : (p2 * p4 * p8);
            int m2 = iter == 0 ? (p4 * p6 * p8) : (p2 * p6 * p8);

            if (A == 1 && (B >= 2 && B <= 6) && m1 == 0 && m2 == 0)
                marker.at<uchar>(i,j) = 1;
        }
    }

    im &= ~marker;
}


// Function for thinning any given binary image within the range of
0-255. If not you should first make sure that your image has this
range preset and configured!
void thinning(Mat& im)
{
    // Enforce the range to be in between 0 - 255
    im /= 255;

    Mat prev = Mat::zeros(im.size(), CV_8UC1);
    Mat diff;

    do {
        thinningIteration(im, 0);
        thinningIteration(im, 1);
        absdiff(im, prev, diff);
        im.copyTo(prev);
    }
```

```
    while (countNonZero(diff) > 0);

    im *= 255;
}
```

The code above can then simply be applied to our previous steps by calling the thinning function on top of our previous binary-generated image. The code for this is:

```
// Apply thinning algorithm
Mat input_thinned = input_binary.clone();
thinning(input_thinned);
```

This will result in the following output:

Comparison of binarized and thinned fingerprint images using skeletization techniques

When we get this skeleton image, the next step is to look for crossing points on the ridges of the fingerprint, called minutiae points. We can do this with a keypoint detector that looks for large changes in local contrast, like the Harris corner detector. Since the Harris corner detector is able to detect strong corners and edges, it is ideal for the fingerprint problem, where the most important minutiae are short edges and bifurcations—the positions where edges come together.

More information about minutiae points and Harris corner detection can be found in the following publications:

Ross Arun A., Jidnya Shah, and Anil K. Jain, *Toward reconstructing fingerprints from minutiae points*, Defense and Security. International Society for Optics and Photonics, 2005.

Harris Chris and Mike Stephens, *A combined corner and edge detector*, Alvey vision conference, Vol. 15, 1988.

Calling the Harris Corner operation on a skeletonized and binarized image in OpenCV is quite straightforward. The Harris corners are stored as positions corresponding with their cornerness response value in the image. If we want to detect points with a certain cornerness, then we should simply threshold the image.

```
Mat harris_corners, harris_normalised;
harris_corners = Mat::zeros(input_thinned.size(), CV_32FC1);
cornerHarris(input_thinned, harris_corners, 2, 3, 0.04, BORDER_
DEFAULT);
normalize(harris_corners, harris_normalised, 0, 255, NORM_MINMAX,
CV_32FC1, Mat());
```

We now have a map with all the available corner responses rescaled to the range of [0 255] and stored as float values. We can now manually define a threshold which will generate a good number of keypoints for our application. Playing around with this parameter could improve performance in other cases. This can be done by using the following code snippet:

```
float threshold = 125.0;
vector<KeyPoint> keypoints;
Mat rescaled;
convertScaleAbs(harris_normalised, rescaled);
Mat harris_c(rescaled.rows, rescaled.cols, CV_8UC3);
Mat in[] = { rescaled, rescaled, rescaled };
int from_to[] = { 0,0, 1,1, 2,2 };
mixChannels( in, 3, &harris_c, 1, from_to, 3 );
for(int x=0; x<harris_normalised.cols; x++){
    for(int y=0; y<harris_normalised.rows; y++){
        if ( (int)harris_normalised.at<float>(y, x) > threshold ){
            // Draw or store the keypoint location here, just like
            //you decide. In our case we will store the location of
            // the keypoint
            circle(harris_c, Point(x, y), 5, Scalar(0,255,0), 1);
            circle(harris_c, Point(x, y), 1, Scalar(0,0,255), 1);
            keypoints.push_back( KeyPoint (x, y, 1) );
        }
    }
}
```

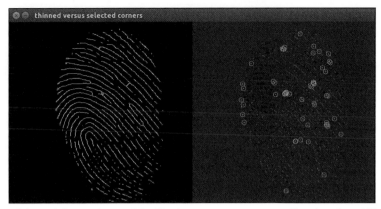

Comparison of thinned fingerprints and the Harris corner response, as well as the selected Harris corners

Now that we have a list of keypoints, we need to create some sort of formal descriptor of the local region around each keypoint to be able to uniquely identify it from other keypoints.

> *Chapter 3, Recognizing Facial Expressions with Machine Learning*, discusses in more detail the wide range of keypoints out there. In this chapter, we will mainly focus on the process. Feel free to adapt the interface to other keypoint detectors and descriptors out there, for better or for worse performance.

Since we have an application where the orientation of the thumb can differ (since it is not in a fixed position), we want a keypoint descriptor that is good at handling these slight differences. One of the most common descriptors for this is the SIFT descriptor, which stands for **scale invariant feature transform**. However, SIFT is not under a BSD license, which can pose problems when used in commercial software. A good alternative in OpenCV is the ORB descriptor. You can implement it in the following way:

```
Ptr<Feature2D> orb_descriptor = ORB::create();
Mat descriptors;
orb_descriptor->compute(input_thinned, keypoints, descriptors);
```

This enables us to calculate only the descriptors using the ORB approach, since we already retrieved the location of the keypoints using the Harris corner approach.

At this point, we can retrieve a descriptor for each detected keypoint of any given fingerprint. The descriptors matrix contains a row for each keypoint containing the representation.

Let's start with the example in which we have just one reference image for each fingerprint. We then have a database containing a set of feature descriptors for the training persons in the database. We have a single new entry, consisting of multiple descriptors for the keypoints found at registration time. We now have to match these descriptors to the descriptors stored in the database, to see which one has the best match.

The simplest way to do this is to perform brute-force matching using the hamming distance criteria between descriptors of different keypoints.

```
// Imagine we have a vector of single entry descriptors as a database
// We will still need to fill those once we compare everything, by
using the code snippets above
vector<Mat> database_descriptors;
Mat current_descriptors;
// Create the matcher interface
Ptr<DescriptorMatcher> matcher = DescriptorMatcher::create("BruteFor
ce-Hamming");
// Now loop over the database and start the matching
vector< vector< DMatch > > all_matches;
for(int entry=0; i<database_descriptors.size();entry++){
    vector< DMatch > matches;
    matcheràmatch(database_descriptors[entry], current_descriptors,
matches);
    all_matches.push_back(matches);
}
```

We now have all the matches stored as DMatch objects. This means that, for each matching couple, we will have the original keypoint, the matched keypoint, and a floating point score between both matches, representing the distance between the matched points.

This seems pretty straightforward. We take a look at the number of matches that have been returned by the matching process and weigh them by their Euclidean distance in order to add some certainty. We then look for the matching process that yielded the biggest score. This will be our best match, and the match we want to return as the selected one from the database.

If you want to avoid an imposter getting assigned to the best matching score, you can add a manual threshold on top of the scoring to avoid matches and ignore those that are not good enough. However, it is possible that, if you increase the score too much, people with little change will be rejected from the system, if, for example, someone cuts their finger and thus changes their pattern drastically.

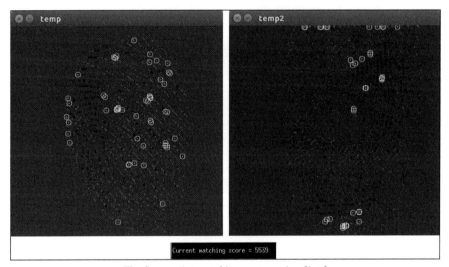

The fingerprint matching process visualized

Iris identification, how is it done?

The last biometric that we will use is the output of an iris scan. Considering our setup, there might be several ways to grab iris data:

- We can separate the face and apply an eye detector using face detection, which can be done with a high-resolution camera. We can use the resulting regions to perform iris segmentation and classification.
- We can use a specific eye camera, which grabs an eye image to be classified. This can be done either with RGB or NIR.

Since the first approach is prone to a lot of problems, such as the resulting eye image having a low resolution, a more common approach is to use a separate eye camera that grabs the eye. This is the method that we will use in this chapter. An example of a captured eye in both the RGB (visible colors) and NIR (near infra-red) spectrums is visualized below:

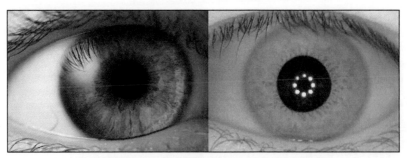

An example of both a RGB and a NIR iris-based image

Using NIR images helps us in several ways:

- First of all, color information is omitted, since a lot of conditions like external sources of light can influence color information when grabbing the iris image.

- Secondly, the pupil center becomes clearer and fully black, which allows us to use techniques that depend on this for segmenting the pupil center.

- Thirdly, the available structure is maintained, under different lighting conditions, due to the NIR spectrum.

- Finally, the outer border of the iris region is clearer, and thus more easily separable.

We will use data from the CASIA eye dataset for the iris recognition, which can be found at http://biometrics.idealtest.org/. This dataset is publicly available for research and non-commercial purposes, and access can be requested through the site. A small part of it can be found in our software repository, where we have a right and a left eye from one individual, which we can now treat as two people since no two irises are identical. We have 10 samples for each eye, of which we will use eight to train and two to test.

The approach that we will implement for iris recognition is based on the technique suggested by John Daugman. The technique is widely accepted and used in commercial systems, and has thus proven its quality.

 The original paper written by John Daugman can be found at: `http://www.cl.cam.ac.uk/~jgd1000/irisrecog.pdf`

Implementing the approach in OpenCV 3

The first step in getting the iris information is segmenting out the actual eye region, containing both the iris and the pupil. We apply a series of operations on top of our data to achieve the desired result. This process is necessary to keep only the desired data and remove all the redundant eye data that is still around.

We first try to get the pupil. The pupil is the darkest area in NIR images, and this information can be used to our advantage. The following steps will lead us to the pupil area in an eye image:

- First, we need to apply segmentation to the darkest regions. We can use the `inRange()` image, since the values in which the pupil lie are specific to the capturing system. However, due to the fact that they all use NIR, the end result will be identical for each separate system.

- Then, we apply contour detection to get the outer border of the pupil. We make sure that we get the biggest contour from just the outer contours so that we only keep one region.

 If you want to improve performance, you can also look for the bright spots of the IR LED first, remove them from the region, and then run the contour detection. This will improve robustness when IR LED spots are close to the pupil border.

The code for the complete process of a single iris can be found at: `https://github.com/OpenCVBlueprints/OpenCVBlueprints/tree/master/chapter_6/source_code/iris/iris_processing/`

This behavior can be achieved by using the following code snippet:

```
// Read in image and perform contour detection
Mat original = imread("path/to/eye/image.png", IMREAD_GRAYSCALE);
Mat mask_pupil;
inRange(original, Scalar(30,30,30), Scalar(80,80,80), mask_pupil);
vector< vector<Point> > contours;
findContours(mask_pupil.clone(), contours, RETR_EXTERNAL, CHAIN_
APPROX_NONE);
// Calculate all the corresponding areas which are larger than
vector< vector<Point> > filtered;
for(int i=0; i<contours.size(); i++){
    double area = contourArea(contours[i]);
    // Remove noisy regions
    if(area > 50.0){
        filtered.push_back(contours[i]);
    }
}
// Now make a last check, if there are still multiple contours left,
take the one that has a center closest to the image center
vector<Point> final_contour=filtered[0];
if(filtered.size() > 1){
    double distance = 5000;
    int index = -1;
    Point2f orig_center(original.cols/2, original.rows/2);
    for(int i=0; i<filtered.size(); i++){
        Moments temp = moments(filtered[i]);
        Point2f current_center((temp.m10/temp.m00), (temp.m01/temp.
m00));
        // Find the Euclidean distance between both positions
        double dist = norm(Mat(orig_center), Mat(current_center));
        if(dist < distance){
            distance = dist;
            index = i;
        }
    }
    final_contour = filtered[index];
}
// Now finally make the black contoured image;
vector< vector<Point> > draw;
draw.push_back(final_contour);
Mat blacked_pupil = original.clone();
drawContours(blacked_pupil, draw, -1, Scalar(0,0,0), FILLED);
```

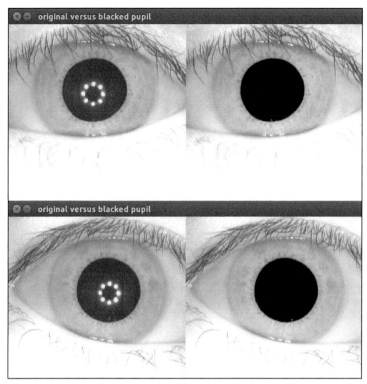

Blacked out pupil region for both left and right eyes

This gives us the ability to black out the eye region when needed, based on the returned contour, as shown in the above figure. The second thing that we need to do is define the outer border of the iris region. This can be done by applying the Hough circle transform on the edge pixels of the iris itself. The following code snippet should perform this.

 Sometimes, the Hough circle detection will not yield a single circle. This is not the case with the proposed database, but if you encounter this, then looking at other techniques like the Laplacian of Gaussians should help you to find and reconstruct the iris region.

```
// Make sure that the input image is gray, we took care of that while
reading in the original image and making sure that the blacked pupil
image is a clone of that.
// Apply a canny edge filter to look for borders
// Then clean it a bit by adding a smoothing filter, reducing noise
Mat preprocessed;
```

```
Canny(blacked_pupil, blacked_pupil, 5, 70);
GaussianBlur(blacked_pupil, preprocessed, Size(7,7));
// Now run a set of HoughCircle detections with different parameters
// We increase the second accumulator value until a single circle is
left and take that one for granted
int i = 80;
vector<Point3f> found_circle;
while (i < 151){
    vector< vector<Point3f> > storage;
    // If you use other data than the database provided, tweaking of
these parameters will be necessary
    HoughCircles(preprocessed, storage, HOUGH_GRADIENT, 2, 100.0, 30,
i, 100, 140);
    if(storage.size() == 1){
        found_circle = storage[0];
        break;
    }
    i++;
}
// Now draw the outer circle of the iris
int radius = found_circle[2];
Mat mask = Mat::zeros(blacked_pupil.rows, blacked_pupil.cols, CV_8UC1);
// The centroid value here must be the same as the one of the inner
pupil so we reuse it back here
Moments temp = Moments(final_contour);
Point2f centroid((temp.m10/temp.m00), (temp.m01/temp.m00));
Circle(mask, centroid, radius, Scalar(255,255,255), FILLED);
bitwise_not(mask, mask);
Mat final_result;
subtract(blacked_pupil, blacked_pupil.clone(), final_result, mask);
// Visualize the final result
imshow("final blacked iris region", final_result);
```

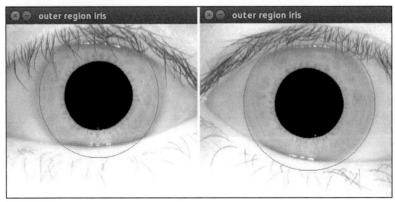

An example of the retrieved Hough Circle result, which gives us the outer border of the iris region, for both the left and right eyes.

Once we have succeeded in finding the outer contour, it is pretty straightforward to mask the iris region from the original input, as shown in the figure below:

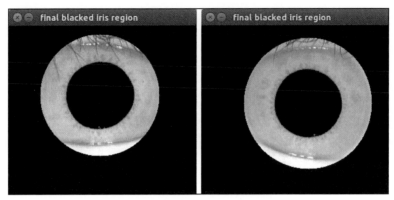

An example of the masked iris image

We now have our region of interest, meaning only the iris region, as shown in the above figure. We acknowledge that there could still be some partial whiskers inside the region, but for now we will simply ignore them. Now, we want to encode this iris image into a feature vector for comparison. There are two steps still to take to reach that level:

- Unwrapping of the iris pattern from a polar coordinate system to a Cartesian coordinate system for further processing
- Applying encoding to the iris image and matching it against a database of known representations

We start by providing a code snippet that will unwrap the desired iris region from the retrieved final result:

```
// Lets first crop the final iris region from the image
int x = int(centroid[0] - radius);
int y = int(centroid[1] - radius);
int w = int(radius * 2);
int h = w;
Mat cropped_region = final_result( Rect(x,y,w,h) ).clone();
// Now perform the unwrapping
// This is done by the logpolar function who does Logpolar to
Cartesian coordinates, so that it can get unwrapped properly
Mat unwrapped;
int center = (float(cropped_region.cols/2.0), float(cropped_region.
cols /2.0));
LogPolar(image, unwrapped, c, 60.0, INTER_LINEAR +  WARP_FILL_
OUTLIERS);
imshow("unwrapped image", unwrapped); waitKey(0);
```

This will result in the following conversion, which gives us the radial unwrapping of the iris region, as shown in the figure below:

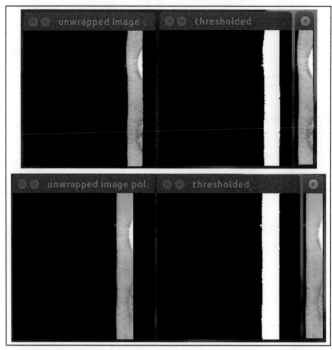

An example of the radially unwrapped iris image for both the left and right eyes

This radial unwrapping is done for all the eight training images that we have for each eye and for two testing images that we also have for each eye. The Daugman approach applies phase quadrant modulation to encode the iris pattern. However, this is not yet implemented in OpenCV and is too complex for this chapter. Therefore, we decided to look for an available OpenCV implementation that could be used to match the irises. A good approach is to use the local binary pattern histogram comparison, since we are looking for something that can identify local textures, and this was also used for face recognition.

Software for unwrapping a complete set of iris images can be found at:

```
https://github.com/OpenCVBlueprints/OpenCVBlueprints/
tree/master/chapter_6/source_code/iris/iris_
processing_batch/
```

Software for creating the matching interface can be found at:

```
https://github.com/OpenCVBlueprints/OpenCVBlueprints/
tree/master/chapter_6/source_code/iris/iris_
recognition/
```

Finally, encoding works as follows in OpenCV 3:

```
// Try using the facerecognizer interface for these irises
// Choice of using LBPH --> local and good for finding texture
Ptr<LBPHFaceRecognizer> iris_model = createLBPHFaceRecognizer();
// Train the facerecognizer
iris_model->train(train_iris, train_labels);
// Loop over test images and match their labels
int total_correct = 0, total_wrong = 0;
for(int i=0; i<test_iris.size(); i ++){
        int predict = iris_model->predict(test_iris[i]);
        if(predict == test_labels[i]){
            total_correct++;
        }else{
            total_wrong++;
        }
}
```

We count the testing results again, which yields the result shown in the figure below:

Total correct: 4 / Total wrong: 0

Encoded iris image and the corresponding iris code visualized.

Combining the techniques to create an efficient people-registration system

The previous sections each discussed a specific biometric property. Now, let's combine all this information to create an efficient identification system. The approach that we will implement follows the structure described in the figure below:

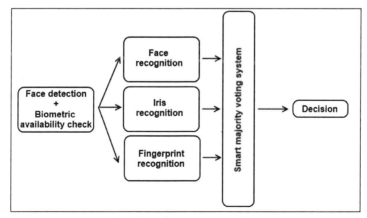

People authentication pipeline

As shown above, the first step is to use a camera interface to check if there actually is a person in front of the camera. This is done by performing face detection on the input image. We also test to see if the other biometric systems are active. This leaves us two checks that need to be performed:

- Check if the iris scanner is in use. This, of course, depends on the system used. If it depends on the eye retrieved from the face detection, this check should be ignored. If the eye is retrieved using an actual eye scanner, then there should at least be an eye detected to give a positive signal.

- Check if the fingerprint scanner is active. Do we actually have a finger available for taking a fingerprint picture? This is checked by applying background subtraction to the empty scene. If a finger is in place, then there should be a response to the background-foreground subtraction.

Of course, we are aware that some of these systems use pressure-based detection to find a hand or finger. In such cases, you do not have to perform this check yourself, but let the system decide whether to proceed or not.

Once we have all the systems, we can start the individual recognition systems described in previous sections. They will all output the identity of a known person from the common database that was constructed for this purpose. Then, all these outcomes are given to the smart majority voting. This system checks for several things:

- It checks if the biometric system checks actually succeeded, by returning their match from the database. If not, a person is not granted access and the system asks to reconfirm the failing biometrics.

- If the system has to measure biometrics more than three times in a row, the system jams and doesn't work until the owner of the system unlocks it. This is to avoid a bug in the current interface that exploits the system and tries to get in.

- If the biometric checks work, a smart majority voting is applied to the results. This means that if two biometrics identify person A but one biometric identifies person B, then the output result will still be person A. If that person is marked as the owner, then the system will allow access.

- Based on the individual software provided with the separate subtopics, it should be quite straightforward to combine them into a single interface.

- If the system still fails (this is a case study, not a 100% failproof system), there are several things that can be done to achieve the desired results.

- ° You should try to improve the detection and matching quality of each separate biometric. This can be done by supplying better training data, experimenting with different feature extraction methods or different feature comparison methods, as discussed in the introduction to the chapter. The variety of combinations is endless, so go ahead and give it a try.

- ° You should try to give each biometric a certainty score on its output. Since we have multiple systems voting for the identity of a person, we could take into account their certainty on single classifications. For example, when running a database, matching the distance to the best match can be wrapped to a scale range of [0 100] to give a certainty percentage. We can then multiply the vote of each biometric by its weight and do a smart-weighted majority voting.

Summary

In this chapter, you learned that an authentication system can be more than a simple face recognition interface by using multiple biometric properties of the person trying to authenticate. We showed you how to perform iris and fingerprint recognition using the OpenCV library to make a multi-biometric authentication system. One can add even more biometrics to the system, since the possibilities are endless.

The focus of the chapter was to get people interested in the power of biometrics and the endless possibilities of the OpenCV library. If you feel inspired by this, do experiment further and share your thoughts with the community.

 I would like to thank the users of the OpenCV Q&A discussion forum who helped me to push the limits when I hit brick walls. I would explicitly like to thank the following users for their directions: Berak, Guanta, Theodore, and GilLevi.

7
Gyroscopic Video Stabilization

Video stabilization is a classic problem in computer vision. The idea is simple – you have a video stream that's shaky, and you're trying to identify the best way to negate the motion of the camera to produce a smooth motion across images. The resulting video is easier to view and has a cinematic look.

Over the years, there have been a number of approaches being tried to solve this. Videos have traditionally been stabilized by using data available only from images, or using specialized hardware to negate physical motion in the camera. Gyroscopes in mobile devices are the middle ground between these two approaches.

In this chapter, we'll cover the following:

- An Android camera application to record media and gyroscope traces
- Using the video and gyroscope trace to find mathematical unknowns
- Using the physical camera unknowns to compensate for camera motion
- Identifying rolling shutter in the camera

 Rolling shutter on a camera sensor produces unwanted effects. We'll cover this in detail in a later section. Also, refer to *Chapter 1, Getting the Most out of Your Camera System*, for a detailed discussion.

Before we get started, let's take a look at some techniques that were used in the past to solve this problem.

Stabilization with images

Video stabilization with images alone seems like the first logical step. Indeed, initial research on stabilizing video captured by cameras was based on using information readily available from the camera sensors to understand how they move image by image.

The idea is to find keypoints in an image sequence to understand how they move image by image. Keypoints are pixel locations on an image that match these criteria:

- Keypoints should be easily recognizable and distinguishable from each other. Corners of objects are good keypoints while a point on a blank wall is not.

- It should be possible to track keypoints across multiple images to calculate motion. You should be able to tell exactly where the keypoint has moved from one frame to another.

- For performance, identifying these keypoints should be fast and memory-efficient. This is usually a bottleneck on low memory and low power devices.

Research with these criteria led to several unique approaches like including some famous algorithms such as SIFT, SURF, ORB, FREAK, and so on. These techniques often work well.

OpenCV comes with several common keypoint detectors. These include ORB, FAST, BRISK, SURF, and so on. Check the 2D Features Framework documentation page for more information on how to use these at: `http://docs.opencv.org/3.0-beta/modules/features2d/doc/feature_detection_and_description.html`.

The keypoint detectors, however, have their own set of drawbacks. Firstly, the results of stabilization are highly dependent on the quality of the images. For example, a low resolution image might not produce the best set of features. Out of focus and blurry images are another concern. This puts a constraint on the types of sequences that can be stabilized. A scene with a clear blue sky and yellow sand might not contain enough features.

A surface with a repetitive pattern will confuse the algorithm because the same features keep showing up in different positions.

The image above is taken from: `https://d2v9y0dukr6mq2.cloudfront.net/video/thumbnail/kG-5Wkc/crowd-of-people-walking-crossing-street-at-night-in-times-square-slow-motion-30p_ekqzvese__S0000.jpg`

Secondly, if there is a large amount of motion in the image (such as people walking in the background or a truck moving across the road), the stabilization will be skewed because of it. The keypoint is tracking the moving object and not the motion of the camera itself. This limits the types of videos that can be successfully stabilized with such an approach. There are ways of getting around such constraints – however, it makes the algorithm more complex.

Stabilization with hardware

Certain industries, such as the movie industry and the military, expect high quality video stabilization. Using just images in those varied environments would not work. This led industries to create hardware-based image stabilization rigs. For example, a quadcopter with a camera needs to have a high quality video output despite (potentially) bad lighting conditions, wind, and so on.

The image above is taken from `http://g01.a.alicdn.com/kf/HTB1.ogPIpXXXXaXXVXXq6xXFXXXw/GH4-A7S-SUMMER-DYS-3-axis-3-Axis-Gimbal-dslr-camera-Stabilizer-gyro-brushless-gimbal-steadicam.jpg`

These devices use a gyroscope to physically move and rotate the camera so that the image sequence stays stable. The results look excellent since you're actually compensating for the motion of the camera.

These devices tend to be on the more expensive side and thus unaffordable for the common consumer. They also tend to be quite bulky. The average person would not want to carry a two kilogram rig on his vacation.

A hybrid of hardware and software

This chapter covers a hybrid solution between the original software-only approach and hardware devices. This became possible only recently, with the advent of the smartphone. People now had a high quality camera and a gyroscope in a small form.

The idea behind this approach is to use the gyroscope to capture motion and the camera sensor to capture light. These two streams are then fused so that the image is always stable.

As the sensors' density increases and we head to 4K cameras, selecting a (stable) subregion of the image becomes an increasingly viable option as we can discard more of the image without compromising on the quality.

The math

Before we jump into the code, let's take an overview of the algorithm. There are four key components.

- The first is the pinhole camera model. We try and approximate real world positions to pixels using this matrix.
- The second is the camera motion estimate. We need to use data from the gyroscope to figure out the orientation of the phone at any given moment.
- The third is the rolling shutter computation. We need to specify the direction of the rolling shutter and estimate the duration of the rolling shutter.
- The fourth is the image warping expression. Using all the information from the previous calculations, we need to generate a new image so that it becomes stable.

The camera model

We use the standard pinhole camera model. This model is used in several algorithms and is a good approximation of an actual camera.

$$x = KX$$

$$K^{-1} = \begin{pmatrix} 1 & 0 & -o_x \\ 0 & 1 & -o_y \\ 0 & 0 & f \end{pmatrix}$$

There are three unknowns. The o variables indicate the origin of the camera axis in the image plane (these can be assumed to be 0). The two 1s in the matrix indicate the aspect ratio of the pixels (we're assuming square pixels). The f indicates the focal length of the lens. We're assuming the focal length is the same in both horizontal and vertical directions.

Using this model, we can see that:

$$X = qK^{-1}x$$

Here, X is the point in the real world. There is also an unknown scaling factor, q, present.

 Estimating this unknown is not possible for monocular vision unless the physical dimensions of an object are known.

K is the intrinsic matrix and x is the point on the image.

The Camera motion

We can assume that the world origin is the same as the camera origin. Then, the motion of the camera can be described in terms of the orientation of the camera. Thus, at any given time t:

$$x = KR(t)X$$

The rotation matrix R can be calculated by integrating the angular velocity of the camera (obtained from the gyroscope).

$$\Delta\theta(t) = (\omega(t + t_d) + \omega_d) * \delta t$$

Here, ω_d is the gyroscope drift and t_d is the delay between the gyroscope and frame timestamps. These are unknowns as well; we need a mechanism to calculate them.

Rolling shutter compensation

When you click a picture, the common assumption is that the entire image is captured in one go. This is indeed the case for images captured with CCD sensors (which were prevalent a while back). With the commercialization of CMOS image sensors, this is no longer the case. Some CMOS sensors support a global shutter too but, in this chapter, we'll assume the sensor has a rolling shutter.

Images are captured one row at a time — usually the first row is captured first, then the second row, and so on. There's a very slight delay between the consecutive rows of an image.

This leads to strange effects. This is very visible when we're correcting camera shake (for example if there's a lot of motion in the camera).

The fan blades are the same size; however due to the fast motion, the rolling shutter causes artifacts in the image recorded by the sensor.

To model the rolling shutter, we need to identify at what time a specific row was captured. This can be done as follows:

$$t(i, y) = t_i + t_s * \frac{y}{h}$$

Here, t_i is the time when the ith frame was captured, h is the height of the image frame, and t_s is the duration of the rolling shutter, that is, the time it takes to scan from top to bottom. Assuming each row takes the same time, the yth row would take $t_s * y / h$ additional time to get scanned.

> This assumes the rolling shutter happens from top to bottom. A rolling shutter from bottom to top can be modeled with a negative value for t_s. Also, a rolling shutter from left to right can be modeled by replacing y / h with x / w where w is the width of the frame.

Image warping

So far, we have the estimated camera motion and a model for correcting the rolling shutter. We'll combine both and identify a relationship across multiple frames:

- $x_i = KR_1(t(i, y_i))X$ (for frame i with rotation configuration 1)
- $x_j = KR_2(t(j, y_j))X$ (for frame j with rotation configuration 2)

We can combine these two equations:

$$x_j = KR_2(t(j, y_j))R_1^T(t(i, y_i))K^{-1}x_i$$

From here, we can calculate a warping matrix:

$$W(t_1, t_2) = KR_2(t_2)R_1^T(t_1)K^{-1}$$

Now, the relationship between points x_i and x_j can be more succinctly described as:

$$x_j = W(t(j, y_j), t(i, y_i))x_i$$

This warp matrix simultaneously corrects both the video shake and the rolling shutter.

Now we can map the original video to an artificial camera that has smooth motion and a global shutter (no rolling shutter artifacts).

This artificial camera can be simulated by low-pass filtering the input camera's motion and setting the rolling shutter duration to zero. A low pass filter removes high frequency noise from the camera orientation. Thus, the artificial camera's motion will appear much smoother.

Ideally, this matrix can be calculated for each row in the image. However, in practice, subdividing the image into five subsections produces good results as well (with better performance).

Project overview

Let's take a moment to understand how the code in this chapter is organized. We have two moving pieces. One is the mobile application and the second is the video stabilizer.

The mobile app only records video and stores the gyroscope signals during the video. It dumps this data into two files: a `.mp4` and a `.csv` file. These two files are the input for the next step. There is no computation on the mobile device. In this chapter, we'll use Android as our platform. Moving to any other platform should be fairly easy — we are doing only basic tasks that any platform should support.

The video stabilizer runs on a desktop. This is to help you figure out what's happening in the stabilization algorithm much more easily. Debugging, stepping through code and viewing images on a mobile device is relatively slower than iterating on a desktop. We have some really good scientific modules available for free (from the Python community. In this project, we will use Scipy, Numpy, and Matplotlib).

Capturing data

First, we need to create an app for a mobile device that can capture both images and gyroscope signals simultaneously. Interestingly, these aren't readily available (at least on Android).

Once we have a video and gyro stream, we'll look at how to use that data.

Create a standard Android application (I use Android Studio). We'll start by creating a blank application. The goal is to create a simple app that starts recording video and gyro signals on touching the screen. On touching again, the recording stops and a video file and a text file are saved on the phone. These two files can then be used by OpenCV to compute the best stabilization.

 Code in this section is available in the GitHub repository for this book: `https://github.com/OpenCVBlueprints/` `OpenCVBlueprints/tree/master/chapter_7`

Recording video

We'll start by implementing a simple video recording utility. Create a new blank project in Android Studio (I named it GyroRecorder and named the activity Recorder). First, we start by adding permissions to our app. Open `AndroidManifest.xml` in your project and add these permissions:

```
<manifest ...>
    <uses-permission android:name="android.permission.CAMERA" />
    <uses-permission android:name="android.permission.WRITE_EXTERNAL_
STORAGE" />
    <application ...>
```

This simply lets our app access the camera and write to storage (the gyro file and the video). Next, open the main activity visual editor and add a TextureView and a Button element inside a vertical LinearLayout.

Change the names of these elements to `texturePreview` and `btnRecord` respectively.

Now we start with some code. In the main activity class, add these lines:

```
public class Recorder extends AppCompatActivity {
    private TextureView mPreview;   // For displaying the live camera
preview
    private Camera mCamera;          // Object to contact the camera
hardware
    private MediaRecorder mMediaRecorder;    // Store the camera's
image stream as a video

    private boolean isRecording = false; // Is video being recoded?
    private Button btnRecord;             // Button that triggers
recording
```

These objects will be used to communicate with Android to indicate when to start recording.

 Android Studio automatically adds imports to your code as you type. For example, the above piece results in the addition of:

```
import android.hardware.Camera;
import android.media.MediaRecorder;
import android.view.TextureView;
```

Next, we need to initialize these objects. We do that in the onCreate event.

```
protected void onCreate(Bundle savedInstanceState) {
    super.onCreate(savedInstanceState);
    setContentView(R.layout.activity_recorder);

    mPreview = (TextureView)findViewById(R.id.texturePreview);
    btnRecord = (Button)findViewById(R.id.btnRecord);

    btnRecord.setOnClickListener(new View.OnClickListener() {
        @Override
        public void onClick(View view) {
            onCaptureClick(view);
        }
    });
```

The onCreate method already contains some methods (super.onCreate, setContentView, and so on; we will add a few lines after that). Now, we need to define what onCaptureClick does.

```
public void onCaptureClick(View view) {
    if (isRecording) {
        // Already recording? Release camera lock for others
        mMediaRecorder.stop();
        releaseMediaRecorder();
        mCamera.lock();

        isRecording = false;
        releaseCamera();
        mGyroFile.close();
        mGyroFile = null;
        btnRecord.setText("Start");
        mStartTime = -1;
    } else {
        // Not recording - launch new "thread" to initiate!
        new MediaPrepareTask().execute(null, null, null);
    }
}
```

 If you want to explore strings.xml, refer to *Chapter 2, Working with Camera Frames*, of the PacktPub book *Android Application Programming with OpenCV*.

Here, we use the internal isRecording variable to notify the media recorder and camera to start saving the stream. We need to create a new thread because initializing the media recorder and camera usually takes a few milliseconds. This lag would be noticeable on the UI if we did it in the main thread.

Once we're done recording (the user taps the Stop button and we need to release the media recorder. This happens in the releaseMediaRecorder method:

```
private void releaseMediaRecorder() {
    if(mMediaRecorder != null) {
        mMediaRecorder.reset();
        mMediaRecorder.release();
        mMediaRecorder = null;
        mCamera.lock();
    }
}
```

Now, we look at creating a new thread. Create this class in your main activity class.

```
class MediaPrepareTask extends AsyncTask<Void, Void, Boolean>{
    @Override
    protected Boolean doInBackground(Void... voids) {
        if(prepareVideoRecorder()) {
            mMediaRecorder.start();
            isRecording = true;
        } else {
            releaseMediaRecorder();
            return false;
        }
        return true;
    }

    @Override
    protected void onPostExecute(Boolean result) {
        if(!result) {
            Recorder.this.finish();
        }

        btnRecord.setText("Stop");
    }
}
```

This creates an object of the type `AsyncTask`. Creating a new object of this class automatically creates a new thread and runs `doInBackground` in that thread. We want to prepare the media recorder in this thread. Preparing the media recorder involves identifying supported image sizes from the camera, finding the suitable height, setting the bitrate of the video and specifying the destination video file.

In your main activity class, create a new method called `prepareVideoRecorder`:

```
@TargetApi(Build.VERSION_CODES.HONEYCOMB)
private boolean prepareVideoRecorder() {
    mCamera = Camera.open();

    Camera.Parameters parameters = mCamera.getParameters();
    List<Camera.Size> mSupportedPreviewSizes =
                        parameters.getSupportedPreviewSizes();
```

Now that we have supported video sizes, we need to find the optimal image size for the camera. This is done here:

```
Camera.Size optimalSize = getOptimalPreviewSize(
                                mSupportedPreviewSizes,
                                mPreview.getWidth(),
                                mPreview.getHeight());
parameters.setPreviewSize(optimalSize.width,
                                optimalSize.height);
```

With the optimal size in hand, we can now set up the camera recorder settings:

```
CamcorderProfile profile = CamcorderProfile.get(
                                CamcorderProfile.QUALITY_HIGH);
profile.videoFrameWidth = optimalSize.width;
profile.videoFrameHeight = optimalSize.height;
```

Now, we try to contact the camera hardware and set up these parameters:

```
mCamera.setParameters(parameters);
try {
        mCamera.setPreviewTexture(
                        mPreview.getSurfaceTexture());
} catch(IOException e) {
        Log.e(TAG,"Surface texture is unavailable or unsuitable" +
e.getMessage());
        return false;
}
```

Here, along with setting the camera parameters, we also specify a preview surface. The preview surface is used to display what the camera sees live.

With the camera setup done, we can now set up the media recorder:

```
mMediaRecorder = new MediaRecorder();
    mCamera.unlock();
    mMediaRecorder.setCamera(mCamera);

    mMediaRecorder.setVideoSource(
                        MediaRecorder.VideoSource.CAMERA);

    mMediaRecorder.setOutputFormat(profile.fileFormat);
    mMediaRecorder.setVideoFrameRate(profile.videoFrameRate);
    mMediaRecorder.setVideoSize(profile.videoFrameWidth,
                        profile.videoFrameHeight);
```

```
mMediaRecorder.setVideoEncodingBitRate(
                            profile.videoBitRate);

mMediaRecorder.setVideoEncoder(profile.videoCodec);
mMediaRecorder.setOutputFile(
                            getOutputMediaFile().toString());
```

This just sets whatever we already know about the video stream — we're simply passing information from what we've gathered into the media recorder.

 This configuration does not record audio. In this project, we're not concerned with the audio signals. However, it should be straightforward to configure the media recorder to store audio as well.

With everything in place, we try to start the media recorder:

```
try {
    mMediaRecorder.prepare();
} catch (IllegalStateException e) {
    Log.d(TAG, "IllegalStateException preparing MediaRecorder:
" + e.getMessage());
    releaseMediaRecorder();
    return false;
} catch (IOException e) {
    Log.d(TAG, "IOException preparing MediaRecorder: " +
e.getMessage());
    releaseMediaRecorder();
    return false;
}
return true;
}
```

And that's the end of the `prepareVideoRecorder` method. We've referenced a bunch of variables and functions that do not exist yet, so we'll define some of them now.

The first is `getOptimalPreviewSize`. Define this method in your activity's class:

```
private Camera.Size getOptimalPreviewSize(List<Camera.Size> sizes,
int w, int h) {
    final double ASPECT_TOLERANCE = 0.1;
    double targetRatio = (double)w / h;
```

```
    if(sizes == null) {
        return null;
    }

    Camera.Size optimalSize = null;

    double minDiff = Double.MAX_VALUE;

    int targetHeight = h;

    for (Camera.Size size : sizes) {
        double ratio = (double)size.width / size.height;
        double diff = Math.abs(ratio - targetRatio);

        if(Math.abs(ratio - targetRatio) > ASPECT_TOLERANCE)
            continue;

        if(Math.abs(size.height - targetHeight) < minDiff) {
            optimalSize = size;
            minDiff = Math.abs(size.height - targetHeight);
        }
    }

    if(optimalSize == null) {
        minDiff = Double.MAX_VALUE;
        for(Camera.Size size : sizes) {
            if(Math.abs(size.height-targetHeight) < minDiff) {
                optimalSize = size;
                minDiff = Math.abs(size.height-targetHeight);
            }
        }
    }

    return optimalSize;
}
```

This function simply tries to match all possible image sizes against an expected aspect ratio. If it cannot find a close match, it returns the closest match (based on the expected height).

The second is `getOutputMediaFile`. This function uses the Android API to find an acceptable location to store our videos. Define this method in the main activity class as well:

```
private File getOutputMediaFile() {
      if(!Environment.getExternalStorageState().
equalsIgnoreCase(Environment.MEDIA_MOUNTED)) {
            return null;
      }


      File mediaStorageDir = new File(Environment.getExternalStorage
PublicDirectory(Environment.DIRECTORY_PICTURES), "Recorder");

      if(!mediaStorageDir.exists()) {
          if(!mediaStorageDir.mkdirs()) {
              Log.d("Recorder", "Failed to create directory");
              return null;
          }
      }

      String timeStamp = new SimpleDateFormat("yyyyMMdd_HHmmss").
format(new Date());
      File mediaFile;
      mediaFile = new File(mediaStorageDir.getPath() + File.
separator + "VID_" + timeStamp + ".mp4");

      return mediaFile;
}
```

It finds the media storage location for pictures and appends a timestamp to the filename.

Now we have almost everything to start recording videos. Two more method definitions and we'll have a working video recorder.

```
private void releaseCamera() {
    if(mCamera != null) {
        mCamera.release();
        mCamera = null;
    }
}
@Override
```

```
protected void onPause() {
    super.onPause();

    releaseMediaRecorder();
    releaseCamera();
}
```

The `onPause` method is called whenever the user switches to another app. It's being a good citizen to release hardware dependencies when you're not using them.

Recording gyro signals

In the previous section, we only looked at recording video. For this project, we also need to record gyroscope signals. With Android, this is accomplished by using a sensor event listener. We'll modify the main activity class for this. Add this `implements` clause:

```
public class Recorder extends Activity implements SensorEventListener
{
    private TextureView mPreview;
    private Camera mCamera;
    ...
```

Now, we need to add a few new objects to our class:

```
    ...
    private Button btnRecord;

    private SensorManager mSensorManager;
    private Sensor mGyro;
    private PrintStream mGyroFile;
    private long mStartTime = -1;

    private static String TAG = "GyroRecorder";

    @Override
    protected void onCreate(Bundle savedInstanceState) {
    ....
```

The `SensorManager` object manages all sensors on the hardware. We're only interested in the gyroscope, so we have a `Sensor` object for it. `PrintStream` writes a text file with the gyroscope signals. We now need to initialize these objects. We do that in the `onCreate` method. Modify the method so that it looks like this:

```
                onCaptureClick(view);
            }
        });


        mSensorManager = (SensorManager)getSystemService(Context.
SENSOR_SERVICE);
        mGyro = mSensorManager.getDefaultSensor(Sensor.TYPE_
GYROSCOPE);
        mSensorManager.registerListener(this, mGyro, SensorManager.
SENSOR_DELAY_FASTEST);
    }
```

Here, we're fetching the gyroscope sensor and registering that this class should receive events (`registerListener`). We're also mentioning the frequency we want data to flow in.

Next, we initialize the `PrintStream` in the `prepareVideoRecorder` method:

```
    private boolean prepareVideoRecorder() {
        mCamera = Camera.open();
        ...
        mMediaRecorder.setOutputFile(getOutputMediaFile().toString());

        try {
            mGyroFile = new PrintStream(getOutputGyroFile());
            mGyroFile.append("gyro\n");
        } catch(IOException e) {
            Log.d(TAG, "Unable to create acquisition file");
            return false;
        }

        try {
            mMediaRecorder.prepare();
        ...
```

This tries to open a new stream to a text file. We fetch the text file name using:

```
private File getOutputGyroFile() {
    if(!Environment.getExternalStorageState().
equalsIgnoreCase(Environment.MEDIA_MOUNTED)) {
        return null;
    }

    File gyroStorageDir = new File(Environment.getExternalStorageP
ublicDirectory(Environment.DIRECTORY_PICTURES), "Recorder");

    if(!gyroStorageDir.exists()) {
        if(!gyroStorageDir.mkdirs()) {
            Log.d("Recorder", "Failed to create directory");
            return null;
        }
    }

    String timeStamp = new SimpleDateFormat("yyyyMMdd_HHmmss").
format(new Date());
    File gyroFile;
    gyroFile = new File(gyroStorageDir.getPath() + File.separator
+ "VID_" + timeStamp + "gyro.csv");

    return gyroFile;
}
```

This is almost the same code as getOutputMediaFile, except that it returns a .csv file (instead of an .mp4) in the same directory.

One last thing and we'll be recording gyroscope signals as well. Add this method to the main activity class:

```
@Override
public void onAccuracyChanged(Sensor sensor, int accuracy) {
    // Empty on purpose
    // Required because we implement SensorEventListener
}

@Override
public void onSensorChanged(SensorEvent sensorEvent) {
    if(isRecording) {
```

```
        if(mStartTime == -1) {
            mStartTime = sensorEvent.timestamp;
        }
        mGyroFile.append(sensorEvent.values[0] + "," +
                         sensorEvent.values[1] + "," +
                         sensorEvent.values[2] + "," +
                         (sensorEvent.timestamp-mStartTime) +
    "\n");
        }
    }
```

The idea is to store values returned by the sensor into the file as soon as possible.

Android specifics

In this section, we'll look at some Android-specific tasks: one is rendering an overlay on top of the camera view and the second is reading media files on Android.

The overlay is helpful for general information and debugging, and looks nice too! Think of it like the heads up display on a consumer camera.

The reading media files section is something we don't use in this chapter (we read media files using Python). However, if you decide to write an Android app that processes videos on the device itself, this section should get you started.

Threaded overlay

Now that we have the camera preview working, we want to render some additional information on top of it. We'll be drawing three things; first, a red circle to indicate whether recording is active, second, the current gyroscope values (angular velocity and estimated theta) just for information, and third, a safety rectangle. When stabilizing, we'll probably be cropping the image a bit. The rectangle will guide your video recording to stay within a relatively safe zone.

Along with this, we'll also be setting it up so that you can create buttons on this overlay. Simple touch events can be used to execute specific functions.

You don't need this section for the application to work, but it's a good idea to know how to render on top of an OpenCV camera view while recording.

Before we start working on the overlay widget, let's define a supporting class, `Point3`. Create a new class called `Point3` with three double attributes:

```
public class Point3 {
    public double x;
    public double y;
    public double z;
}
```

We start by defining a new class, `CameraOverlayWidget`.

```
public class CameraOverlayWidget extends SurfaceView implements
GestureDetector.OnGestureListener, SurfaceHolder.Callback {
    public static String TAG= "SFOCV::Overlay";
    protected Paint paintSafeExtents;
    protected Button btn;
    protected GestureDetector mGestureDetector;
```

We've subclassed this from `SurfaceView` to be able to render things on it. It also implements the gesture detector class so that we'll be able to monitor touch events on this widget.

```
    private long sizeWidth = 0, sizeHeight = 0;

    // Stuff required to paint the recording sign
    protected boolean mRecording = false;
    protected Paint paintRecordCircle;
    protected Paint paintRecordText;

    // Calibrate button
    private Paint paintCalibrateText;
    private Paint paintCalibrateTextOutline;

    private Paint paintTransparentButton;

    private RenderThread mPainterThread;
    private boolean bStopPainting = false;

    private Point3 omega;
    private Point3 drift;
    private Point3 theta;

    public static final double SAFETY_HORIZONTAL = 0.15;
    public static final double SAFETY_VERTICAL = 0.15;
```

We define a bunch of variables to be used by the class. Some of them are `Paint` objects – which are used by the `SurfaceView` to render things. We've created different paints for the safety rectangle, the red recording circle, and the text.

Next, there are variables that describe the current state of the recorder. These variables answer questions like, is it currently recording? What's the size of the video? What is the latest gyro reading? We'll use these state variables to render the appropriate overlay.

We also define some safety fractions – the safety rectangle will have a margin of 0.15 on each edge.

```
    protected GestureDetector.OnGestureListener mCustomTouchMethods =
null;
    protected OverlayEventListener mOverlayEventListener = null;
```

And finally, we add a few event listeners – we'll use these to detect touches in specific areas of the overlay (we won't be using these though).

Let's look at the constructor for this class:

```
    public CameraOverlayWidget(Context ctx, AttributeSet attrs) {
        super(ctx, attrs);

        // Position at the very top and I'm the event handler
        setZOrderOnTop(true);
        getHolder().addCallback(this);

        // Load all the required objects
        initializePaints();

        // Setup the required handlers/threads
        mPainterThread = new RenderThread();
        mGestureDetector = new GestureDetector(ctx, this);
    }
```

Here, we set up some basics when the object is initialized. We create the paint objects in `initializePaints`, create a new thread for rendering the overlay and also create a gesture detector.

```
    /**
     * Initializes all paint objects.
     */
    protected void initializePaints() {
        paintSafeExtents = new Paint();
```

```
        paintSafeExtents.setColor(Color.WHITE);
        paintSafeExtents.setStyle(Paint.Style.STROKE);
        paintSafeExtents.setStrokeWidth(3);

        paintRecordCircle = new Paint();
        paintRecordCircle.setColor(Color.RED);
        paintRecordCircle.setStyle(Paint.Style.FILL);

        paintRecordText = new Paint();
        paintRecordText.setColor(Color.WHITE);
        paintRecordText.setTextSize(20);

        paintCalibrateText = new Paint();
        paintCalibrateText.setColor(Color.WHITE);
        paintCalibrateText.setTextSize(35);
        paintCalibrateText.setStyle(Paint.Style.FILL);

        paintCalibrateTextOutline = new Paint();
        paintCalibrateTextOutline.setColor(Color.BLACK);
        paintCalibrateTextOutline.setStrokeWidth(2);
        paintCalibrateTextOutline.setTextSize(35);
        paintCalibrateTextOutline.setStyle(Paint.Style.STROKE);

        paintTransparentButton = new Paint();
        paintTransparentButton.setColor(Color.BLACK);
        paintTransparentButton.setAlpha(128);
        paintTransparentButton.setStyle(Paint.Style.FILL);
    }
```

As you can see, paints describe the physical attributes of the things to draw. For example, `paintRecordCircle` is red and fills whatever shape we draw. Similarly, the record text shows up white with a text size of 20.

Now let's look at the `RenderThread` class—the thing that does the actual drawing of the overlay. We start by defining the class itself and defining the `run` method. The `run` method is executed when the thread is spawned. On returning from this method, the thread stops.

```
    class RenderThread extends Thread {
        private long start = 0;
        @Override
```

```
        public void run() {
            super.run();

            start = SystemClock.uptimeMillis();

            while(!bStopPainting && !isInterrupted()) {
                long tick = SystemClock.uptimeMillis();
                renderOverlay(tick);
            }
        }
```

Now let's add the `renderOverlay` method to `RenderThread`. We start by getting a lock on the canvas and drawing a transparent color background. This clears anything that already exists on the overlay.

```
        /**
         * A renderer for the overlay with no state of its own.
         * @returns nothing
         */
        public void renderOverlay(long tick) {
            Canvas canvas = getHolder().lockCanvas();

            long width = canvas.getWidth();
            long height = canvas.getHeight();

            // Clear the canvas
            canvas.drawColor(Color.TRANSPARENT, PorterDuff.Mode.
    CLEAR);
```

Now, we draw the safety bounds of the camera view. While stabilizing the video, we'll inevitably have to crop certain parts of the image. The safe lines mark this boundary. In our case, we take a certain percentage of the view as safe.

```
            // Draw the bounds
            long lSafeW = (long)(width * SAFETY_HORIZONTAL);
            long lSafeH = (long)(height * SAFETY_VERTICAL);
            canvas.drawRect(lSafeW, lSafeH, width-lSafeW, height-
    lSafeH, paintSafeExtents);
```

If we're recording, we want to blink the red recording circle and the recording text. We do this by taking the current time and the start time.

```
if(mRecording) {
    // Render this only on alternate 500ms intervals
    if(((tick-start) / 500) % 2 == 1) {
        canvas.drawCircle(100, 100, 20,
paintRecordCircle);
        final String s = "Recording";
        canvas.drawText(s, 0, s.length(), 130, 110,
paintRecordText);
    }
}
```

Now we draw a button that says "Record" on it.

```
canvas.drawRect((float)(1-SAFETY_HORIZONTAL)*sizeWidth,
(float)(1-SAFETY_VERTICAL)*sizeHeight, sizeWidth , sizeHeight,
paintTransparentButton);

final String strCalibrate = "Calibrate";
canvas.drawText(strCalibrate, 0, strCalibrate.length(),
width-200, height-200, paintCalibrateText);
canvas.drawText(strCalibrate, 0, strCalibrate.length(),
width-200, height-200, paintCalibrateTextOutline);
```

While recording the video, we will also display some useful information—the current angular velocity and estimated angle. You can verify if the algorithm is working as expected or not.

```
if(omega!=null) {
    final String strO = "O: ";
    canvas.drawText(strO, 0, strO.length(), width - 200,
200, paintCalibrateText);
    String strX = Math.toDegrees(omega.x) + "";
    String strY = Math.toDegrees(omega.y) + "";
    String strZ = Math.toDegrees(omega.z) + "";
    canvas.drawText(strX, 0, strX.length(), width - 200,
250, paintCalibrateText);
    canvas.drawText(strY, 0, strY.length(), width - 200,
300, paintCalibrateText);
```

```
                     canvas.drawText(strZ, 0, strZ.length(), width - 200,
          350, paintCalibrateText);
                  }

                  if(theta!=null) {
                      final String strT = "T: ";
                      canvas.drawText(strT, 0, strT.length(), width - 200,
          500, paintCalibrateText);
                      String strX = Math.toDegrees(theta.x) + "";
                      String strY = Math.toDegrees(theta.y) + "";
                      String strZ = Math.toDegrees(theta.z) + "";
                      canvas.drawText(strX, 0, strX.length(), width - 200,
          550, paintCalibrateText);
                      canvas.drawText(strY, 0, strY.length(), width - 200,
          600, paintCalibrateText);
                      canvas.drawText(strZ, 0, strZ.length(), width - 200,
          650, paintCalibrateText);
                  }
```

And, with this, the render overlay method is complete!

```
                  // Flush out the canvas
                  getHolder().unlockCanvasAndPost(canvas);
              }

          }
```

This class can be used to spawn a new thread and this thread simply keeps the overlay updated. We've added a special logic for the recording circle so that it makes the red circle blink.

Next, let's look at some of the supporting functions in `CameraOverlayWidget`.

```
          public void setRecording() {
              mRecording = true;
          }

          public void unsetRecording() {
              mRecording = false;
          }
```

Two simple set and unset methods enable or disable the red circle.

```
          @Override
          public void onSizeChanged(int w,int h,int oldw,int oldh) {
```

```
        super.onSizeChanged(w, h, oldw, oldh);

        sizeWidth = w;
        sizeHeight = h;
    }
```

If the size of the widget changes (we'll be setting it fullscreen on the preview pane), we should know about it and capture the size in these variables. This will affect the positioning of the various elements and the safety rectangle.

```
    public void setCustomTouchMethods(GestureDetector.
SimpleOnGestureListener c){
        mCustomTouchMethods = c;
    }


    public void setOverlayEventListener(OverlayEventListener listener)
{
        mOverlayEventListener = listener;
    }
```

We also have a few set methods that let you change the values to be displayed on the overlay.

```
    public void setOmega(Point3 omega) {
        this.omega = omega;
    }

    public void setDrift(Point3 drift) {
        this.drift = drift;
    }

    public void setTheta(Point3 theta) {
        this.theta = theta;
    }
```

There are other functions that can be used to modify the overlay being displayed. These functions set the gyroscope values.

Now, let's look at some Android-specific lifecycle events such as pause, resume, and so on.

```
    /**
     * This method is called during the activity's onResume. This
ensures a wakeup
     * re-instantiates the rendering thread.
     */
```

```
    public void resume() {
        bStopPainting = false;
        mPainterThread = new RenderThread();
    }

    /**
     * This method is called during the activity's onPause method.
This ensures
     * going to sleep pauses the rendering.
     */
    public void pause() {
        bStopPainting = true;

        try {
            mPainterThread.join();
        }
        catch(InterruptedException e) {
            e.printStackTrace();
        }
        mPainterThread = null;
    }
```

These two methods ensure we're not using processor cycles when the app isn't in the foreground. We simply stop the rendering thread if the app goes to a paused state and resume painting when it's back.

```
    @Override
    public void surfaceCreated(SurfaceHolder surfaceHolder) {
        getHolder().setFormat(PixelFormat.RGBA_8888);

        // We created the thread earlier - but we should start it only
when
        // the surface is ready to be drawn on.
        if(mPainterThread != null && !mPainterThread.isAlive()) {
            mPainterThread.start();
        }
    }

    @Override
    public void surfaceChanged(SurfaceHolder holder, int format, int
width, int height) {
        // Required for implementation
    }
    @Override
```

```
public void surfaceDestroyed(SurfaceHolder holder) {
    // Required for implementation
}
```

When the surface is created, we set up the pixel format (we want it to be transparent, we make the surface of the type RGBA). Also, we should spawn a new thread to get the overlay rendering going.

With that, we're almost ready with our overlay display. One last thing remains—responding to touch events. Let's do that now:

```
@Override
public boolean onTouchEvent(MotionEvent motionEvent) {
    boolean result = mGestureDetector.onTouchEvent(
                                        motionEvent);

    return result;
}


@Override
public boolean onDown(MotionEvent motionEvent) {
    MotionEvent.PointerCoords coords =
                        new MotionEvent.PointerCoords();

    motionEvent.getPointerCoords(0, coords);

    // Handle these only if there is an event listener
    if(mOverlayEventListener!=null) {
        if(coords.x >= (1-SAFETY_HORIZONTAL)*sizeWidth &&
            coords.x<sizeWidth &&
            coords.y >= (1-SAFETY_VERTICAL)*sizeHeight &&
            coords.y<sizeHeight) {
            return mOverlayEventListener.onCalibrate(
                                        motionEvent);
        }
    }

    // Didn't match? Try passing a raw event - just in case
    if(mCustomTouchMethods!=null)
        return mCustomTouchMethods.onDown(motionEvent);

    // Nothing worked - let it bubble up
    return false;
}


@Override
```

```java
public void onShowPress(MotionEvent motionEvent) {
    if(mCustomTouchMethods!=null)
        mCustomTouchMethods.onShowPress(motionEvent);
}


@Override
public boolean onFling(MotionEvent motionEvent,
                       MotionEvent motionEvent2,
                       float v, float v2) {
    Log.d(TAG, "onFling");

    if(mCustomTouchMethods!=null)
        return mCustomTouchMethods.onFling(motionEvent,
                                           motionEvent2,
                                           v, v2);

    return false;
}


@Override
public void onLongPress(MotionEvent motionEvent) {
    Log.d(TAG, "onLongPress");

    if(mCustomTouchMethods!=null)
        mCustomTouchMethods.onLongPress(motionEvent);
}


@Override
public boolean onScroll(MotionEvent motionEvent,
                        MotionEvent motionEvent2,
                        float v, float v2) {
    Log.d(TAG, "onScroll");

    if(mCustomTouchMethods!=null)
        return mCustomTouchMethods.onScroll(motionEvent,
                                            motionEvent2,
                                            v, v2);

    return false;
}


@Override
public boolean onSingleTapUp(MotionEvent motionEvent) {
```

```
        Log.d(TAG, "onSingleTapUp");

        if(mCustomTouchMethods!=null)
            return mCustomTouchMethods.onSingleTapUp(motionEvent);

        return false;
    }
```

These functions do nothing but pass on events to the event listener, if there is any. We're responding to the following events: `onTouchEvent`, `onDown`, `onShowPress`, `onFlight`, `onLongPress`, `onScroll`, `onSingleTapUp`.

One final piece of code remains for the overlay class. We've used something called `OverlayEventListener` at certain places in the class but have not yet defined it. Here's what it looks like:

```
    public interface OverlayEventListener {
        public boolean onCalibrate(MotionEvent e);
    }

}
```

With this defined, we will now be able to create event handlers for specific buttons being touched on the overlay (the calibrate and record buttons).

Reading media files

Once you've written the media file, you need a mechanism to read individual frames from the movie. We can use Android's Media Decoder to extract frames and convert them into OpenCV's native Mat data structure. We'll start by creating a new class called `SequentialFrameExtractor`.

Most of this section is based on Andy McFadden's tutorial on using the MediaCodec at bigflake.com.

 As mentioned earlier, you don't need this class to get through this chapter's project. If you decide to write an Android app that reads media files, this class should get you started. Feel free to skip this if you like!

We will be using the Android app only to record the video and gyro signals.

```
public class SequentialFrameExtractor {
    private String mFilename = null;
```

```
    private CodecOutputSurface outputSurface = null;
    private MediaCodec decoder = null;

    private FrameAvailableListener frameListener = null;

    private static final int TIMEOUT_USEC = 10000;
    private long decodeCount = 0;
}
```

mFilename is the name of the file that's being read, it should only be set when an object of SequentialFrameExtractor is created. CodecOutputSurface is a construct borrowed from http://bigflake.com that encapsulates logic to render a frame using OpenGL and fetches raw bytes for us to use. It is available on the website and also in the accompanying code. The next is MediaCodec—Android's way of letting you access the decoding pipeline.

FrameAvailableListener is an interface we'll create in just a moment. It allows us to respond whenever a frame becomes available.

What is TIMEOUT_USEC and decodeCount?

```
    private long decodeCount = 0;
    public SequentialFrameExtractor(String filename) {
        mFilename = filename;
    }

    public void start() {
        MediaExtractor mediaExtractor = new MediaExtractor();
        try {
            mediaExtractor.setDataSource(mFilename);
        } catch(IOException e) {
            e.printStackTrace();
        }
    }
```

We've created a constructor and a new start method. The start method is when the decoding begins and it will start firing the onFrameAvailable method as new frames become available.

```
            e.printStackTrace();
        }
        MediaFormat format = null;
        int numTracks = mediaExtract.getTrackCount();
        int track = -1;
```

```
for(int i=0;i<numTracks;i++) {
    MediaFormat fmt = mediaExtractor.getTrackFormat(i);
    String mime = fmt.getString(MediaFormat.KEY_MIME);
    if(mime.startswith("video/")) {
        mediaExtractor.selectTrack(i);
        track = i;
        format = fmt;
        break;
    }
}
if(track==-1) {
    // Did the user select an audio file?
}
```

Here, we loop over all the tracks available in the given file (audio, video, and so on) and identify a video track to work with. We're assuming this is a mono-video file, so we should be good to select the first video track that shows up.

With the track selected, we can now start the actual decoding process. Before that, we must set up a decoding surface and some buffers. The way MediaCodec works is that it keeps accumulating data into a buffer. Once it accumulates an entire frame, the data is passed onto a surface to be rendered.

```
int frameWidth = format.getInteger(
                            MediaFormat.KEY_WIDTH);
int frameHeight = format.getInteger(
                            MediaFormat.KEY_HEIGHT);
outputSurface = new CodecOutputSurface(frameWidth,
                                        frameHeight);


String mime = format.getString(MediaFormat.KEY_MIME);
decoder = MediaCodec.createDecoderByType(mime);
decoder.configure(format,
                outputSurface.getSurface(),
                null,
                0);
decoder.start();

ByteBuffer[] decoderInputBuffers =
                            decoder.getInputBuffers();
MediaCodec.BufferInfo info = new MediaCodec.BufferInfo();
int inputChunk = 0;
boolean outputDone = false, inputDone = false;
long presentationTimeUs = 0;
```

With the initial setup done, we now get into the decoding loop:

```
while(!outputDone) {
    if(!inputDone) {
        int inputBufIndex =
                decoder.dequeueInputBuffer(TIMEOUT_USEC);
        if(inputBufIndex >= 0) {
            ByteBuffer inputBuf =
                    decoderInputBuffers[inputBufIndex];
            int chunkSize = mediaExtractor.readSampleData(
                                        inputBuf, 0);
            if(chunkSize < 0) {
                decoder.queueInputBuffer(inputBufIndex,
                                    0, 0, 0L,
                        mediaCodec.BUFFER_FLAG_END_OF_STREAM);
                inputDone = true;
            } else {
                if(mediaExtractor.getSampleTrackIndex()
                                            != track) {
                    // We somehow got data that did not
                    // belong to the track we selected
                }
                presentationTimeUs =
                        mediaExtractor.getSampleTime();
                decoder.queueInputBuffer(inputBufIndex,
                                    0, chunkSize,
        presentationTimeUs, 0);
                inputChunk++;
                mediaExtractor.advance();
            }
        }
    } else {
        // We shouldn't reach here - inputDone, protect us
    }
}
```

This is the input half of the media extraction. This loop reads the file and queues chunks for the decoder. As things get decoded, we need to route it to the places we need:

```
    } else {
        // We shouldn't reach here - inputDone, protect us
    }
    if(!outputDone) {
        int decoderStatus = decoder.dequeueOutputBuffer(
```

```
                                            info, TIMEOUT_USEC);
            if(decoderStatus ==
                        MediaCodec.INFO_TRY_AGAIN_LATER) {
                // Can't do anything here
            } else if(decoderStatus ==
                    MediaCodec.INFO_OUTPUT_BUFFERS_CHANGED) {
                // Not important since we're using a surface
            } else if(decoderStatus ==
                        MediaCodec.INFO_OUTPUT_FORMAT_CHANGED) {
                MediaFormat newFormat = decoder.getOutputFormat();
                // Handled automatically for us
            } else if(decoderStatus < 0) {
                // Something bad has happened
            } else {
                if((info.flags & MediaCodec.BUFFER_FLAG_END_OF_
STREAM) != ) {

                    outputDone = true;

                }
            }

            boolean doRender = (info.size != 0);
            decoder.releaseOutputBuffer(decoderStatus, doRender);
            if(doRender) {
                outputSurface.awaitNewImage();
                outputSurface.drawImage(true);

                try {
                    Mat img = outputSurface.readFrameAsMat();
                    if(frameListener != null) {
                        Frame frame = new Frame(img,
presentationTimeUs,
                                                new Point3(), new
Point());
                        frameListener.onFrameAvailable(frame);
                    }
                } catch(IOException e) {
                    e.printStackTrace();
                }
                decodeCount++;
                if(frameListener!=null)
                    frameListener.onFrameComplete(decodeCount);
            }
        }
```

```
            }

        medaiExtractor.release();
        mediaExtractor = null;
    }
```

This completes the output half of the decode loop. Whenever a frame is complete, it converts the raw data into a Mat structure and creates a new `Frame` object. This is then passed to the `onFrameAvailable` method.

Once the decoding is complete, the media extractor is released and we're done!

The only thing left is to define what `FrameAvailableListener` is. We shall do that now:

```
    public void setFrameAvailableListener(FrameAvailableListener
listener) {
        frameListener = listener;
    }

    public interface FrameAvailableListener {
        public void onFrameAvailable(Frame frame);
        public void onFrameComplete(long frameDone);
    }
}
```

This is a common pattern in Java when defining such listeners. The listeners contain methods that are fired on specific events (in our case, when a frame is available, or when the processing of a frame is complete).

Calibration

In the section that discusses the mathematical basis, we found several unknown camera parameters. These parameters need to be figured out so we can process each image and stabilize it. As with any calibration process, we need to use a predefined scene. Using this scene and a relative handshake, we will try to estimate the unknown parameters.

The unknown parameters are:

- Focal length of the lens
- Delay between gyroscope and frame timestamps

- Bias in the gyroscope
- Duration of the rolling shutter

It is often possible to detect the focal length of a phone camera (in terms of millimeters) using the platform API (getFocalLength() for Android). However, we're interested in the camera space focal length. This number is a product of the physical focal length and a conversion ratio that depends on the image resolution and the physical size of the camera sensor, which might differ across cameras. It is also possible to find the conversion ratio by trigonometry if the field of view (getVerticalViewAngle() and getHorizontalViewAngle() for Android) is known for a sensor and lens setup. However, we'll just leave it as an unknown and let the calibration find it for us.

> If you're interested in more information on this, refer to *Chapter 5,
> Combining Image Tracking with 3D Rendering*, of PacktPub's *Android
> Application Programming with OpenCV*.

We need to estimate the delay between gyro and frame timestamps to improve the quality of the output on sharp turns. This also offsets any lag introduced by the phone when recording the video.

Rolling shutter effects are visible at high speed and the estimated parameter tries to correct these.

It is possible to calculate these parameters with a short clip that's shaky. We use a feature detector from OpenCV to do this.

> During this phase, we'll be using Python. The SciPy library provides
> us with mathematical functions that we can use out of the box. It is
> possible to implement these on your own, but that would require a
> more in-depth explanation of how mathematical optimization works.
> Along with this, we'll use Matplotlib to generate graphs.

Data structures

We'll set up three key data structures: first, the unknown parameters, second, something to read the gyro data file generated by the Android app, and third, a representation of the video being processed.

The first structure is to store the estimates from the calibration. It contains four values:

- An estimate of the focal length of the camera (in camera units, not physical units)
- The delay between the gyroscope timestamps and the frame timestamps
- The gyroscope bias
- The rolling shutter estimated

Let's start by creating a new file called `calibration.py`.

```python
import sys, numpy

class CalibrationParameters(object):
    def __init__(self):
        self.f = 0.0
        self.td = 0.0
        self.gb = (0.0, 0.0, 0.0)
        self.ts = 0.0
```

Reading the gyroscope trace

Next, we'll define a class to read in the `.csv` file generated by the Android app.

```python
class GyroscopeDataFile(object):
    def __init__(self, filepath):
        self.filepath = filepath
        self.omega = {}

    def getfile_object(self):
        return open(self.filepath)
```

We initialize the class with two main variables: the file path to read, and a dictionary of angular velocities. This dictionary will store mappings between the timestamp and the angular velocity at that instant. We'll eventually need to calculate actual angles from the angular velocity, but that will happen outside this class.

Now we add the `parse` method. This method will actually read the file and populate the Omega dictionary.

```python
    def parse(self):
        with self._get_file_object() as fp:
            firstline = fp.readline().strip()
```

```
if not firstline == 'utk':
    raise Exception("The first line isn't valid")
```

We validate that the first line of the csv file matches our expectation. If not, the csv file was probably not compatible and will error out over the next few lines.

```
for line in fp.readlines():
    line = line.strip()
    parts = line.split(",")
```

Here, we initiate a loop over the entire file. The `strip` function removed any additional whitespace (tabs, spaces, newline characters, among others) that might be stored in the file.

After removing the whitespace, we split the string with commas (this is a comma-separated file!).

```
timestamp = int(parts[3])
ox = float(parts[0])
oy = float(parts[1])
oz = float(parts[2])
print("%s: %s, %s, %s" % (timestamp,
                                    ox,
                                    oy,
                                    oz))
self.omega[timestamp] = (ox, oy, oz)
return
```

Information read from the file is plain strings so we convert that into the appropriate numeric type and store it in `self.omega`. We're now ready to parse the csv files and get started with numeric calculations.

Before we do that, we'll define a few more useful functions.

```
def get_timestamps(self):
    return sorted(self.omega.keys())

def get_signal(self, index):
    return [self.omega[k][index] for k in self.get_timestamps()]
```

The `get_timestamps` method on this class will return a sorted list of timestamps. Building on this, we also define a function called `get_signal`. The angular velocity is composed of three signals. These signals are packed together in `self.omega`. The `get_signal` function lets us extract a specific component of the signal.

For example, `get_signal(0)` returns the X component of angular velocity.

```
def get_signal_x(self):
    return self.get_signal(0)

def get_signal_y(self):
    return self.get_signal(1)

def get_signal_z(self):
    return self.get_signal(2)
```

These utility functions return only the specific signal we're looking at. We'll be using these signals to smooth out individual signals, calculate the angle, and so on.

Another issue we need to address is that the timestamps are discrete. For example, we might have angular velocities at timestamp N and the next reading might exist at N+500000 (remember, the timestamps are in nanoseconds). However, the video file might have a frame at N+250000. We need a way to interpolate between two angular velocity readings.

We'll use simple linear interpolation to estimate the angular velocity at any given moment.

```
def fetch_approximate_omega(self, timestamp):
    if timestamp in self.omega:
        return self.omega[timestamp]
```

This method takes in a timestamp and returns the estimated angular velocity. If the exact timestamp already exists, there is no estimation to do.

```
i = 0
sorted_timestamps = self.get_timestamps()
for ts in sorted_timestamps:
    if ts > timestamp:
        break
    i += 1
```

Here we're walking over the timestamps and finding the timestamp that is closest to the one requested.

```
t_previous = sorted_timestamps[i]
t_current = sorted_timestamps[i+1]
dt = float(t_current - t_previous)
slope = (timestamp - t_previous) / dt

est_x = self.omega[t_previous][0]*(1-slope) + self.omega[t_
current][0]*slope
```

```
        est_y = self.omega[t_previous][1]*(1-slope) + self.omega[t_
current][1]*slope
        est_z = self.omega[t_previous][2]*(1-slope) + self.omega[t_
current][2]*slope
        return (est_x, est_y, est_z)
```

Once we have the two closest timestamps (i and i+1 in the list `sorted_timestamps`), we're ready to start linear interpolation. We calculate the estimated X, Y, and Z angular velocities and return these values.

This finishes our work on reading the gyroscope file!

The training video

We'll also create a new class that lets us treat the entire video sequence as a single entity. We'll extract useful information from the video in a single pass and store it for future reference, making our code both faster and more memory efficient.

```
class GyroVideo(object):
    def __init__(self, mp4):
        self.mp4 = mp4
        self.frameInfo = []
        self.numFrames = 0
        self.duration = 0
        self.frameWidth = 0
        self.frameHeight = 0
```

We initialize the class with some variables we'll be using throughout. Most of the variables are self-explanatory. `frameInfo` stores details about every frame—like the timestamp of a given frame and keypoints (useful for calibration).

```
    def read_video(self, skip_keypoints=False):
        vidcap = cv2.VideoCapture(self.mp4)
        success, frame = vidcap.read()
        prev_frame = None
        previous_timestamp = 0
        frameCount = 0
```

We define a new method that will do all the heavy lifting for us. We start by creating the OpenCV video reading object (`VideoCapture`) and try to read a single frame.

```
        while success:
            current_timestamp = vidcap.get(0) * 1000 * 1000
            print "Processing frame#%d (%f ns)" % (frameCount,
current_timestamp)
```

The `get` method on a `VideoCapture` object returns information about the video sequence. Zero (0) happens to be the constant for fetching the timestamp in milliseconds. We convert this into nanoseconds and print out a helpful message!

```
if not prev_frame:
    self.frameInfo.append({'keypoints': None,
                                   'timestamp': current_
timestamp})
    prev_frame = frame
    previous_timestamp = current_timestamp
    continue
```

If this is the first frame being read, we won't have a previous frame. We're also not interested in storing keypoints for the first frame. So we just move on to the next frame.

```
if skip_keypoints:
    self.frameInfo.append({'keypoints': None,
                                   'timestamp': current_
timestamp})
    continue
```

If you set the `skip_keypoints` parameter to `true`, it'll just store the timestamps of each frame. You might then use this parameter to read a video after you've already calibrated your device and already have the values of the various unknowns.

```
old_gray = cv2.cvtColor(prev_frame, cv2.COLOR_BGR2GRAY)
new_gray = cv2.cvtColor(frame, cv2.COLOR_BGR2GRAY)

old_corners = cv2.goodFeaturesToTrack(old_gray, 1000, 0.3,
30)
```

We convert the previous and the current frame into grayscale and extract some good features to track. We'll use these features and track them in the new frame. This gives us a visual estimate of how the orientation of the camera changed. We already have the gyroscope data for this; we just need to calibrate some unknowns. We achieve this by using the visual estimate.

```
if old_corners == None:
    self.frameInfo.append({'keypoints': None,
                                   'timestamp': current_
timestamp})
    frameCount += 1
```

```
previous_timestamp = current_timestamp
prev_frame = frame
success, frame = vidcap.read()
continue
```

If no corners were found in the old frame, that's not a good sign. Was it a very blurry frame? Were there no good features to track? So we simply skip processing it.

If we did find keypoints to track, we use optical flow to identify where they are in the new frame:

```
new_corners, status, err = cv2.calcOpticalFlowPyrLK(old_gray,
                                        new_gray,
                                        old_corners,
                                        None,
                                        winSize=(15,15)
                                        maxLevel=2,
                                        criteria=(cv2.TERM_
CRITERIA_EPS
                                            | cv2.TERM_
CRITERIA_COUNT,
                                            10, 0.03))
```

This gives us the position of the corners in the new frame. We can then estimate the motion that happened between the previous frame and the current, and correlate it with the gyroscope data.

A common issue with `goodFeaturesToTrack` is that the features aren't robust. They often move around, losing the position they were tracking. To get around this, we add another test just to ensure such random outliers don't make it to the calibration phase. This is done with the help of RANSAC.

RANSAC stands for **Ran**dom **Sam**ple **C**onsensus. The key idea of RANSAC is that the given dataset contains a set of inliers that fit perfectly to a given model. It gives you the set of points that most closely satisfy a given constraint. In our case, these inliers would account for the points moving from one set of positions to another. It does not matter how numerous the outliers of the data set are.

OpenCV comes with a utility function to calculate the perspective transform between two frames. While the transform is being estimated, the function also tries to figure out which points are outliers. We'll hook into this functionality for our purposes too!

```
            if len(old_corners) > 4:
                    homography, mask = cv2.findHomography(old_corners,
        new_corners,

                                                    cv2.RANSAC, 5.0)
                    mask = mask.ravel()
                    new_corners_homography = [new_corners[i] for i in
        xrange(len(mask)) if mask[i] == 1])
                    old_corners_homography = [old_corners[i] for i in
        xrange(len(mask)) if mask[i] == 1])
                    new_corners_homography = numpy.asarray(new_corners_
        homography)
                    old_corners_homography = numpy.asarray(old_corners_
        homography)
              else:
                    new_corners_homography = new_corners
                    old_corners_homography = old_corners
```

We need at least four keypoints to calculate the perspective transform between two frames. If there aren't enough points, we just store whatever we have. We get a better result if there are more points and some are eliminated.

```
            self.frameInfo.append({'keypoints': (old_corners_
        homography,
                                                    new_corners_
        homography),
                                            'timestamp': current_timestamp})
                    frameCount += 1
                    previous_timestamp = current_timestamp
                    prev_frame = frame
                    success, frame = vidcap.read()
              self.numFrames = frameCount
              self.duration = current_timstamp
              return
```

Once we have everything figured out, we just store it in the frame information list. And this marks the end of our method!

Handling rotations

Let's take a look at how we rotate frames to stabilize them.

Rotating an image

Before we get into how images can be rotated for our project, let's look at rotating images in general. The goal is to produce images like the one below:

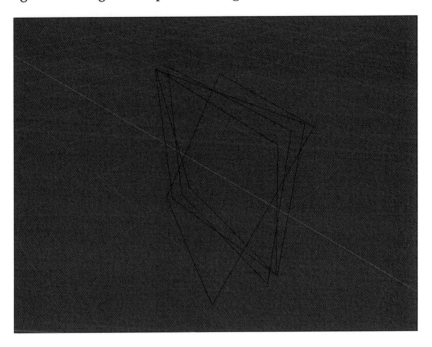

Rotating an image in 2D is simple, there's only one axis. A 2D rotation can be achieved by using an affine transform.

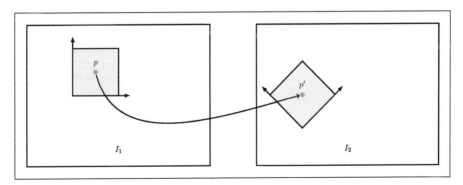

In our project, we need to rotate images around all three axes. An affine transform is not sufficient to produce these, so we need to go towards a perspective transform. Also, rotations are linear transformations; this means we can split an arbitrary rotation into its component X, Y, and Z rotations and use that to compose the rotation.

To achieve this, we'll use the OpenCV Rodrigues function call to generate these transformation matrices. Let's start by writing a function that arbitrarily rotates an image.

```
def rotateImage(src, rx, ry, rz, f, dx=0, dy=0, dz=0,
convertToRadians=False):
    if convertToRadians:
        rx = (rx) * math.pi / 180
        ry = (ry) * math.pi / 180
        rz = (rz) * math.pi / 180

    rx = float(rx)
    ry = float(ry)
    rz = float(rz)
```

This method accepts a source image that needs to be rotated, the three rotation angles, an optional translation, the focal length in pixels, and whether the angles are in radians or not. If the angles are in degrees, we need to convert them to radians. We also force convert these into `float`.

Next, we'll calculate the width and the height of the source image. These, along with the focal length, are used to transform the rotation matrix (which is in real world space) into image space.

```
w = src.shape[1]
h = src.shape[0]
```

Now, we use the Rodrigues function to generate the rotation matrix:

```
smallR = cv2.Rodrigues(np.array([rx, ry, rz]))[0]
R = numpy.array([ [smallR[0][0], smallR[0][1], smallR[0][2], 0],
                  [smallR[1][0], smallR[1][1], smallR[1][2], 0],
                  [smallR[2][0], smallR[2][1], smallR[2][2], 0],
                  [0,            0,            0,            1]])
```

The Rodrigues function takes a vector (a list) that contains the three rotation angles and returns the rotation matrix. The matrix returned is a 3x3 matrix. We'll convert that into a 4x4 homogeneous matrix so that we can apply transformations to it.

It's usually a good idea to keep dz equal to the focal length. This implies that the image was captured at just the right focal length and needs to be rotated about that point. You are free to change dz to other values, but usually setting it equal to F gives good results.

We now apply a simple translation to the matrix. The translation matrix is easily evaluated as follows:

```
x = numpy.array([[1.0, 0,   0,   dx],
                 [0,   1.0, 0,   dy],
                 [0,   0,   1.0, dz],
                 [0,   0,   0,   1]])
T = numpy.asmatrix(x)
```

Until now, all transformations have happened in world space. We need to change these into image space. This is accomplished by the simple pinhole model of a camera.

```
c = numpy.array([[f, 0, w/2, 0],
                 [0, f, h/2, 0],
                 [0, 0, 1,   0]])
cameraMatrix = numpy.asmatrix(c)
```

Combining these transforms is straightforward:

```
transform = cameraMatrix * (T*R)
```

This matrix can now be used in OpenCV's `warpPerspective` method to rotate the source image.

```
output = cv2.warpPerspective(src, transform, (w, h))
return output
```

The output of this isn't exactly what you want though, the images are rotated about (0, 0) in the image. We need to rotate the image about the center. To achieve this, we need to insert an additional translation matrix right *before* the rotations happen.

```
w = src.shape[1]
h = src.shape[0]

# New code:
```

```
      x = numpy.array([ [1,  0,  -w/2],
                        [0,  1,  -h/2],
                        [0,  0,  0],
                        [0,  0,  1]])
   A1 = numpy.asmatrix(x)
   ...
```

Now, we insert the matrix A1 at the very beginning:

```
   transform = cameraMatrix * (T*(R*A1))
```

Now images should rotate around the center; this is exactly what we want and is a self-contained method that we can use to rotate images arbitrarily in 3D space using OpenCV.

Accumulated rotations

Rotating an image with a single rotation vector is quite straightforward. In this section, we'll extend that method so it is better suited for our project.

We have two data sources active when recording a video: the image capture and the gyroscope trace. These are captured at different rates—images every few milliseconds and gyroscope signals every few microseconds. To calculate the exact rotation required to stabilize an image, we need to accumulate the rotation of dozens of gyroscope signals. This means that the rotation matrix needs to have information on several different gyroscope data samples.

Also, the gyroscope and image sensors are not in sync; we will need to use linear interpolation on the gyroscope signals to bring them in sync.

Let's write a function that returns the transformation matrix.

```
   def getAccumulatedRotation(w, h,
                             theta_x, theta_y, theta_z, timestamps,
                             prev, current,
                             f,
                             gyro_delay=None, gyro_drift=None, shutter_
   duration=None):
       if not gyro_delay:
           gyro_delay = 0

       if not gyro_drift:
           gyro_drift = (0, 0, 0)

       if not shutter_duration:
           shutter_duration = 0
```

This function takes a lot of parameters. Let's go over each of them:

- w, h: We need to know the size of the image to convert it from world space to image space.
- theta_*: Currently, we have access to angular velocity. From there, we can evaluate actual angles and that is what this function accepts as parameters.
- Timestamps: The time each sample was taken.
- prev, current: Accumulate rotations between these timestamps. This will usually provide the timestamp of the previous frame and the current frame.
- f, gyro_delay, gyro_drift, and shutter_duration are used to improve the estimate of the rotation matrix. The last three of these are optional (and they get set to zero if you don't pass them).

From the previous section, we know that we need to start by translating (or we'll get rotations about (0, 0)).

```
x = numpy.array([[1, 0, -w/2],
                 [0, 1, -h/2],
                 [0, 0, 0],
                 [0, 0, 1]])
A1 = numpy.asmatrix(x)
transform = A1.copy()
```

We'll use the "transform" matrix to accumulate rotations across multiple gyroscope samples.

Next, we offset the timestamps by using gyro_delay. This is just adding (or subtracting, based on the sign of its value) to the timestamp.

```
prev = prev + gyro_delay
current = current + gyro_delay
if prev in timestamps and current in timestamps:
    start_timestamp = prev
    end_timestamp = current
else:
    (rot, start_timestamp, t_next) = fetch_closest_trio(theta_x,
                                                        theta_y,
                                                        theta_z,

timestamps,
```

```
                                                        prev)
(rot, end_timestamp, t_next) = fetch_closest_trio(theta_x,
                                                  theta_y,
                                                  theta_z,
                                                  timestamps,
                                                  current)
```

If the updated `prev` and `current` values exist in the timestamps (meaning we have values captured from the sensor at that time instant) – great! No need to interpolate. Otherwise, we use the function `fetch_closest_trio` to interpolate the signals to the given timestamp.

This helper function returns three things:

- The interpolated rotation for the requested timestamp
- The closest timestamp in the sensor data
- The timestamp right after it

We use `start_timestamp` and `end_timestamp` for iterating now.

```
    for time in xrange(timestamps.index(start_timestamp), timestamps.
index(end_timestamp)):
        time_shifted = timestamps[time] + gyro_delay
        trio, t_previous, t_current = fetch_closest_trio(theta_x,
theta_y, theta_z, timestamps, time_shifted)
        gyro_drifted = (float(trio[0] + gyro_drift[0]),
                        float(trio[1] + gyro_drift[1]),
                        float(trio[2] + gyro_drift[2]))
```

We iterate over each timestamp in the physical data. We add the gyroscope delay and use that to fetch the closest (interpolated) signals. Once that's done, we add the gyroscope drift per component. This is just a constant that should be added to compensate for errors in the gyroscope.

Using these rotation angles, we now calculate the rotation matrix, as in the previous section.

```
        smallR = cv2.Rodrigues(numpy.array([[-float(gyro_drifted[1]),
                                             -float(gyro_drifted[0]),
                                             -float(gyro_drifted[2])]]))
    [0]
```

```
        R = numpy.array([[smallR[0][0], smallR[0][1], smallR[0][2],
0],
                         [smallR[1][0], smallR[1][1], smallR[1][2],
0],
                         [smallR[2][0], smallR[2][1], smallR[2][2],
0],
                         [0,            0,             0,
1]])
        transform = R * transform
```

This piece of code is almost the same as that in the previous section. There are a few key differences though. Firstly, we're providing negative values to Rodrigues. This is to negate the effect of motion. Secondly, the X and Y values are swapped. (gyro_drifted[1] comes first, followed by `gyro_drifted[0]`). This is required because the axes of the gyroscope and the ones used by these matrices are different.

This completes the iteration over the gyroscope samples between the specified timestamps. To complete this, we need to translate in the Z direction just like in the previous section. Since this can be hardcoded, let's do that:

```
    x = numpy.array([[1, 0, 0, 0],
                     [0, 1, 0, 0],
                     [0, 0, 1, f],
                     [0, 0, 0, 1]])
    T = numpy.asmatrix(x)
```

We also need to use the camera matrix to convert from world space to image space.

```
    x = numpy.array([[f, 0, w/2, 0],
                     [0, f, h/2, 0],
                     [0, 0, 1,   0]])
    A2 = numpy.asmatrix(x)
    transform = A2 * (T*transform)
    return transform
```

We first translate in the Z direction and then convert to image space. This section essentially lets you rotate frames of your video with the gyroscope parameters.

The calibration class

With our data structures ready, we're in a good place to start the key piece of this project. The calibration builds on all the previously mentioned classes.

As always, we'll create a new class which encapsulates all the calibration-related tasks.

```
class CalibrateGyroStabilize(object):
    def __init__(self, mp4, csv):
        self.mp4 = mp4
        self.csv = csv
```

The object requires two things: the video file and the gyroscope data file. These get stored in the object.

Before jumping directly into the calibration method, let's create some utility functions that will be helpful when calibrating.

```
def get_gaussian_kernel(sigma2, v1, v2, normalize=True):
    gauss = [math.exp(-(float(x*x) / sigma2)) for x in range(v1,
v2+1)]

    if normalize:
        total = sum(guass)
        gauss = [x/total for x in gauss]

    return gauss
```

This method generates a Gaussian kernel of a given size. We'll use this to smooth out the angular velocity signals in a bit.

```
def gaussian_filter(input_array):
    sigma = 10000
    r = 256
    kernel = get_gaussian_kernel(sigma, -r, r)
    return numpy.convolve(input_array, kernel, 'same')
```

This function does the actual smoothing of a signal. Given an input signal, it generates the Gaussian kernel and convolves it with the input signal.

Convolutions are a mathematical tool to produce new functions. You can think of the gyroscope signal as a function; you give it a timestamp and it returns a value. To smooth it out, we need to combine it with another function. This function, called the Gaussian function, is a smooth bell curve. Both these functions have different time ranges on which they operate (the gyroscope function might return values between a time of 0 seconds and 50 seconds while the Gaussian function might just work for a time of 0 seconds to 5 seconds). Convolving these two functions produces a third function that behaves a bit like both, thereby effectively smoothing out the minor variations in the gyroscope signal.

Next, we write a function that calculates an error score giving two sets of points. This will be a building block in estimating how good the calibration has been.

```
def calcErrorScore(set1, set2):
    if len(set1) != len(set2):
        raise Exception("The given sets need to have the exact
same length")

    score = 0
    for first, second in zip(set1.tolist(), set2.tolist()):
        diff_x = math.pow(first[0][0] - second[0][0], 2)
        diff_y = math.pow(first[0][1] - second[0][1], 2)
        score += math.sqrt(diff_x + diff_y)

    return score
```

This error score is straightforward: you have two lists of points and you calculate the distance between the corresponding points on the two lists and sum it up. A higher error score means the points on the two lists don't correspond perfectly.

This method, however, only gives us the error on a single frame. We're concerned about errors across the whole video. We therefore write another method.

```
def calcErrorAcrossVideo(videoObj, theta, timestamp, focal_length,
gyro_delay=None, gyro_drift=None, rolling_shutter=None):
    total_error = 0
    for frameCount in xrange(videoObj.numFrames):
        frameInfo = videoObj.frameInfo[frameCount]
        current_timestamp = frameInfo['timestamp']

        if frameCount == 0:
            previous_timestamp = current_timestamp
            continue
        keypoints = frameInfo['keypoints']

        if not keypoints:
            continue
```

We pass in the video object and all the details we have estimated (the theta, timestamps, focal length, gyroscope delay, and so on). With these details, we try to do the video stabilization and see what differences exists between the visually tracked keypoints and the gyroscope-based transformations.

Since we're calculating the error across the whole video, we need to iterate over each frame. If the frame's information does not have any keypoints in it, we simply ignore the frame. If the frame does have keypoints, here's what we do:

```
            old_corners = frameInfo['keypoints'][0]
            new_corners = frameInfo['keypoints'][1]
            transform = getAccumulatedRotation(videoObj.frameWidth,
                                    videoObj.frameHeight,
                                    theta[0], theta[1],
theta[2],
                                    timestamps,
                                    int(previous_
timestamp),
                                    int(current_timestamp),
                                    focal_length,
                                    gyro_delay,
                                    gyro_drift,
                                    rolling_shutter)
```

The `getAccumulatedRotation` function is something we'll write soon. The key idea of the function is to return a transformation matrix for the given theta (the angles we need to rotate to stabilize the video). We can apply this transform to `old_corners` and compare it to `new_corners`.

Since `new_corners` was obtained visually, it is the ground truth. We want `getAccumulatedRotation` to return a transformation that matches the visual ground truth perfectly. This means the error between `new_corners` and the transformed `old_corners` should be minimal. This is where `calcErrorScore` helps us:

```
            transformed_corners = cv2.perspectiveTransform(old_
corners, transform)
            error = calcErrorScore(new_corners, transformed_corners)
            total_error += error
            previous_timestamp = current_timestamp
        return total_error
```

We're ready to calculate the error across the whole video! Now let's move to the calibration function:

```
        def calibrate(self):
            gdf = GyroscopeDataFile(csv)
            gdf.parse()
```

```
signal_x = gdf.get_signal_x()
signal_y = gdf.get_signal_y()
signal_z = gdf.get_signal_z()
timestamps = gdf.get_timestamps()
```

The first step is to smooth out the noise in the angular velocity signals. This is the desired signal with smooth motion.

```
smooth_signal_x = self.gaussian_filter(signal_x)
smooth_signal_y = self.gaussian_filter(signal_y)
smooth_signal_z = self.gaussian_filter(signal_z)
```

We'll be writing the `gaussian_filter` method soon; for now, let's just keep in mind that it returns a smoothed out signal.

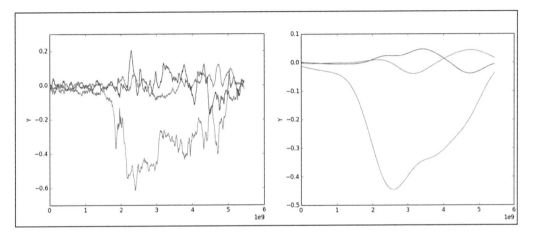

Next, we calculate the difference between the physical signal and the desired signal. We need to do this separately for each component.

```
g = [ [], [] [] ]
g[0] = numpy.subtract(signal_x, smooth_signal_x).tolist()
g[1] = numpy.subtract(signal_y, smooth_signal_y).tolist()
g[2] = numpy.subtract(signal_z, smooth_signal_z).tolist()
```

We also need to calculate the delta between the timestamps. We'll be using this for integration.

```
dgt = self.diff(timestamps)
```

Next, we integrate the angular velocities to get actual angles. Integration introduces errors into our equations but that's okay. It is good enough for our purposes.

```
theta = [ [], [], [] ]
for component in [0, 1, 2]:
        sum_of_consecutives = numpy.add( g[component][:-1],
g[component][1:])
        dx_0 = numpy.divide(sum_of_consecutives, 2 * 1000000000)
        num_0 = numpy.multipy(dx_0, dgt)
        theta[component] = [0]
        theta[component].extend(numpy.cumsum(num_0))
```

And that's it. We have calculated the amount of theta that will stabilize the image! However, this is purely from the gyroscope's view. We still need to calculate the unknowns so that we can use these thetas to stabilize the image.

To do this, we initialize some of the unknowns as variables with an arbitrary initial value (0 in most cases). Also, we load the video and process the keypoint information.

```
focal_length = 1080.0
gyro_delay = 0
gyro_drift = (0, 0, 0)
shutter_duration = 0

videoObj = GyroVideo(mp4)
videoObj.read_video()
```

Now, we use SciPy's optimize method to minimize the error. To do this, we must first convert these unknowns into a Numpy array.

```
parameters = numpy.asarray([focal_length,
                            gyro_delay,
                            gyro_drift[0], gyro_drift[1],
gyro_drift[2]])
```

Since we've not yet incorporated fixing the rolling shutter, we ignore that in the parameters list. Next, we call the actual optimization function:

```
result = scipy.optimize.minimize(self.
calcErrorAcrossVideoObjective,
                                 parameters,
                                 (videoObj, theta,
timestamps),
                                 'Nelder-Mead')
```

Executing this function takes a few seconds, but it produces the values of the unknowns for us. We can then extract these from the result as follows:

```
focal_length = result['x'][0]
gyro_delay = result['x'][1]
gyro_drift = ( result['x'][2], result['x'][3], result['x'][4]
)

print "Focal length = %f" % focal_length
print "Gyro delay   = %f" % gyro_delay
print "Gyro drift   = (%f, %f, %f)" % gyro_drift
```

With this, we're done with calibration! All we need to do is return all the relevant calculations we've done just now.

```
    return (delta_theta, timestamps, focal_length, gyro_delay, gyro_
drift, shutter_duration)
```

And that's a wrap!

Undistorting images

In the previous section, we calculated all the unknowns in our equations. Now, we can go ahead with fixing the shaky video.

We'll start off by creating a new method called `stabilize_video`. This method will take a video file and a corresponding csv file.

```
def stabilize_video(mp4, csv):
    calib_obj = CalibrateGyroStabilize(mp4, csv)
```

We create an object of the calibration class we just defined and pass it the required information. Now, we just need to call the calibrate function.

```
    delta_theta, timestamps, focal_length, gyro_delay, gyro_drift,
shutter_duration = calib_obj.calibrate()
```

This method call may take a while to execute, but we need to run this only once for every device. Once calculated, we can store these values in a text file and read them from there.

Once we have estimated all the unknowns, we start by reading the video file for each frame.

```
    vidcap = cv2.VideoCapture(mp4)
```

Now we start iterating over each frame and correcting the rotations.

```
frameCount = 0
success, frame = vidcap.read()
previous_timestamp = 0
while success:
    print "Processing frame %d" % frameCount
```

Next, we fetch the timestamp from the video stream and use that to fetch the closest rotation sample.

```
current_timestamp = vidcap.get(cv2.CAP_PROP_POS_MSEC) * 1000 *
1000
```

The `VideoCapture` class returns timestamps in milliseconds. We convert that into nanoseconds to keep consistent units.

```
rot, prev, current = fetch_closest_trio(delta_theta[0],
                                        delta_theta[1],
                                        delta_theta[2],
                                        timestamps,
                                        current_timestamps)
```

With these pieces, we now fetch the accumulated rotation.

```
rot = accumulateRotation(frame, delta_theta[0],
                         delta_theta[1],
                         delta_theta[2],
                    timestamps, previous_timestamp,
                    prev,
                    focal_length,
                    gyro_delay,
                    gyro_drift,
                    shutter_duration)
```

Next, we write the transformed frame into a file and move on to the next frame:

```
cv2.imwrite("/tmp/rotated%04d.png" % frameCount, rot)
frameCount += 1
previous_timestamp = prev
success, frame = vidcap.read()
    return
```

And this finishes our simple function to negate the shakiness of the device. Once we have all the images, we can combine them into a single video with `ffmpeg`.

```
ffmpeg -f image2 -i image%04d.jpg output.mp4
```

Testing calibration results

The effectiveness of the calibration depends on how accurately it can replicate motion on the video. For any frame, we have matching keypoints in the previous and current frames. This gives a sense of the general motion of the scene.

Using the estimated parameters, if we are able to use previous frames' keypoints to generate the current frames' keypoints, we can assume the calibration has been successful.

Rolling shutter compensation

At this point, our video is stable, however, when objects in the scene are moving quickly, the rolling shutter effects become more pronounced.

To fix this, we'll need to do a few things. First, incorporate the rolling shutter speed into our calibration code. Second, when warping images, we need to unwarp the rolling shutter as well.

Calibrating the rolling shutter

To start calibrating the rolling shutter duration, we need to tweak the error function to incorporate another term. Let's start by looking at the `calcErrorAcrossVideo` method. The part we're interested in is:

```
def calcErrorAcrossVideo(videoObj, theta, timestamp, focal_length,
gyro_delay=None, gyro_drift=None, rolling_shutter=None):
    total_error = 0
    ...
        transform = getAccumulatedRotation(...)
        transformed_corners =
          cv2.perspectiveTransform(old_corners, transform)
    ...
```

Also, we'll need to add logic to transform a corner based on its location—a corner in the upper part of the image is transformed differently from a corner in the lower half.

So far, we have had a single transformation matrix and that was usually sufficient. However, now, we need to have multiple transformation matrices, one for each row. We could choose to do this for every row of pixels, however that is a bit excessive. We only need transforms for rows that contain a corner we're tracking.

We'll start by replacing the two lines mentioned above. We need to loop over each corner individually and warp it. Let's do this with a simple `for` loop:

```
for pt in old_corners:
    x = pt[0][0]
    y = pt[0][1]

    pt_timestamp = int(current_timestamp) + rolling_shutter *
(y-frame_height/2) / frame_height
```

Here, we extract the x and y coordinates of the old corner and try to estimate the timestamp when this particular pixel was captured. Here, I'm assuming the rolling shutter is in the vertical direction, from the top of the frame to the bottom.

We use the current estimate of the rolling shutter duration and estimate subtract and add time based on the row the corner belongs to. It should be simple to adapt this for a horizontal rolling shutter as well. Instead of using y and `frameHeight`, you would have to use x and `frameWidth`—the calculation would stay the same. For now, we'll just assume this is going to be a vertical rolling shutter.

Now that we have the estimated timestamp of capture, we can get the rotation matrix for that instant (remember, the gyroscope produces a higher resolution data than the camera sensor).

```
transform = getAccumulatedRotation(videoObj.frameWidth, videoObj.
frameHeight, theta[0], theta[1], theta[2], timestamps, int(previous_
timestamp), int(pt_timestamp), focal_length, gyro_delay, gyro_drift,
doSub=True)
```

This line is almost the same as the original we had; the only difference is that we've replaced `current_timestamp` with `pt_timestamp`.

Next, we need to transform this point based on the rolling shutter duration.

```
output = transform * np.matrix("%f;%f;1.0" % (x, y)).tolist()
tx = (output[0][0] / output[2][0]).tolist()[0][0]
ty = (output[1][0] / output[2][0]).tolist()[0][0]
transformed_corners.append( np.array([tx, ty]) )
```

After transforming, we simply append it to the `transformed_corners` list (just like we did earlier).

With this, we're done with the calibration part. Now, we move onto warping images.

Warping with grid points

Let's start by writing a function that will do the warping for us. This function takes in these inputs:

- The original image
- A bunch of points that should ideally line up in a perfect grid

The size of the point list gives us the number of rows and columns to expect and the function returns a perfectly aligned image.

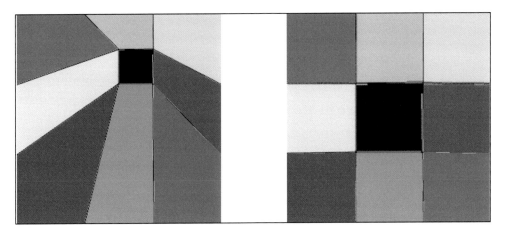

Let's define the function:

```
def meshwarp(src, distorted_grid):
    """
    src: The original image
    distorted_grid: The list of points that have been distorted
    """
    size = src.shape
```

As mentioned earlier, this takes in an image and the list of control points. We store the size of the image for future reference.

```
    mapsize = (size[0], size[1], 1)
    dst = np.zeros(size, dtype=np.uint8)
```

The size we stored earlier will most likely have three channels in it. So we create a new variable called `mapsize`; this stores the size of the image but only one channel. We'll use this later for creating matrices for use by the remap function in OpenCV.

We also create a blank image of the same size as the original. Next, we look at calculating the number of rows and columns in the grid.

```
quads_per_row = len(distorted_grid[0]) - 1
quads_per_col = len(distorted_grid) - 1
pixels_per_row = size[1] / quads_per_row
pixels_per_col = size[0] / quads_per_col
```

We'll use the variables in some loops soon.

```
pt_src_all = []
pt_dst_all = []
```

These lists store all the source (distorted) points and the destination (perfectly aligned) points. We'll have to use `distorted_grid` to populate `pt_src_all`. We'll procedurally generate the destination based on the number of rows and columns in the input data.

```
for ptlist in distorted_grid:
    pt_src_all.extend(ptlist)
```

The distorted grid should be a list of lists. Each row is a list that contains its points.

Now, we generate the procedural destination points using the `quads_per_*` variables we calculated earlier.

```
for x in range(quads_per_row+1):
    for y in range(quads_per_col+1):
        pt_dst_all.append( [x*pixels_per_col,
                            y*pixels_per_row])
```

This generates the ideal grid based on the number of points we passed to the method.

We then have all the required information to calculate the interpolation between the source and destination grids. We'll be using `scipy` to calculate the interpolation for us. We then pass this to OpenCV's remap method and that applies it to an image.

To begin with, `scipy` needs a representation of the expected output grid so we need to specify a dense grid that contains all the pixels of the image. This is done with:

```
gx, gt = np.mgrid[0:size[1], 0:size[0]]
```

Once we have the base grid defined, we can use Scipy's `interpolate` module to calculate the mapping for us.

```
g_out = scipy.interpolate.griddata(np.array(pt_dst_all),
                                   np.array(pt_src_all),
                                   (gx, gy), method='linear')
```

`g_out` contains both the x and y coordinates of the remapping; we need to split this into individual components for OpenCV's `remap` method to work.

```
mapx = np.append([], [ar[:,0] for ar in g_out]).reshape(mapsize).
astype('float32')
mapy = np.append([], [ar[:,1] for ar in g_out]).reshape(mapsize).
astype('float32')
```

These matrices are exactly what remap expects and we can now simply run it with the appropriate parameters.

```
        dst = cv2.remap(src, mapx, mapy, cv2.INTER_LINEAR)
        return dst
```

And that completes our method. We can use this in our stabilization code and fix the rolling shutter as well.

Unwarping with calibration

Here, we discuss how to warp images given a mesh for stabilizing the video. We split each frame into a 10x10 mesh. We warp the mesh and that results in warping the image (like control points). Using this approach, we should get good results and decent performance as well.

The actual unwarp happens in the `accumulateRotation` method:

```
def accumulateRotation(src, theta_x, theta_y, theta_z, timestamps,
prev, current, f, gyro_delay=None, gyro_drift=None, shutter_
duration=None):
    ...
    transform = getAccumulatedRotation(src.shape[1], src.shape[0],
theta_x, theta_y, theta_z, timestamps, prev, current, f, gyro_delay,
gyro_drift)
    o = cv2.warpPerspective(src, transform (src.shape[1], src.
shape[0]))
    return o
```

Here, there's a single perspective transform happening. Now, instead, we have to do a different transform for each of the 10x10 control points and use the `meshwarp` method to fix the rolling shutter. So replace the `transform` = line with the contents below:

```
    . . .
    pts = []
    transformed_pts = []
    for x in range(10):
        current_row = []
        current_row_transformed = []
        pixel_x = x * (src.shape[1] / 10)
        for y in range(10):
            pixel_y = y * (src.shape[0] / 10)
            current_row.append( [pixel_x, pixel_y] )
        pts.append(current_row)
```

We have now generated the original grid in the `pts` list. Now, we need to generate the transformed coordinates:

```
    . . .
    for y in range(10):
        pixel_y = y * (src.shape[0] / 10
        if shutter_duration:
            y_timestamp = current + shutter_duration*(pixel_y -
src.shape[0]/2)
        else:
            y_timestamp = current
    . . .
```

If a shutter duration is passed, we generate the timestamp at which this specific pixel was recorded. Now we can transform (`pixel_x`, `pixel_y`) based on the shutter rotation and append that to `current_row_transformed`:

```
    . . .
    transform = getAccumulatedRotation(src.shape[1], src.shape[0],
theta_x, theta_y, theta_z, timestamps, prev, y_timestamp, f, gyro_
delay, gyro_drift)
    output = cv2.perspectiveTransform(np.array([[pixel_x,
pixel_y]], transform)
    current_row_transformed.append(output)
    pts.append(current_row)
    pts_transformed.append(current_row_transformed)
    . . .
```

This completes the grid for `meshwarp`. Now all we need to do is generate the warped image. This is simple since we already have the required method:

```
o = meshwarp(src, pts_transformed)
return o
```

And this completes our transformation. We now have rolling shutter incorporated into our undistortion as well.

What's next?

What we have right now is a very barebones implementation of video stabilization. There are a few more things you can add to it to make it more robust, more automated and the output more pleasing to the eye. Here are a few things to get you started.

Identifying gyroscope axes

In this chapter, we've hard-coded the axes of the gyroscope. This might not be the case for all mobile phone manufacturers. Using a similar calibration technique, you should be able to find an axes configuration that minimizes errors across the video.

Estimating the rolling shutter direction

We've hard-coded the direction of the rolling shutter. Using specific techniques (like blinking an LED really fast at the camera), it is possible to estimate the direction of the rolling shutter and incorporate that into the calibration code. Certain camera sensors don't have the rolling shutter artifacts at all. This test can also identify if such a sensor is being used.

Smoother timelapses

Now that we've stabilized the video, we can speed up (or slow down) the video much better. There are commercial packages that do similar tasks – now your OpenCV code can do it too!

Repository of calibration parameters

You will have to calibrate every new device type you come across. If you move from one device type (say, a Samsung S5 to an iPhone 6), you'll have to run a calibration for this combination of lens and sensor. However, moving between different devices of the same kind does not require a re-calibration (such as moving from one iPhone 6 to another). If you're able to collect enough calibration results, your code can run perfectly on pretty much any device.

[You could also figure out a fallback mechanism if the repository does not have the required parameters.]

Incorporating translations

Currently, we're only using rotations. This means that if you shake the camera in a single plane, the algorithm won't do much. By using inputs from the accelerometer and using the translation of keypoints, it should be possible to compensate for translation as well. This should produce higher quality video.

Additional tips

Here are some additional things to keep in mind while working with Python and computer vision in general. They should help speed up your work and keep you safe from unexpected crashes!

Use the Python pickle module

Python gives us a neat way to store Python objects as files on disk. In our project, we have the gyroscope calibration class. This class stores information like the video dimensions and keypoints across different frames. Calculating this information from scratch everytime you want to test your code is cumbersome. You can easily pickle this object into a file and read back the data when required.

Here is some sample code for pickling the video object in our code:

```
import pickle
fp = open("/path/to/file.data", "w")
videoObj = GyroVideo(mp4)
pickle.dump(videoObj, fp)
fp.close()
```

To read the object back into the script:

```
import pickle
fp = open("/path/to/file.data", "r")
videoObj = pickle.load(fp)
fp.close()
```

This saves time when iterating on code and verifying if something works as expected.

Write out single images

When working with videos, you most often end up using something like the VideoWriter class from OpenCV. You feed it frames and it writes out a video file. While this is a perfectly valid way to get things done, you have more control if you write out individual frames to disk and then use a video encoder to combine the images into a video stream.

A simple way to combine multiple images is to use `ffmpeg`.

```
ffmpeg -i /tmp/image%04d.png -f image2 output.mp4
```

Testing without the delta

In the project, we're trying to stabilize video – thus we're calculating the delta between the actual gyroscope signal and a smoothed out version of the signal.

You might want to try it out with just the actual gyroscope signal; this will totally keep the video still. This might be useful for situations where you want the camera to appear completely still.

Summary

In this chapter, we've covered quite a bit: talking to your gyroscope, using that to find unknowns, negating the effects of camera shake and rolling shutter.

We started out by creating an Android app that uses background tasks to initiate recording media into a video file. While doing this, we figured out how to extend OpenCV's camera view class to incorporate custom UI and responsiveness. With this, you can now create very sophisticated UIs with an OpenCV backend. Along with this, we also captured the gyroscope trace and stored it in a single file. The sampling rate of the gyroscope and the media were different – however, we did not care about it at this stage. We'll let the app store a higher density of gyroscope traces (every few hundred microseconds versus every few dozen milliseconds for the media).

Once we had the media/csv pair, we used Python and the numpy/scipy libraries to calibrate the system. We had three unknowns initially: the pixel focal length of the camera, the gyroscope delay (the offset between the gyroscope recordings and the media timestamps) and the gyroscope drift.

We devised an error function that takes the expected keypoints and the transformed keypoints and returns the amount of errors. We then used this to calculate errors across the whole video. Using this, and Scipy's optimize method, we were able to find the values for these unknowns. This calibration needs to happen only once for each device type.

Then we added another parameter to our calibration—the rolling shutter. Estimating the value of this unknown was similar to the previous three, however, incorporating the undistortion was a bit tricky. We had to create a new method called `meshwarp` that takes a distorted grid. This method rectifies the grid and removes artifacts due to the rolling shutter. We worked on a vertical rolling shutter, however it should be easy to convert it to a horizontal rolling shutter.

We touched upon a lot of different areas: sensors, calibration, and geometric distortions. I hope this chapter gives you an insight into designing your own pipelines for working with images.

Index

Symbols

2D Features Framework documentation
  URL 280
2D scale space relation 222-224
-h parameter 194
-info parameter 193
-num parameter 193
-vec parameter 193
-w parameter 194

A

active illumination or structured light
  URL 20
active imaging systems 6
Active Shape Model
  URL 147
actual model training 185
Android NDK
  URL 170
Android-specific tasks
  defining 300
  media files, reading 311-316
  threaded overlay 300-311
Android Studio
  OpenCV, integrating into 164
  setting up, with OpenCV 167
Android Studio project
  OpenCV Android SDK, compiling
    to 164-166
aperture priority (A) 71
aperture setting 10

application showcase 176-178
application specific training data
  amount of training data 186-188
  object annotation files, creating for positive
    samples 189-192
  positive dataset, parsing into OpenCV
    data vector 193-195
  preparing 186
  selecting 186
application user interface, Android section
  camera frame, capturing 155, 156
  Capture button, implementing 160-162
  defining 152
  Save button, implementing 163, 164
  setup activity layout 154, 155
ASCII codes
  reference 191
ASUS Xtion PRO Live
  supercharging 19-30
automatic facial expression recognition
  problems 104

B

biometrics
  about 236
  application-specific normalization,
    applying 236, 237
  authentication process 240
  descriptor of recorded biometric,
    creating 238
  machine learning, for matching
    retrieved feature vector 238-240
  training dataset, obtaining 236, 237
bootstrapping process 216

C

calibration
about 316, 317
calibration class 331-337
data structures 317
images, undistorting 337, 338
results, testing 339
rotations, handling 325
unknown parameters 316
camera frame
capturing 155, 156
obtaining, Camera API used 157-159
Camera Sensor Review publications
URL 32
camera trap
about 61
planning 62-65
URL 62
cascade classification process
about 200, 201
boosting process, firing up 204, 205
features, precalculation 203
HAAR-like wavelet feature
models 207, 208
integral image, precalculation 203
local binary pattern models 209
negative samples, grabbing 203
positive samples, grabbing 203
temporary result, saving to stage
file 205-207
visualization tool, for object
models 210, 211
cascade classification training tool
reference 196
CASIA eye dataset
reference 268
catalogue
URL 51
classification
defining 125
process 126
CodecOutputSurface
URL 312
Code Laboratories (CL)
URL 14

colorful images
references 88
convolutions 332

D

data
capturing 288
gyro signals, recording 297-299
video, recording 288-297
data collection 185
data normalization, on detected face regions
about 244-247
Eigenface decomposition, through
PCA 249-251
face recognition approaches 247-249
linear discriminant analysis, Fisher
criterion used 252-254
local binary pattern histograms 255-257
dataset
splitting 126, 127
data structures
about 317
gyroscope trace, reading 318-321
training video 321-324
depth map 19
depth of field 9
descriptors
URL 120
detection result
false positive detections, reducing 215, 216
influencing, with parameters of
detection command 212-214
object instance detection,
increasing 215-217
optimizing, with scene specific
knowledge and constraints 212
digital single-lens reflex (DSLR) camera 65
dimensionality reduction
defining 123
distribution, of feature representation
computing, over k clusters 121
do-it-yourself (DIY) kits
URL 18
dynamic scene
and static scene, comparing 79

E

electromagnetic radiation types
  far infrared (FIR) light 4
  gamma rays 5
  microwaves 4
  near infrared (NIR) light 4
  radio waves 4
  ultraviolet (UV) light 5
  visible light 5
  x-rays 5
evaluation
  defining 138-140
  different number of clusters 143
  with different features 143
  with different learning algorithms 140
exposure bracketing
  about 63
  shell script, writing for 70, 72
exposure compensation 70
exposure value (EV) 70
extension tube 54

F

Face Alignment
  URL 147
face detection
  about 241
  data normalization, on detected face
    region 245-247
  data normalization, on detected face
    regions 244
  reference 244
  Viola and Jones boosted cascade
    classifier algorithm used 242, 243
face detection algorithm
  used, for extracting face region 106-108
face region
  extracting 112
  extracting, face detection algorithm
    used 106-108
  facial landmarks, extracting from 108
  finding, in image 105
facial expression dataset 105

facial expression recognition
  defining 103, 104
facial landmarks
  about 146
  defining 146
  detecting 147
  extracting, from face region 108
  URL 146
  using 147
facial recognition
  problems 258
feature extraction
  defining 114, 115
  improving 147
final feature
  computing, for each image 123
fingerprint identification
  about 259
  approach, implementing in
    OpenCV 3 260-266
  performing 259
fingerprint software
  reference 260
flandmark library
  compiling 110
  defining 108, 109
  downloading 110
  facial landmarks, detecting with 111
  URL 108
Flickr
  URL 50
focal length 11
focus distance 11
foreground mask 83
f-stop 11

G

general face detector 241
glass
  defining 49-59
global shutter 10
Gnome Virtual File System (GVFS) 67
gPhoto2
  about 65
  photo camera, controlling with 65, 66

setting up 69
testing 69
URL 66
wrapping 72-76
gPhoto2-compatible camera
URL 77
GPU optimizations
about 225
performing 228-232
GS3-U3-23S6M-C model
supercharging 31-48
using 54
gyroscope axes
identifying 345

H

HAAR-like wavelet feature models
about 207
node feature index 208
node left and node right 208
node threshold 208
hard negative mining 216
HDR images
creating 98, 99
HDR imaging and tone mapping
references 99
helper function 330
high dynamic range (HDR) 63
high quality object samples 187
histogram equalization 242
hybrid solution
defining, of hardware and software 283
hyper parameter optimization
techniques 239

I

image features
advanced features 116-120
contributed features 116-118
extracting, from facial component
regions 115, 116
key points, visualizing 120
image features space
clustering, into k clusters 121, 122

image formats
packed image 7
planar image 8
raw image 7
image matching comparison
URL 120
images
HDR images, creating 98, 99
processing 98
landmarks, visualizing 111
reference 98
time-lapse videos, creating 100, 101
iris identification
about 267
approach, implementing in
OpenCV 3 269-275
performing 267, 268
ISO speed 9

J

Japanese Female Facial Expression (JAFFE)
about 105
URL 105
Java and C++ interaction
creating, with JNI 168-170
Java Native Interface (JNI) 168
JNI documentation
URL 169
JNI tips, from API guides
URL 169

K

Kaggle
about 145, 146
URL 145
k clusters
image features space, clustering
into 121, 122
K-fold cross validation
defining 148
K-Nearest Neighbors (KNN)
about 135
testing stage 136
training stage 136

L

LBP feature-based model
about 209
eight 32-bit values 209
node feature index 209
node left and node right 209
learning rate 84
lenses
examples 55
libgphoto2
finding 77
URL 77
light
coloring 4-7

M

macam
URL 14
machine learning techniques
artificial neural networks 240
boosting and random forests 239
K-Nearest Neighbors search 239
Naïve Bayes classifiers 239
similarity matching 239
support vector machines 239
machine vision camera 4
MacPorts
URL 69
macropixels 7
manual exposure (M) 74
math
about 283
camera model 284
camera motion 284
image warping 286
shutter compensation, rolling 285, 286
Mathias Appel
URL 94
memcpy
URL 46
MFlenses
URL 50
mirror lock-up (MLU) 65

modules, OpenCV
URL 3
monochrome (gray) images 6
motion analysis and object tracking
URL 84
Motion Sensors API documentation
URL 178
multi-layer perceptron
defining 130-132
network, defining 132
network, training 133, 134
testing stage 134, 135
training stage 132
multiprocessing module
URL 72

N

Native Development Kit (NDK) 149
natural occurring samples 187
NDK/JNI
OpenCV C++, compiling with 170, 171
negative sample generation
reference 188
Normal Bayes classifier
about 137
testing stage 137
training stage 137
normal lens 54

O

object annotation
reference 189
object categorization 183-185
object detection 183-185
object recognition 183
omitted sections, script
URL 90
OpenCV
integrating, into Android Studio 164
OpenCV 3
URL 113
OpenCV Android SDK
compiling, to Android Studio
project 164-166
importing 167, 168

OpenCV C++
  compiling, with NDK/JNI 170-172
OpenCV C++ code
  implementing 174, 175
opencv_contrib module
  compiling 145
OpenCV, for Android
  URL 165
OpenCV Java code
  implementing 173, 174
OpenNI
  URL 20
OpenNI2
  references 22
OpenNI-compliant depth cameras
  supercharging 19-30
OpenSUSE, gPhoto2
  URL 69

P

Panorama
  Android section 152
  defining 149-152
  OpenCV section 152
panorama application 178, 179
parameters, accumulated rotations 329
parameter selection, for training
      object model
  about 195, 196
  cascade classification process 200
  cross-validation, using 212
  parameters, training 196-200
  resulting object model 205
parameters training, in object model
  -bg 199
  -data 197
  -featureType 199
  -maxFalseAlarmRate 200
  -minHitRate 199
  -numNeg 198
  -numPos 198
  -numStages 198
  -precalcIdxBufSize 199
  -precalcValBufSize 199
  -vec 199
  about 196

passive imaging systems 6
people registration system
  creating, by combining techniques 275, 276
performance evaluation
  about 225
  object detection performance
      testing 226-228
PGR
  about 33
  URL 33
photo camera
  controlling, with gPhoto2 65, 66
photogenic subject presence
  colorful subject, detecting 87-92
  detecting 77-81
  face of mammal, detecting 93-98
  moving subject, detecting 81-87
photosites 6
Picture Transfer Protocol (PTP) 66
PlayStation Eye
  supercharging 14-18
Point Grey Research cameras
  supercharging 31-48
practical applications 232, 233
precision 226
Principle Component Analysis (PCA) 123
project
  defining 287
PS3EYEDriver
  URL 14
python-gphoto2
  URL 77
Python pickle module
  using 346
Python script
  writing, to wrap gPhoto2 72-76

R

RANSAC 323
recall 226
recognition 182
region of interest (ROI) 34
repository, of calibration parameters 346
resolution 9
rolling shutter 10

rolling shutter direction
  estimating 345
rotation invariance object detection
  obtaining 217-222
rotations
  accumulated rotations 328-331
  image, rotating 325-327

S

sample counting tool
  reference 193
sample creation tool
  reference 193
SensorKinect
  URL 20
sensor sizes, in machine vision cameras
  URL 53
shell script
  writing, for exposure bracketing 70, 71
  writing, to unmount camera drives 67, 68
shutter compensation
  rolling 339
  rolling shutter, calibrating 339, 340
  unwarping, with calibration 343, 344
  warping, with grid points 341-343
shutter speed 10
Simple DirectMedia Layer 2 (SDL2)
  about 36
  URL 36
single images
  writing 347
smoother timelapses 345
software usage guide
  defining 113-138
source code and build files, Infravision
  URL 22
source code, driver
  URL 14
source code, LookSpry
  URL 36
source code, Unblinking Eye
  URL 15

spectral response 6
spherical aberrations 49
stabilization
  with hardware 282
  with hardware, reference 282
  with images 280, 281
  with images, reference 281
Stitcher class
  URL 179
Stitching module
  URL 179
stump weak classifiers 200
subject
  capturing, in moment 8-12
subprocess module
  URL 72
supported methods, of histogram
      comparison
  URL 88
Support Vector Machine (SVM)
  defining 127, 128
  testing stage 130
  training stage 128-130
system overview 143

T

Technical Application Note (TAN)
  URL 35
Technical Reference Manual
  URL 34
testing
  without delta 347
throughput
  about 10
  factors 10
time-lapse videos
  creating 100, 101
T-number 12
tone mapping 98
translations
  incorporating 346
transmittance 12
T-stop 12

U

unusual suspects
  rounding up 13

V

validation 185
video stabilization 279
vignetting 53
Viola and Jones algorithm 181

W

white paper, PGR
  URL 32
wrappers
  finding 77

X

Xtion devices
  URL 21
Xtion PRO Live
  URL 21

Y

YUV channels 7

Thank you for buying
OpenCV 3 Blueprints

About Packt Publishing

Packt, pronounced 'packed', published its first book, *Mastering phpMyAdmin for Effective MySQL Management*, in April 2004, and subsequently continued to specialize in publishing highly focused books on specific technologies and solutions.

Our books and publications share the experiences of your fellow IT professionals in adapting and customizing today's systems, applications, and frameworks. Our solution-based books give you the knowledge and power to customize the software and technologies you're using to get the job done. Packt books are more specific and less general than the IT books you have seen in the past. Our unique business model allows us to bring you more focused information, giving you more of what you need to know, and less of what you don't.

Packt is a modern yet unique publishing company that focuses on producing quality, cutting-edge books for communities of developers, administrators, and newbies alike. For more information, please visit our website at www.packtpub.com.

About Packt Open Source

In 2010, Packt launched two new brands, Packt Open Source and Packt Enterprise, in order to continue its focus on specialization. This book is part of the Packt Open Source brand, home to books published on software built around open source licenses, and offering information to anybody from advanced developers to budding web designers. The Open Source brand also runs Packt's Open Source Royalty Scheme, by which Packt gives a royalty to each open source project about whose software a book is sold.

Writing for Packt

We welcome all inquiries from people who are interested in authoring. Book proposals should be sent to author@packtpub.com. If your book idea is still at an early stage and you would like to discuss it first before writing a formal book proposal, then please contact us; one of our commissioning editors will get in touch with you.

We're not just looking for published authors; if you have strong technical skills but no writing experience, our experienced editors can help you develop a writing career, or simply get some additional reward for your expertise.

Learning OpenCV 3 Computer Vision with Python
Second Edition

ISBN: 978-1-78528-384-0   Paperback: 266 pages

Unleash the power of computer vision with Python using OpenCV

1. Create impressive applications with OpenCV and Python.

2. Familiarize yourself with advanced machine learning concepts.

3. Harness the power of computer vision with this easy-to-follow guide.

OpenCV Essentials

ISBN: 978-1-78398-424-4   Paperback: 214 pages

Acquire, process, and analyze visual content to build full-fledged imaging applications using OpenCV

1. Create OpenCV programs with a rich user interface.

2. Develop real-world imaging applications using free tools and libraries.

3. Understand the intricate details of OpenCV and its implementation using easy-to-follow examples.

Please check **www.PacktPub.com** for information on our titles

OpenCV for Secret Agents

ISBN: 978-1-78328-737-6   Paperback: 302 pages

Use OpenCV in six secret projects to augment your home, car, phone, eyesight, and any photo or drawing

1. Build OpenCV apps for the desktop, the Raspberry Pi, Android, and the Unity game engine.

2. Learn real-time techniques that can be used to classify images, detecting and recognizing any person or animal, and studying motion and distance with superhuman precision.

3. Design hands-free interfaces that are practical in home automation, in cars, and in discrete surveillance.

Learning Image Processing with OpenCV

ISBN: 978-1-78328-765-9   Paperback: 232 pages

Exploit the amazing features of OpenCV to create powerful image processing applications through easy-to-follow examples

1. Learn how to build full-fledged image processing applications using free tools and libraries.

2. Take advantage of cutting-edge image processing functionalities included in OpenCV v3.

3. Understand and optimize various features of OpenCV with the help of easy-to-grasp examples.

Please check **www.PacktPub.com** for information on our titles

Printed in Poland
by Amazon Fulfillment
Poland Sp. z o.o., Wrocław